GOLDENEYE
GUIDEBOOKS
AF348407
THE
LAKE DISTRICT
WRITTEN AND PHOTOGRAPHED BY WILLIAM FRICKER

To My Siblings: Julia, Penny, Rosalind, Mark & Lucy who all share a love of wild places, and for their continued love and encouragement.

Research & Text: William Fricker

Photography: William Fricker (unless credited with an initial- see page 217)

First published in the United Kingdom, in 2009, by Goldeneye, Unit 10, Chivenor Business Park, Barnstaple, North Devon EX31 4AY www.goldeneyeguides.co.uk

Cartographic Consultants: Cox Cartographic Ltd

Maps taken from Goldeneye's Digital Database

Book design and layout: Chris Dyer Design

Sub Editor: Caroline Patterson

Mountain Bike routes: Al Churcher

Car Tours: JF Kearney

Abbreviations in Text

C14 14th Century Mar-Oct 1 March to 31 October (inclusive) NT National Trust property EH English Heritage property BHs Bank Holidays W/Es Weekends East Easter E/C Early Closing TIC Tourist Information Centre M Monday Tu Tuesday W Wednesday Th Thursday F Friday Sa Saturday Su Sunday SS Supplied by Subject (reference illustrations)

All Rights Reserved

Correct Information

The contents of this publication were believed to be correct and accurate at the time of printing. However, Goldeneye accepts no responsibility for any errors, omissions or changes in the details given, or for the consequences arising thereto, from the use of this book. However, the publishers would greatly appreciate your time in notifying us of any changes or new attractions (or places to eat, drink and stay) that you consider merit inclusion in the next edition. Your comments are most welcome, for we value the views and suggestions of our readers. Please write to: The Editor, Goldeneye, 10 Chivenor Business Park, Barnstaple EX31 4AY, United Kingdom.

ISBN Number 1-85965 168 2

EAN Number 9 781859 651681

Printed and bound in the UK by Butler Tanner & Dennis Ltd

I wandered lonely as a Cloud
That floats on high o'er Vales and Hills
When all at once I saw a crowd
A host of dancing Daffodils
Along the Lake, beneath the trees
Ten thousand dancing in the breeze
The waves beside them danced, but they
Outdid the sparkling waves In glee
A poet could not but be gay
In such a laughing company
I gazed and gazed but little thought
What wealth the show to me had brought
For oft when on my couch I lie
In vacant or in pensive mood
They flash upon that inward eye
Which is the bliss of solitude
And then my heart with pleasure fills
And dances with the Daffodils

William Wordsworth

It has been a humbling experience to produce this book. To follow in the footsteps of William Wordsworth, Thomas Gray and others has been a challenge and an education. It can be a thankless task to compare ones meagre efforts with these fellows and some would consider it an arrogance to even attempt it. I would agree with them (half-way) but then I would have to agree with my wife's argument that I in fact was not trying to emulate, compete or better what had gone before.

Goldeneye Guidebooks have grown out of the Goldeneye Map-Guide series, a series that I have written and researched, and provided photography for over twenty years. In this time I have visited the Lakes in many guises, as writer, photographer, climber and walker, and as a holidaymaker with wife and children. So one sees the area in differing lights.

My intention has been to produce a practical and easy to use book - one that is clear to navigate, fun to read and a pleasure to turn the page, and one that will highlight and enthuse you to delve beneath the surface. I have recommended other guidebooks and maps to use too, to help you gain further, more detailed knowledge than I can provide in a portable book.

I would hope that once you have trawled the pages you will agree this is more than a guidebook. It is meant to be a souvenir, an object to treasure. And, in this regard, I have tried to be different from the norm and have illustrated the lakes with more than one image and have portrayed them in all weathers and seasons. I have also taken you beyond the lakes, streams and mountains, and to the estuaries and coast that lie a short distance beyond the tourist spots. And, to provide a different visual perspective, I have included contemporary and traditional paintings. The touring maps add value and provide an immense amount of detail, rarely found in similar guide books. This, thankfully, saves unnecessary descriptive prose. But the major difference of this guidebook, compared to many others on the market (who first commission a writer, then gather the images from various picture libraries), is that I have researched and written it, and produced 95% of the photography. This, I believe, has given me a greater insight into my subject, and the opportunity to create an intense labour of love. Goldeneye Guides believe in using small teams to produce each guidebook. This ensures an undiluted passion for each subject. So, thank you Chris (designer), Caroline (editor) and Dave (cartographer) for sharing this incredible journey.

I realise that for many this may be your first time in the Lake District. It may also be your only ever visit given the thousands of other destinations available to you. I want you to be made aware of the best on offer. It is home to some remarkable hotels and restaurants and some luxurious inns and B&Bs. I have illustrated the finest. Not all are excessively pricey but the top hotels are not cheap. They will be an experience to live with you forever and are thus worthy of a special occasion.

William Fricker

CONTENTS

John Ruskin's rowing boat and carriage, Brantwood

The Lake District is arguably the most beautiful corner of England. It is compact and varied and has a landscape of such intense beauty that it mesmerised the C19 poets leaving them lost for words. Hundreds of thousands visit the popular tourist towns and lakes each year but away from these honey pots lie often deserted and secluded valleys, tarns and dales.

The Lakes has attracted fifty thousand plus publications which if heaped together would create a mountain to rival Scafell. However, the intention of this book is not to compete with the thousands of previous publications but to produce an up to date, up to the minute guide to the many features of interest and beauty, in this area. And this includes accommodation, where to eat and drink, and what to see and do. The text is precise, words describing the position of a place is omitted as our touring maps and town plans pin point these important details.

The classic guide was written by one of Lakeland's most famous sons in 1810, and William Wordsworth's 'Guide to the Lakes' is still in print today. For the fell walker, the most comprehensive companions are Alfred Wainwright's series of Pictorial Guides to the Lakeland Fells, and the Ordnance Survey 1: 25,000 Outdoor Leisure maps.

The area is divided into three areas. The Northern Divide was formed by 5,000 million year old Skiddaw Slate, the substance of the mountains Skiddaw and Blencathra. The Central Zone includes Borrowdale's Volcanic Rock, which moulded the ranges of Scafell, Helvellyn and the Langdale Pikes. Southern Lakeland was created by smoother Silurian rocks, a mere 400 million years old, these provide the softer, wooded landscapes of Coniston and Windermere. The glaciers which followed the Ice Age swept through the valley floors, excavating huge bowls which formed the lakes.

Wind, rain and running water have scarred the landscape, which is forever changing. Man has built dams and created tarns, artificial lakes and forests.

Man has occupied these fells for more than 5,000 years. Neolithic settlers cleared the woodlands and built stone axe factories. Later, Iron Age tribes built strategic hill forts. The Romans occupied the area from AD45 to the 5th Century and built a chain of settlements, forts and roadways which crossed the high fells. They also developed the mining of local minerals. The Norse Invaders in the 8th Century left the legacy of ancient crosses and their language. During the Norman Occupation, the land was divided and managed by the Abbeys at Furness, St. Bees and Holm Cultram, who developed an early woollen industry which later boomed in the Middle Ages, and the local cloth, 'Kendal Green', reached international fame after it was worn by archers at the battle of Flodden Field. Today the colour is still evident in the town's lampposts and litter bins.

In the late 18th Century, and early 19th Century, poets and artists discovered this landscape. Their numbers increased, as did the general population and the numbers of tourists with the coming of the railway so staunchly discouraged by William Wordsworth.

The Lake District is England's only true mountain area. The landscape is grand and spectacular, peaceful and ethereal, and forever changing in mood and tempo. The beauty of the area changes with the seasons but for the active, or passive, enthusiast there is always much to do and see and the best time is always the present. To discover the true lakes, you must travel beyond the photograph or painting and experience the living landscape. Tread a rocky path, get buffeted by wind and rain and dip into a clear mountain beck or pool. Experience the wonderful camaraderie of the fell walker. The thrill of fresh air and exercise will provide a hearty appetite, which can be well catered for in the many excellent hotels, inns and restaurants. In recent years Britain has seen a resurgence in locally-produced food and Lake District farmers have made sure they weren't left behind as consumers became more aware of quality, organic produce and food miles. Their meat and produce are now championed by the Made in Cumbria campaign group, and local shops are proud to sell items grown nearby.

Afternoon tea at a Country House hotel; the Sharrow Bay, Gilpin Lodge, Samling

Circular walk around Tarn Hows

Climb Great Gable for the Remembrance Day Sunday service

Climb Helvellyn on mid-summer's day sunrise

Get up early and visit Wastwater. Lunch at the Wasdale Head Inn

Hire a rowing boat on Derwent Water

Take a trip on the T'all Ratty Railway, Ravenglass

Trip on Steam Yacht Gondola to visit Brantwood

Visit a Literary shrine: Brantwood, Dove Cottage or Rydal Mount

Walk to a waterfall: Aira Force or Galleny Force

Try a section of the Cumbria Way

Steamboat trip on Ullswater or Windermere

Follow one of our Scenic Drives

Follow the Arts & Crafts Movement trail starting from Blackwell

Sail Coniston in the image of Swallows & Amazon

Explore the Duddon Valley that inspired Wordsworth to write 35 sonnets

Explore the Borrowdale valleys

Discover the history of Lakeland at Abbot Hall's Museum of Lakeland Life

There are 463 lakes and tarns in the Lake District. It's not possible to visit them all in a weekend or during a short break. Listed below is a brief description of the most beautiful and most accessible. The choice is yours...

1 Bassenthwaite Lake
Mysterious and haunting. Best viewed from Skiddaw and Thornthwaite Forest.

2 Buttermere
"The Lake of the Dairy Pastures" and considered, by many, to be the most beautiful.

3 Coniston Water
Literary connections galore. Ruskin's home Brantwood overlooks the lake and green pastures, and the south side is the location for many "Swallows and Amazons" adventures.

4 Crummock Water
The crooked lake surrounded by mountains. Good walking area.

5 Derwent Water
"The Queen of the Lakes" is one of the largest and most beautiful. Ringed by towering peaks.

6 Elterwater
"The Swan Lake" – a tranquil and reedy lake. Looks fabulous in a hoar frost.

7 Esthwaite Water
Pretty lake surrounded by fields and woodland.

8 Grasmere
Magical at dawn, and a favourite with the Wordsworths. Best viewed from Loughrigg Terrace.

9 Loweswater
"The Leafy Lake" – remote and sometimes forgotten. Good pub nearby.

10 Rydal Water
Magical at dawn and dusk, and on calm, clear winter days. Circular walk.

11 Tarn Hows
Popular circular walk, so get there early.

12 Ullswater
Grand and scenic with ever-changing moods. Inspired Wordsworth's sonnet "I wandered lonely as a cloud."

13 Wastwater
The deepest and most dramatic of all the lakes. Some say this is Britain's favourite view.

14 Windermere
England's largest lake and the most visited of all of Lakeland's lakes. It grows on you.

5
6
7
8
9
10
11
12
13
14

New House Farm ss

Nab Cottage

Red Bedroom, The Samling ss

This is a selection to make choosing your B&B or hotel an easy and quick process. We suggest you view their websites to find one that suits your budget, style and expectation. It is often the unexpected that will surprise you. Perhaps a stunning bathroom or lakeside view, or a quirky and funny hostess oozing charm who will draw you back again, and again. Your choice may also be determined by the proximity of a recommended eatery. B&Bs rarely provide evening meals and the choice of above average pub cuisine is limited in this region. So please book accordingly.

Country House Hotels

Gilpin Lodge, Windermere. 015394 88818
www.gilpinlodge.com

Holbeck Ghyll, Windermere. 015394 32375
www.holbeckghyll.com

Miller Howe, Windermere. 015394 42536
www.millerhowe.com

Sharrow Bay Ullswater. 01768 486301 www.sharrowbay.co.uk

Winder Hall, Low Lorton. 01900 85107 www.winderhall.co.uk

Country House B&B

Beechmount Country House. Near Sawrey. 015394 36356
www.beechmountcountryhouse.co.uk

Cockenskell Farm, Blawith. 01229 885217
www.cockenskell.co.uk

Cote How Country Guest House, Rydal. 015394 32765
www.cotehow.co.uk

Grange Country House, Keswick. 01768 72500
www.grangekeswick.com

Low Graythwaite Hall, Graythwaite. 015395 31676
www.lowgraythwaitehall.co.uk

Low House, Windermere. 015394 43156 www.lowhouse.co.uk

Boutique Hotels

The Samling, Windermere. 015394 31922
www.thesamling.com

Moss Grove Hotel, Grasmere. 015394 35251
www.mossgrove.com

Country Cottage B&B

Buckle Yeat, Near Sawrey. 015394 36446
www.buckle-yeat.co.uk

Nab Cottage, Rydal. 015394 35311 www.rydalwater.com

Willow Cottage, Bassenthwaite. 01768 776440
www.willowbarncottage.co.uk

Farm House B&B

Bank Ground, Coniston. 015394 41264
www.bankground.com

Highside Farm, Bassenthwaite. 01768 76952
www.highside.co.uk

Hill Farm, Cartmel. 015395 36477 www.hillfarmbb.co.uk

Stonethwaite Farm, Borrowdale. 01768 77234

Tranthwaite Hall, Underbarrow. 015395 68285
www.tranthwaitehall.co.uk

Yew Tree Farm, Coniston. 015394 41433
www.yewtree-farm.co.uk

Yew Tree Farm, Rosthwaite. 01768 77675
www.borrowdaleherdwick.co.uk

Family-Run Hotels

Knoll Country House, Lakeside. 015395 31347
www.theknoll-lakeside.co.uk

Linthwaite House Hotel, Windermere.
015394 88600 www.linthwaite.com

West Vale Country House, Far Sawrey. 015394 42817
www.westvalecountryhouse.co.uk

Abbey House Hotel, Barrow

Gilpin Lodge ss

L'enclume ss

Sharrow Bay ss

Stonethwaite Farm

Guest Accommodation

Brooklands Guest House, Penrith. 01768 863395
www.brooklandsguesthouse.com

Crosthwaite House, Crosthwaite. 015395 68264
www.crosthwaitehouse.co.uk

Low Jock Scar, Selside. 01539 823259 www.lowjockscar.co.uk

Old Vicarage, Ambleside. 015394 33364
www.oldvicarageambleside.co.uk

Plantation Cottage, Sandside. 01524 762069

Seatoller House, Borrowdale. 017687 77218
www.seatollerhouse.co.uk

Luxurious B&B

Fairfield, Windermere. 015394 46565 www.the-fairfield.co.uk

Low Fell, Windermere. 01539 445612 www.low-fell.co.uk

New House Farm, Lorton. 01900 85404
www.newhouse-farm.co.uk

No 43, Arnside. 01524 762761 www.no43.org.uk

The Howbeck, Windermere. 015394 44739
www.howbeck.co.uk

Restaurant With Rooms

Jericho at The Waverley, Windermere. 015394 42522
www.waverleyhotel.com

L'enclume, Cartmel. 01539 536362 www.lenclume.co.uk

The Pheasant, Bassenthwaite Lake. 017687 76234
www.the-pheasant.co.uk

Room With A View

White Moss House, Rydal. 01539 435295 www.whitemoss.com

Fellside Studios, Troutbeck. 015394 34000
www.fellsidestudios.co.uk

Spa Style - The Works

Langdale Hotel & Country Club, Great Langdale.
015394 37302 www.langdale.co.uk

Inns With Rooms

Bay Horse, Canal Foot, Ulverston. 01229 583972
www.thebayhorsehotel.co.uk

Britannia Inn, Elterwater. 015394 37210 www.britinn.co.uk

Drunken Duck Inn, Ambleside. 015394 36347
www.drunkenduckinn.co.uk

Kirkstile Inn, Loweswater. 01900 85219 www.kirkstile.com

Mortal Man, Troutbeck. 015394 33193
www.themortalman.com

Old Dungeon Ghyll, Great Langdale. 01539 437272
www.odg.co.uk

Pennington Hotel, Ravenglass. 01229 717222
www.thepennington.co.uk

Punchbowl Inn, Crosthwaite. 015395 68237
www.the-punchbowl.co.uk

Tower Bank Arms, Near Sawrey. 015394 36334
www.towerbankarms.com

Queens Head Inn, Askham. 01931 712225
www.queensheadaskham.com

Queens Head Inn, Tirril. 01768 863219
www.queensheadinn.co.uk

Queens Head, Troutbeck. 015394 32174
www.queensheadhotel.com

Strands Inn & Brewery, Nether Wasdale. 019467 26237
www.strandshotel.co.uk

Wasdale Head Inn. 019467 26229 www.wasdale.com

The Priory Church of St Mary and St Michael, Cartmel

L'enclune ss

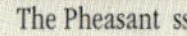

The Pheasant ss

The Samling ss

Jericho ss

Lucy's of Ambleside ss

Holbeck Ghyll ss

Gilpin Lodge ss

Choosing the right café, restaurant or inn can make or break a romantic weekend. It may also determine where you decide to stay. Many will choose a pub or café at the beginning or end of a walk. I hope our selection below will make your life a little easier to plan. All establishments are described in the following guide but not all restaurants/eating places described in the guide are listed below. This is a judicious selection.

Farm Shops with Restaurants

Carleton Farm Shop, Carleton. 01768 210027
www.carletonfarmshop.co.uk

Courtyard Café, Holker Hall, Cark-in-Cartmel. 015395 58328
www.holker-hall.co.uk

Low Sizergh Farm, Sizergh. 015395 60426
www.lowsizerghbarn.co.uk

Plumgarths Farm Shop, Crook Road, Kendal. 01539 736300
www.plumgarths.co.uk

Foodie Inns

Drunken Duck Inn, Ambleside. 015394 36347
www.drunkenduckinn.co.uk

Gate Inn, Yanwath. 01768 862386 www.yanwathgate.com

Kirkstile Inn, Loweswater. 01900 85219 www.kirkstile.com

Queens Head Inn, Tirril. 01768 863219
www.queensheadinn.co.uk

Queens Head, Troutbeck. 015394 32174
www.queensheadhotel.com

Café Bistros

Chesters Café by the River, Skelwith Bridge. 015394 32553
www.chesters-cafebytheriver.co.uk

Fusion Café, Brougham Hall. 07933 177234
www.allfusedglass.co.uk

Jumble Room, Grasmere. 015394 35188
www.thejumbleroom.co.uk

Jumping Jenny at Brantwood. 01539 441715
www.jumpingjenny.com

Lakeland Pedlar, Keswick. 017687 74492
www.lakelandpedlar.co.uk

Lucy's On A Plate, Ambleside. 015394 31191
www.lucysofambleside.co.uk

Merienda Café, Station Street, Cockermouth. 01900 822790
www.merienda.co.uk

Rogan & Company, Cartmel. 015395 35917
www.roganandcompany.co.uk

Waterside Wholefood & Vegetarian Café, Kendal. 01539 729743
www.watersidewholefood.co.uk

Wilf's Café, Staveley. 01539 822329 www.wilfs-cafe.co.uk

Zeffirelli's, Ambleside. 015394 33845 www.zeffirellis.com

Cafés With A View

Bluebird Café, Coniston. 015394 41649 www.thebluebirdcafe.com

Zest, Harbourside, Whitehaven. 01946 692848
www.zestwhitehaven.com

Restaurants With Rooms

Gilpin Lodge, Windermere. 015394 88818 www.gilpinlodge.com

Holbeck Ghyll, Windermere. 015394 32375
www.holbeckghyll.com

L'enclume, Cartmel. 01539 536362 www.lenclume.co.uk

Miller Howe, Windermere. 015394 42536 www.millerhowe.com

Linthwaite House Hotel, Windermere. 015394 88600
www.linthwaite.com

The Pheasant, Bassenthwaite Lake. 017687 76234
www.the-pheasant.co.uk

Sharrow Bay, Ullswater. 01768 486301 www.sharrowbay.co.uk

The Samling, Windermere. 015394 31922 www.thesamling.com

Tea Rooms

Grange Tea Rooms, Borrowdale.

Granny Dowbekin's, Pooley Bridge. 01768 486453

Greystoke Cycle Café Tea Garden, Greystoke. 017684 883984
www.greystokecyclecafe.co.uk

The Flock In, Rosthwaite. 017687 77675
www.borrowdaleherdwick.co.uk

The Old Sawmill Tearoom, Mirehouse. 017687 72287
www.theoldsawmill.co.uk

The Old Stackyard Tea Rooms, Cockermouth. 01900 822777
www.wellingtonjerseys.co.uk

Town Restaurants

Jericho at The Waverley, Windermere. 015394 45026
www.waverleyhotel.com

Glass House, Ambleside. 015394 32137
www.theglasshouserestaurant.co.uk

Unique Dining, Keswick. 017687 73400
www.uniquedinining.co.uk

Quince & Medlar, 13 Castlegate, Cockermouth. 01900 823579
www.quinceandmedlar.co.uk

Zest Restaurant, Whitehaven. 01946 692848
www.zestwhitehaven.com

WESTMORLANDIÆ et Cumberlandiæ Comit: noua vera et Elaborata descriptio. An°. Dni. 1576.
SCOTIÆ
GILSLAN
CARLISLE
KESWICK
EGREMOND
COPELAND
Copeland forest
West warde forst
RAVENGLAS
OCEANVS OCCIDENS
CHRISTOPHORVS SAXTON DESCRIPSIT
Scala Miliarum
AVGVSTINVS RYTHER ANGLVS SCVLPSIT AN° DNI 1576

NORTH VM
BRIÆ
PICTES
PARS
DVNELMEN
SIS EPISCO
PATVS
PARS
EBORA
CEN
SIS
PARS
Elizabeth Regina
DIEV · ET · MON · DROYT
INDVSTRIA · NATVRAM · ORNAT
ORIENS
Barnard cast:

LOCATOR MAP

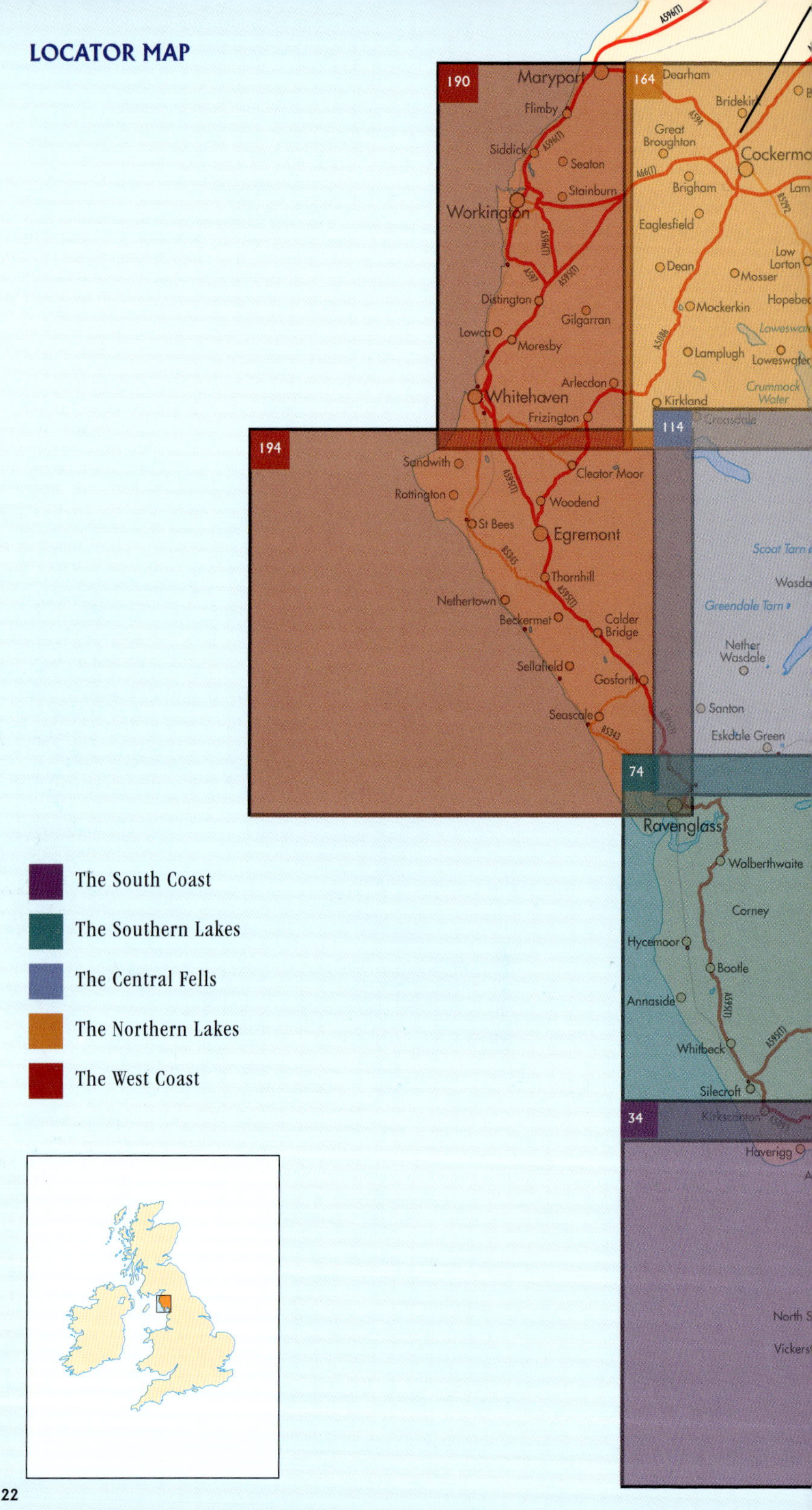

The South Coast

The Southern Lakes

The Central Fells

The Northern Lakes

The West Coast

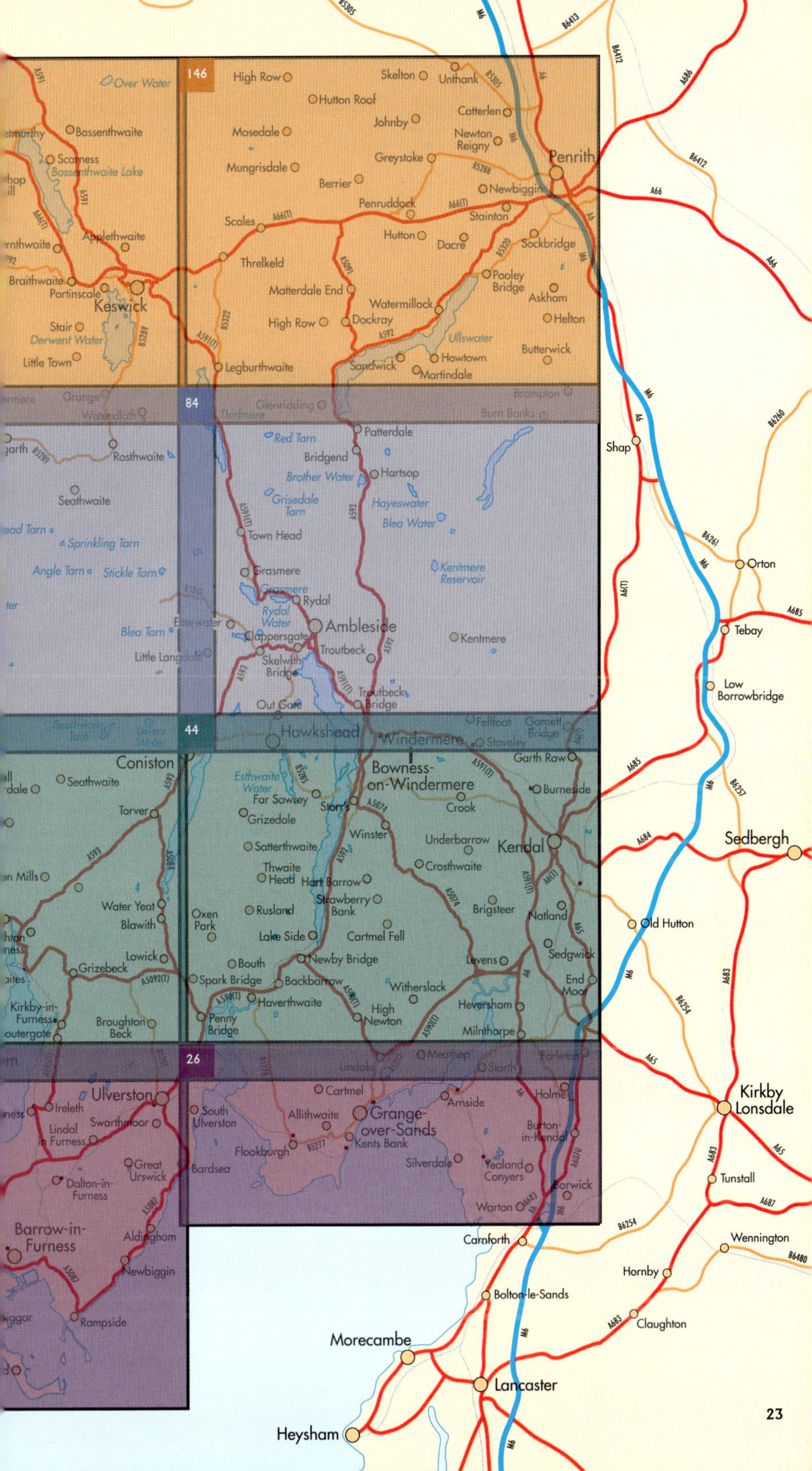

146
84
44
26
Over Water
High Row
Skelton
Unthank
Bassenthwaite
Hutton Roof
Catterlen
Scarness
Mosedale
Johnby
Newton Reigny
Bassenthwaite Lake
Mungrisdale
Greystoke
Penrith
Applethwaite
Berrier
Newbiggin
Penruddock
A66(T)
Scales
A66(T)
Stainton
Threlkeld
Hutton
Dacre
Sockbridge
Braithwaite
Matterdale End
Pooley Bridge
Askham
Portinscale
Watermillock
Helton
Keswick
Stair
High Row
Dockray
Butterwick
Derwent Water
Howtown
Little Town
Legburthwaite
Sandwick
Martindale
Ullswater
Shap
Grange
Glenridding
Burn Banks
Waterdlath
Thirlmere
Patterdale
Rosthwaite
Red Tarn
Bridgend
Hartsop
Seathwaite
Brother Water
Hayeswater
Head Tarn
Grisedale Tarn
Blea Water
Sprinkling Tarn
Town Head
Orton
Angle Tarn
Stickle Tarn
Grasmere
Kentmere Reservoir
Grasmere
Rydal
Blea Tarn
Elterwater
Rydal Water
Ambleside
Tebay
Clappersgate
Troutbeck
Little Langdale
Skelwith Bridge
Kentmere
Low Borrowbridge
Out Gate
Troutbeck Bridge
Seathwaite Tarn
Levers Water
Hawkshead
Windermere
Fellfoot
Garnett Bridge
Coniston
Staveley
Garth Row
Seathwaite
Esthwaite Water
Bowness-on-Windermere
Burneside
Torver
Far Sawrey
Storrs
Crook
Grizedale
Winster
Underbarrow
Kendal
Mills
Satterthwaite
Crosthwaite
Thwaite Head
Hart Barrow
Water Yeat
Rusland
Strawberry Bank
Brigsteer
Natland
Blawith
Oxen Park
Old Hutton
Grizebeck
Lowick
Lake Side
Cartmel Fell
Levens
Sedgwick
Kirkby-in-Furness
Bouth
Newby Bridge
Witherslack
End Moor
Spark Bridge
Backbarrow
Sedbergh
outergate
Haverthwaite
High Newton
Heversham
Broughton Beck
Penny Bridge
Milnthorpe
Lindale
Meathop
Storth
Forton
Ulverston
Cartmel
Arnside
Holme
Ireleth
South Ulverston
Allithwaite
Grange-over-Sands
Swarthmoor
Burton-in-Kendal
Lindal in Furness
Flookburgh
Kents Bank
Great Urswick
Silverdale
Yealand Conyers
Bardsea
Kirkby Lonsdale
Dalton-in-Furness
Warton
Borwick
Barrow-in-Furness
Tunstall
Aldingham
Carnforth
Wennington
Newbiggin
Hornby
Claughton
Rampside
Bolton-le-Sands
Morecambe
Lancaster
Heysham

For beaches, sand dunes, estuaries, wild flowers, shipbuilding, fine cuisine, stately homes and the birthplace of C19 exploration.

This stretch of coastline has a beauty all its own and is a fine contrast to the mountains on the distant, northern horizon. From the treacherous mud flats of Morecambe Bay, home to former fishing villages specialising in the shrimp industry, to the wide open estuaries fed by the rivers, Duddon, Kent and Leven. Here, you will find nesting and breeding grounds for sea birds, and amongst the dunes and marram grass, a wealth of wild flowers.

In the centre of this countryside stands the village of Cartmel. A beautifully constructed village of increasing popularity with one of the finest churches in the North of England and a centre of fine cuisine. Just to the west of Cartmel, the stately home of Holker Hall that could be described as a mini Chatsworth.

Journey a little westward and you come to Ulverston, a Free Trade town, the centre of C19 exploration and home to the founding fathers of Quakerism. But, if you seek some alternative history, for example, industrial or monastic history, or perhaps a solitary walk-through a nature reserve then a visit to Barrow-in-Furness will satisfy your needs.

Sandscale Beach

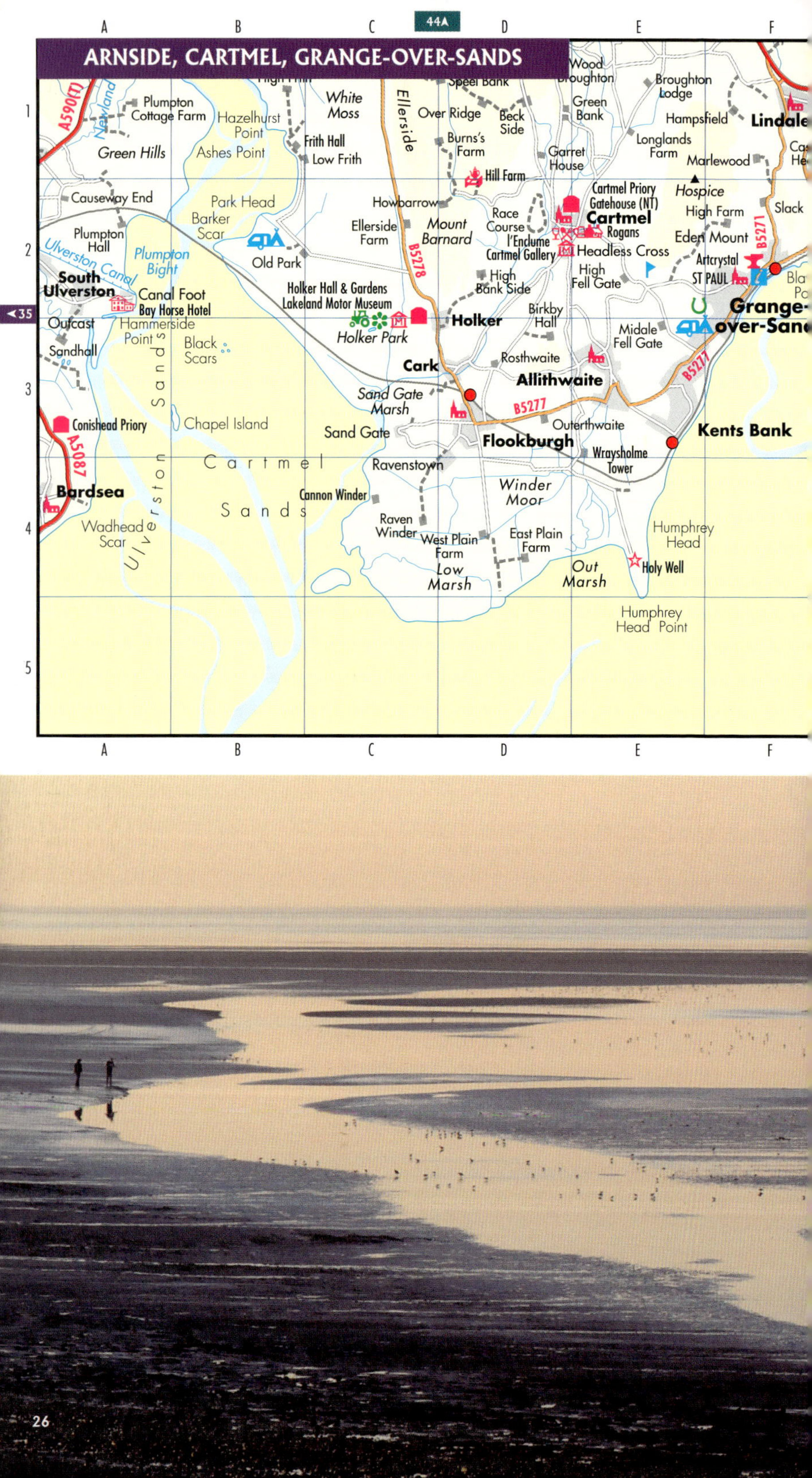
44▲
ARNSIDE, CARTMEL, GRANGE-OVER-SANDS
A590(T)
Newland
Plumpton Cottage Farm
High Frith
Hazelhurst Point
Ashes Point
White Moss
Frith Hall
Low Frith
Ellerside
Speel Bank
Over Ridge
Burns's Farm
Beck Side
Wood Broughton
Green Bank
Broughton Lodge
Hampsfield
Lindale
Green Hills
Causeway End
Hill Farm
Howbarrow
Garret House
Longlands Farm
Marlewood
Cas Hea
Plumpton Hall
Park Head
Barker Scar
Ellerside Farm
Mount Barnard
Race Course
Cartmel Priory Gatehouse (NT)
Cartmel
Rogans
Hospice
High Farm
Eden Mount
Slack
Ulverston Canal
Plumpton Bight
Old Park
B5278
l'Enclume
Cartmel Gallery
Headless Cross
Artcrystal
ST PAUL
B5271
South Ulverston
Canal Foot
Bay Horse Hotel
Holker Hall & Gardens
Lakeland Motor Museum
High Bank Side
High Fell Gate
Bla Po
Outcast
Hammerside Point
Black Scars
Holker Park
Holker
Birkby Hall
Midale Fell Gate
Grange-over-Sand
Sandhall
Conishead Priory
Chapel Island
Cark
Sand Gate Marsh
Rosthwaite
Allithwaite
B5277
B5277
A5087
Cartmel
Sand Gate
Flookburgh
Outerthwaite
Kents Bank
Bardsea
Sands
Cannon Winder
Ravenstown
Winder Moor
Wraysholme Tower
Wadhead Scar
Ulverston Sands
Raven Winder
West Plain Farm
East Plain Farm
Low Marsh
Out Marsh
Holy Well
Humphrey Head
Humphrey Head Point
35

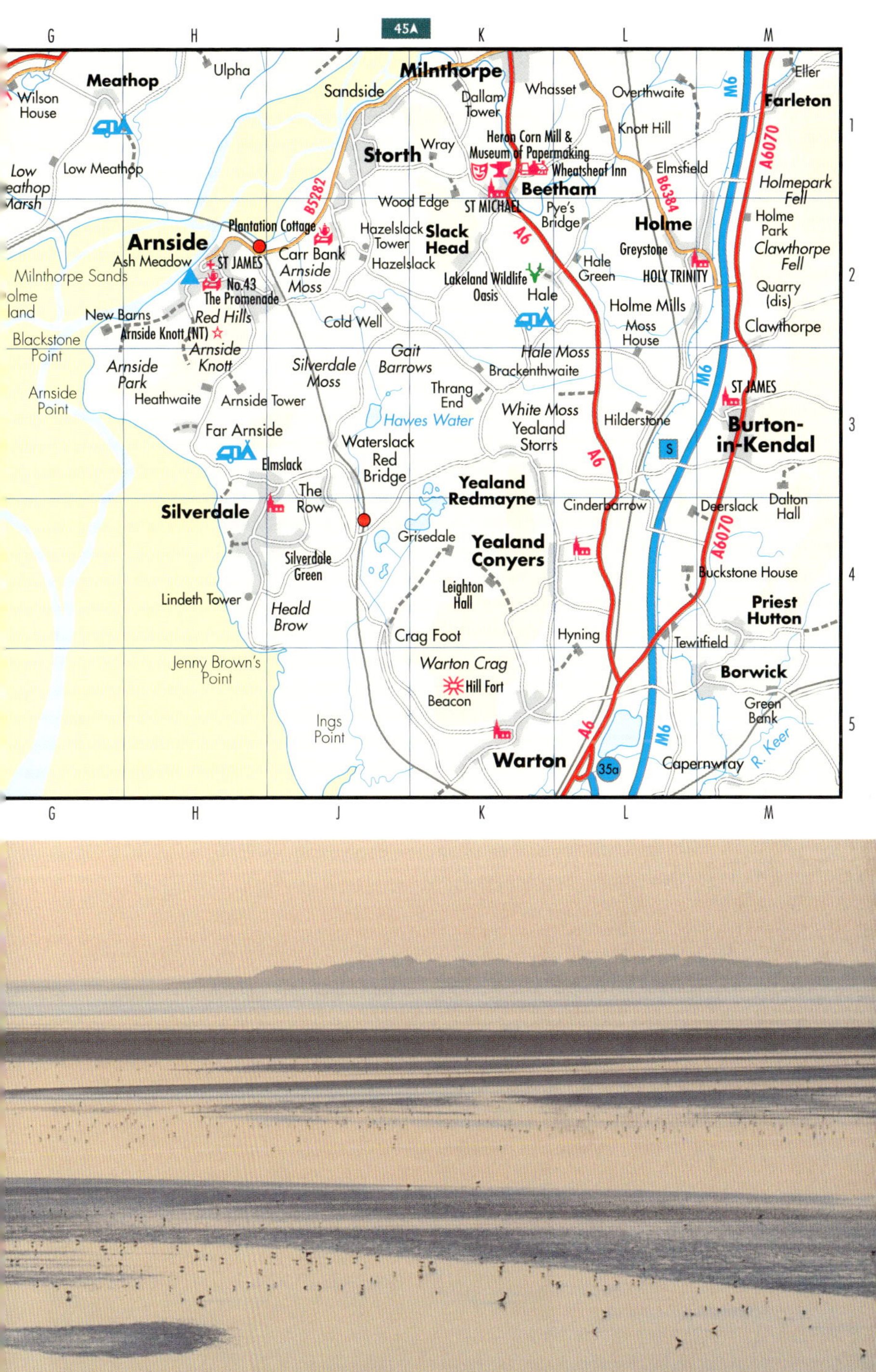

45▲
G   H   J   K   L   M
Meathop
Wilson House
Ulpha
Sandside
Milnthorpe
Whasset
Overthwaite
Eller
M6
Farleton
Low Meathop Marsh
Low Meathop
Storth
Wray
Dallam Tower
Knott Hill
A6070
B5282
Heron Corn Mill & Museum of Papermaking
Wheatsheaf Inn
Elmsfield
Holmepark Fell
Plantation Cottage
Wood Edge
ST MICHAEL
Beetham
B6384
Holme
Holme Park
Arnside
Ash Meadow
ST JAMES
Carr Bank
Hazelslack Tower
Slack Head
Pye's Bridge
A6
Greystone
Clawthorpe Fell
Milnthorpe Sands
No.43
The Promenade
Arnside Moss
Hazelslack
HOLY TRINITY
Holme Mills
Quarry (dis)
Holme land
Red Hills
Lakeland Wildlife Oasis
Hale Green
Clawthorpe
Blackstone Point
New Barns
Arnside Knott (NT) ☆
Cold Well
Hale
Moss House
Arnside Park
Arnside Knott
Gait Barrows
Hale Moss
Arnside Point
Heathwaite
Arnside Tower
Silverdale Moss
Brackenthwaite
ST JAMES
Far Arnside
Hawes Water
Thrang End
White Moss
Hilderstone
Burton-in-Kendal
Elmslack
Waterslack Red Bridge
Yealand Storrs
A6
Deerslack
Dalton Hall
Silverdale
The Row
Yealand Redmayne
Cinderbarrow
M6
Buckstone House
Silverdale Green
Grisedale
Yealand Conyers
Priest Hutton
Lindeth Tower
Heald Brow
Leighton Hall
Hyning
Tewitfield
Borwick
Jenny Brown's Point
Crag Foot
Warton Crag
Hill Fort
Beacon
Green Bank
Ings Point
Warton
A6
35a
Capernwray
R. Keer
G   H   J   K   L   M
Duddon Sands

Railway Viaduct, Arnside

ARNSIDE

When shrimps were abundant on the sand flats of Morecambe Bay, Arnside was a thriving little fishing port. That industry has faded and with the coming of the railways the early Victorian visitors arrived and the village became a seaside resort. The villas look out upon the beautiful Kent Estuary and the long, thin viaduct carries the Carnforth to Barrow railway. The more affluent built larger houses on the hillside to the south. You can walk or drive up to Arnside Knott for a spectacular, panoramic view of the Lakeland fells to the Pennines. (H2)

Where to Stay...

No 43, The Promenade.
Lesley Hornsby describes her venture as a boutique guesthouse. It is chic and smart with comfortable contemporary furnishings. She prides herself on her breakfasts with ingredients from local suppliers. But, call me old fashioned, it's the view you'll remember, with the sun at dusk over the Kent estuary. (H2) 01524 762761 www.no43.org.uk

Plantation Cottage, Arnside Road, Sandside. Set evenly between Sandside and Arnside behind a large garden overlooking the estuary. Your hosts are keen horsemen and have been in the horse racing/training business all their lives. Their home is decorated with memorabilia from their courageous past. Comfy bedrooms. (J2) 01524 762069

Special Places to Visit...

Arnside Knott (NT). It's the views that go on and on across the Kent estuary and the best time is sunset. Don't forget your tripod (and camera). (H3)

Lakeland Wildlife Oasis.
A wildlife centre, home to a range of exotic animals from sealife to monkeys and various endangered species. Hands-on displays for the adventurous. Café/gift shop. Open daily 10-5 (4 in winter). (K2) 015395 63027. www.wildlifeoasis.co.uk

CARTMEL

One of the most popular villages in the Southern Lakes. There is an attractive openness about it, and it's easy to walk around in about twenty minutes. There are some fine C17 and C18 buildings, and pretty cottages huddle around the square. You won't go thirsty or hungry because there's a binful of tearooms and inns, and of course the finest restaurant in this part of the world, the Michelin starred "L'enclume". Art galleries and antique emporia are moving in to take advantage of the new market. If you feel in need of meditation, solitude, prayer or intellectual stimulation then you must visit the Priory Church of St Mary & St Michael. Arguably, the most interesting church in Cumbria. Don't miss the tiny Race Course, maybe the smallest in the country. (E2)

Iguana, Lakeland Wildlfe Oasis ss

| 11,000 BC | Ice sheets melt | 6,000 BC | Langdale Axe Factory started |
| 8,000 BC | Mesolithic hunter-gatherers settle in coastal areas. | 1400-3200 BC | Castlerigg Stone Circle erected |

This church is of great interest and is Cumbria's greatest medieval parish church. The building is massive, and cruciform in shape, and has some late C12 original features with C15 Perpendicular windows. The Renaissance screens are simply magnificent. Note the detail of the carved misericords below in the choir stalls. The stained glass is varied; the great East window has three remaining central panels. Just imagine what it was like when fully in situ. Don't miss the recently restored medieval glass panels in the Piper Choir. C14 Harington monuments. Of more recent interest, some modern sculptures by Josefina de Vasconcellos. And, look out for the curling snake in the South Porch (D2)

Cartmel Gallery, The Square.
A gallery with a personal touch displaying a fine collection of contemporary British design: glass, jewellery, sculpture etc. More than half their artists are Cumbrian. Open Tu-Su 10.30-5. (E2) 01539 536881
www.cartmelgallery.co.uk

Cartmel Priory Gatehouse
(NT). The gatehouse to the C12 Augustinian priory that was fortified after raids by Robert the Bruce. Open daily East-Oct except M & Tu, & winter W/Es, 10-4. (E2)
01524 701178
www.nationaltrust.org.uk

Cartmel Village Shop, The Square. Home of the famous Sticky Toffee Pudding and one of Rick Stein's food heroes. Deli and wine store, and home baked bread. Sandwiches and pastries. Open M-Sa 9-5, Su 10.30-4.30. 015395 36280

Flookburgh (or Fluke-Town).
Formerly the centre of a thriving shrimp industry. The shrimp were cultivated and fished in the shallow waters of Morecambe Bay using tractors and nets. The cockle was another form of seafood farmed here but that industry was decimated by two hard winters in the 1960s, and by the arrival of the oyster-catcher. Flat fish called flukes were also caught by using stake nets during the seasons Oct-Dec, and Apr-May. Hence, the local name, Fluke-Town.

GRANGE-OVER-SANDS

A small, civilised resort overlooking the treacherous tidal flats of Morecambe Bay. The town has a holiday atmosphere but has recently suffered from cheap foreign travel to Spain and Florida. It is a suntrap and is popular with golfers and the retired. The town attracted a great boost to its popularity when the rail link was developed in 1857. A move staunchly opposed by Wordsworth and Ruskin. The mild climate encourages the growth of alpine flowers, shrubs and sub-tropical flowers. The estuary flats are popular resting and breeding grounds for sea birds. The beaches are sandy but swimming is not to be encouraged due to the strong

Cartmel Gallery ss

currents in the estuary. Golf may be a better bet if you have brought your clubs. For the more adventurous it is worth joining one of the guided walks across the sands, and perhaps follow the route developed by the Romans. (F2)

Special Places to Visit...

Artcrystal, 2a Imperial Buildings, Main Street. Patrick McMahon is a unique kind of guy who has plied his trade since 1983. He engraves intricate designs and illustrations on to crystal glass. Watch him at work. Open Tu-Sa 9-5. (F2) 01539 535656 www.artcrystal.co.uk

Holker Hall & Gardens. This is without doubt Cumbria's premier stately home. It is the home of the Cavendish family (of Chatsworth fame) who have lived here for 400 years and is a Chatsworth in miniature. From the outside the Hall cannot be described as an aesthetic gem. It is to the interior and the award-winning gardens that one's eye is drawn. The Hall has some magnificent rooms: the Library, the Gallery, the Drawing Room and various bedrooms, all sumptuously decorated and furnished with antiques, portraits and exquisite wallpaper. The original building was built in the C16 by the Preston family and was passed down the family line: Preston - Lowther -Cavendish. Each generation has left its mark but it was not until after the disastrous fire in 1871 that the incumbent, the 7th Duke of Devonshire, took on the task of rebuilding the west wing and upgrading the overall look of the building. Pevsner describes it as the finest Elizabethan gothic in the north of England.The gardens are an absolute delight. The Cavendish ancestors and generations of gardeners have collected a vast variety of plants, shrubs and trees. No wonder the numerous awards. You can also wander around the Deer park, visit the Lakeland Motor Museum and get lost in the Adventure playground and picnic area. Food Hall & Gift shop. Café. Open daily except Sa, Apr-Oct from 10. (C2) 015395 58328
www.holker-hall.co.uk

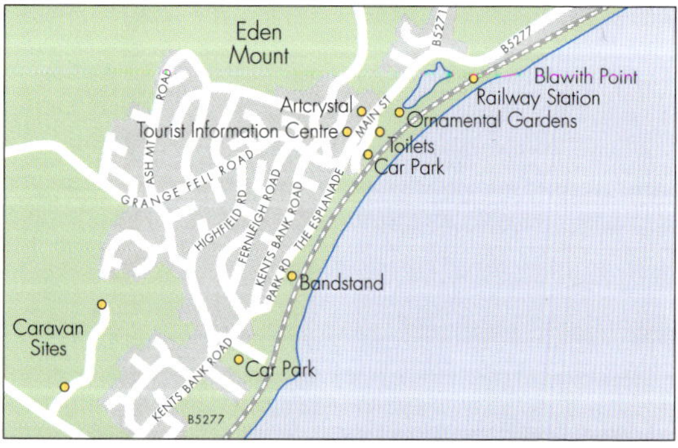

Grange-Over-Sands

71	Roman conquest of Brigantes begins		78	Romans build a fort (naval base) at Ravenglass
78	Agricola advances in Cumbria and erects garrisons between the Solway and Tyne		90	Galava Roman fort built (in today's Ambleside)
			100	Romans arrive in Eskdale and build Hardknott Fort

Lakeland Motor Museum, Holker Hall. Over 150 vintage and classic cars, motorcycles, tractors, cycles and engines. Replica of a 1920s garage. Houses the Campbell Legend Bluebird Exhibition with a full size replica of the 1935 Bluebird Car and the famous Jet Hydroplane in which Donald Campbell was killed on Coniston Water in 1967. Children's activity centre. Open daily 1Feb to 1Nov Su-F 10.30-4.45. (C2) 015395 58328 www.lakelandmotormuseum.co.uk

Special Places to Visit...

Conishead Priory, Priory Rd. Gothic mansion home to the Manjushri Kadampa Meditation Centre. New Buddhist Temple with the largest bronze Buddha statue cast in Europe. Fine plaster ceilings, stained glass and wood panelling. Garden and woodland trails. Cafe. Gift shop. Open East-Oct W/Es & BHs 2-5, M-F by appoint. Closed during summer festivals (A3) 01229 584029 www.manjushri.org

Heron Corn Mill & Museum of Papermaking. Restored working powder type corn mill. Driven by 14ft high breast shot water-wheel. Baking Gallery. The museum illustrates the past and present art of papermaking. Occasional demonstrations. Shop. Open mid-Mar to Oct Wed-Su & BHs 11-4. (K1) 015395 65027 www.heronmill.org

Where to Eat, Drink & Be Merry...

The Bay Horse Hotel & Restaurant, Canal Foot. Not every day does one drive through a massive drug plant (Glaxo) to reach a restaurant of sound reputation. Such are the unique qualities to be found at Canalfoot: an enviable reputation and wonderful views from your bedroom window. A must for all twitchers and gastronomes. (A2) 01229 583972 www.thebayhorsehotel.co.uk

SS Jaguar, Lakeland Motor Museum ss

Courtyard Café, Holker Hall. Building something of a reputation for homemade and locally produced meals. After all, they have all the tenant farmers to supply saltmarsh lamb, venison, cheeses, puddings and a lot more. 015395 58328 www.holker-hall.co.uk

L'enclume, Cartmel. Simon Rogan has established himself as one of the top 15 chefs in the UK and is one of only three Michelin Stars in Cumbria. This is the place to head for if you are looking for that singular, all food enhancing weekend. It is a restaurant with luxurious bedrooms and perhaps for the affluent gastronome the first choice destination for those wishing to be near the coast. 01539 536362 www.lenclume.co.uk

Wheatsheaf Inn at Beetham. A hostelry and traditional coaching inn since 1609 proudly serves up local and seasonal fare. Accommodation. (K2) 015395 62123 www.wheatsheafbeetham.com

Where to Stay...

Hill Farm, Cartmel. A charming C16 farmhouse set in its own 60 acres. The bedrooms are chintzy and comfy, the lounge is cosy with sofas and low ceilings. Panoramic views. 015395 36477 www.hillfarmbb.co.uk

Short, Easy Walks...

Arnside Knott National Trust car park. (H2) 2.5 miles/4 km. Grade is easy on tracks and bridlepath. Circular, waymarked walk around a nature reserve through woodland affording spectacular views of the Lakeland hills, Kent Estuary and Morecambe Bay.

Grange Over Sands to Cross Bay. (H2) 8 miles/15 km. First check with the Grange Tourist Information Centre who will introduce you to an official guide. The route usually goes from Arnside to Kents Bank. It is a magical route watched over by oyster catchers and sweeping ducks but only to be attempted in the summer months when accompanied by an experienced guide. Only the local experts know the safe route through the treacherous quick sands and changing tides. Do not undertake this alone, on any account.

Flookburgh car park to Humphrey Head. (D3) 6 miles/10 km (there & back). An easy walk along country lanes and paths to a popular viewpoint delivering a fine panorama across Morecambe Bay. Half way from Flookburgh, look to your left up lane to the 800 year old Wraysholme Tower. Soon it's a gentle climb up to the bird reserve and Point.

Arnside Promenade to Silverdale. (H2) 4 miles/7 km. An easy stroll along the coastal path taking in tarmac roads and paths through woodland. This linear route follows waymarked signs all the way to Silverdale and affords you fine seaward views. There is a possible extension of the walk by 1.5 miles to the National Trust reserve of Jenny Brown's Point.

BARROW-IN-FURNESS, MILLOM, ULVERSTON

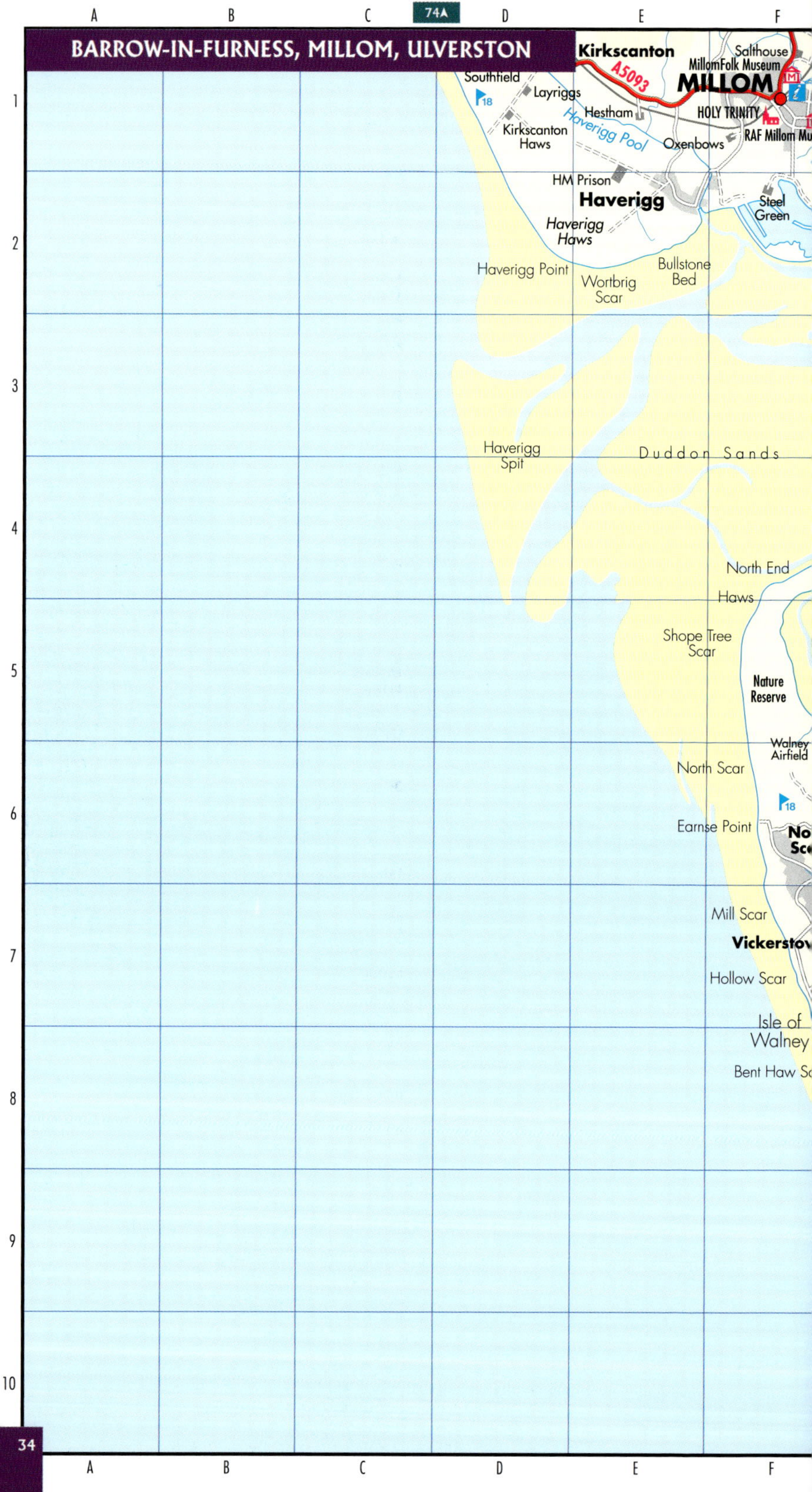

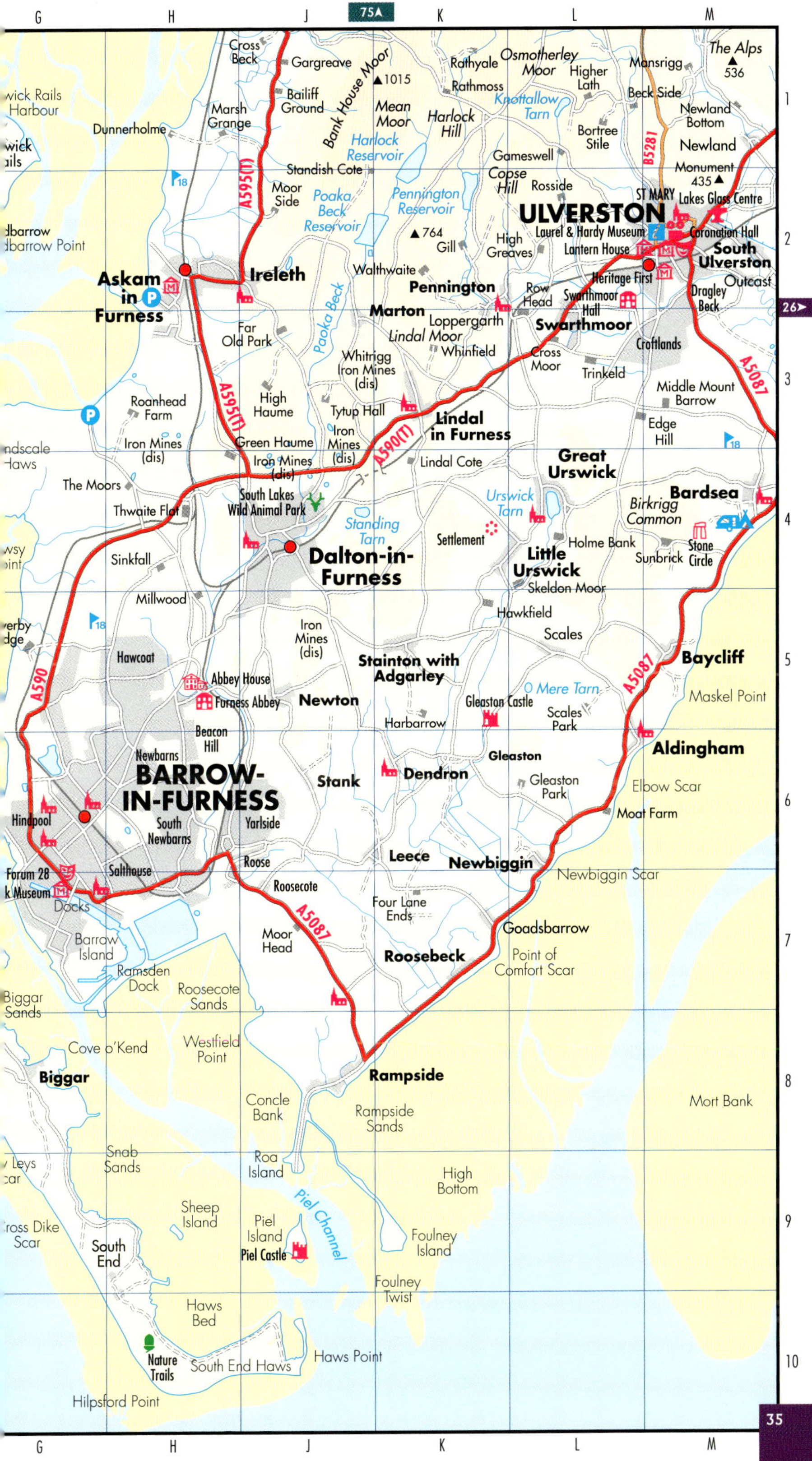
75▲
G H J K L M
Cross Beck
Gargreave
Bank House Moor
▲1015
Rathyale
Osmotherley Moor
Higher Lath
Mansrigg
The Alps
▲536
wick Rails Harbour
Bailiff Ground
Marsh Grange
Mean Moor
Rathmoss
Knottallow Tarn
Beck Side
Newland Bottom
wick ails
Dunnerholme
Harlock Reservoir
Harlock Hill
Bortree Stile
Newland
18
Standish Cote
Gameswell
B5281
Monument 435 ▲
dbarrow
A595(T)
Moor Side
Poaka Beck Reservoir
Pennington Reservoir
Copse Hill
Rosside
ULVERSTON
St MARY
Lakes Glass Centre
dbarrow Point
Ireleth
▲764 Gill
High Greaves
Laurel & Hardy Museum
Coronation Hall
Askam in Furness
P
Walthwaite
Pennington
Row Head
Lantern House
South Ulverston
Marton
Swarthmoor Hall
Heritage First
Dragley Beck
Far Old Park
Loppergarth
Lindal Moor
Whinfield
Swarthmoor
Outcast
Croftlands
A5087
A595(T)
Roanhead Farm
High Haume
Whitrigg Iron Mines (dis)
Tytup Hall
Cross Moor
Trinkeld
Middle Mount Barrow
P
Iron Mines (dis)
Green Haume
Iron Mines (dis)
A590(T)
Lindal in Furness
Edge Hill
18
ndscale Haws
Iron Mines (dis)
Lindal Cote
Great Urswick
The Moors
Thwaite Flat
South Lakes Wild Animal Park
Standing Tarn
Urswick Tarn
Birkrigg Common
Bardsea
wsy int
Settlement
Holme Bank
Stone Circle
Sinkfall
Dalton-in-Furness
Little Urswick
Sunbrick
rby dge
Millwood
Skeldon Moor
18
Iron Mines (dis)
Hawkfield
A590
Hawcoat
Abbey House
Scales
Baycliff
Abbey House
Furness Abbey
Newton
Stainton with Adgarley
Mere Tarn
A5087
Maskel Point
Beacon Hill
Gleaston Castle
Scales Park
Newbarns
BARROW-IN-FURNESS
Stank
Harbarrow
Gleaston
Aldingham
Hindpool
South Newbarns
Dendron
Gleaston Park
Elbow Scar
Yarslide
Moat Farm
Forum 28
Salthouse
Roose
Leece
Newbiggin
Newbiggin Scar
k Museum
Roosecote
Goadsbarrow
Docks
A5087
Four Lane Ends
Barrow Island
Moor Head
Roosebeck
Point of Comfort Scar
Ramsden Dock
Roosecote Sands
Biggar Sands
Cove o'Kend
Westfield Point
Rampside
Mort Bank
Biggar
Concle Bank
Rampside Sands
Leys car
Snab Sands
Roa Island
High Bottom
ross Dike Scar
Sheep Island
Piel Island
Piel Channel
Foulney Island
South End
Piel Castle
Foulney Twist
Haws Bed
Nature Trails
South End Haws
Haws Point
Hilpsford Point
G H J K L M
35

Barrow in Furness, The Dock Museum

BARROW-IN-FURNESS

The name conjures up a vision of heavy industry: filth and smog, steel mills and men with blackened faces dressed in torn clothes stoking giant furnaces. This image is long gone. Barrow was an important C19 port, and exporter of iron ore. In the late C19 under the stewardship of Vickers it was the major shipbuilding centre of the world. The town was prosperous and the elders developed a model town with long, wide, tree-lined streets. The larger buildings were built by James Ramsden, and in Duke Street stands his magnificent Victorian Town Hall. Just off the main streets are rows of neat terraced houses built for the shipyard workers. On the north side of the town within the grounds of Furness Abbey (and on your left hand side, if you arrive by car on the A590) stands The Abbey Hotel designed by Lutyens for the Vickers Board to entertain visiting dignitaries and their potential clients: King George V, The Prince of Wales and the Queen Mother. Today, BAE Systems are the main employer and their massive silos hide the manufacture of nuclear submarines and modern ordnance. The town lies close to the nature reserves, estuary and sea. The added advantage of living in Barrow is the close proximity to Lakeland. For those with an interest in nature and the outdoors it provides a high standard of living. When the order book is full the town takes on an air of humble enthusiasm. Cross the bridge to Walney Island and enter the nature reserve teeming with eider ducks. Beyond that stretches a 12 mile long beach backed by sand dunes. (H6) www.furness.co.uk

Special Places to Visit...

Dock Museum. Discover the history of Barrow-in-Furness, from its beginnings as a small boatyard to its growth as a major industrial power through its Steelworks, Furness Railway and shipyards. Widescreen film show. Coffee shop. Large play area outside. Open daily except Mon Easter to Oct 10-5, Nov to Easter W-F 10.30-4, W/E 11-4.30. (G7) 01229 876400 www.dockmuseum.org.uk

Piel Island. Just the place if you seek solitude, nature and wild birds. (J9)

DALTON-IN-FURNESS.

Former Capital of Furness. The monks from the abbey used to hold court here in the Castle, later to be used as a prison and court house. The birthplace of George Romney, the famous portrait painter. (J4) www.dalton-in-furness.org.uk

Special Places to Visit...

South Lakes Wild Animal Park. Tiger conservation centre plus lemurs, kangaroos, rhinos, giraffes, apes and monkeys. Open daily, all year from 10. (J4) 01229 466086 www.wildanimalpark.co.uk

Where to Stay...

Abbey House Hotel, Abbey Road. This great house was built by an industrialist of style, vision and hospitality. Commander Craven was the Chairman of Vickers Shipbuilding and he commissioned Sir Edwin Lutyens in 1914 to build him a home where he could entertain his potential customers. For all students and lovers of architecture this is a place not to be missed. (H5) 01229 838282 www.abbeyhousehotel.com

Abbey House Hotel, Barrow

410 Official end of Roman Britain, Coel Hen takes over as High King of Northern Britain	450 Ceneu dies; Rheged created by Gwrast Lledlwm
420 Coel Hen dies, Ceneu takes over Northern Britain	490 Gwrast Lledlwm dies; Rheged given to Merchion Gul

WHITE ROSE.

Furness Abbey (EH). The red sandstone ruin of a once prosperous Cistercian abbey sits peacefully beside a wooded combe. Founded by King Stephen in 1123 and originally of the Savigniac Order later passing to the Cistercians in 1147. It became the second most powerful abbey in England but was forever involved in inter border disputes with the Scots and was sacked by Robert Bruce in 1322 with pillaging continuing until about 1346. Its end came in 1537 when Henry VIII dissolved the monasteries and had all its roof tiles removed. A little museum displays gargoyles and knights' tombs. Open daily 10-5, winter (Oct-Mar) weekends 10-4. (H5) 01229 823420 www.english-heritage.org.uk

Sandscale Dunes

ULVERSTON

Former port and market centre with narrow cobbled streets. It is today a Free Trade Town inhabited by forward thinkers. A place for conversation and debate in the many cafes, and once the home of John Barrow who did so much to expand exploration in the C19. Th & Sa market. (L2)

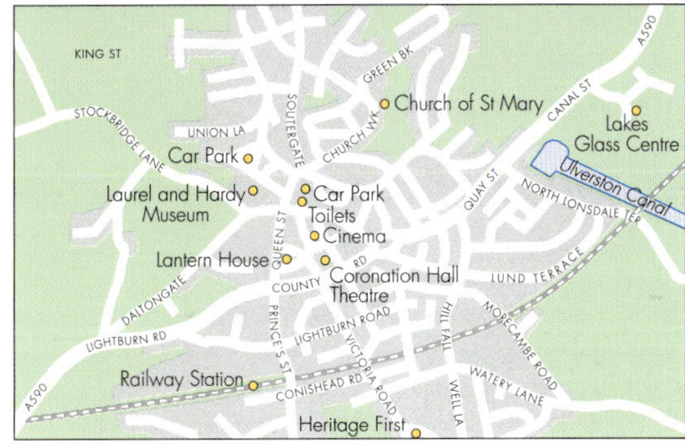

Ulverston

Special Places to Visit...

Colony Country Store.
Leading candle manufacturer, and largest producer of scented candles in Europe. See the traditional craft of candle making. Shop. (L2) 01229 461111 www.colony.com

Lakes Glass Centre, Oubas Hill.
Combination of Cumbria Crystal and Heron Glass. A showcase of master craftsmen. Factory viewing. Exhibition and shop. Coffee shop/Restaurant. Open daily, M-Sa 9-5, Su shop only 10-4.30. (L2) 01229 581385

Lantern House International.
Art organisation producing performing arts, film, dance and plays, plus exhibitions (in Cruck Barn and gallery) to challenge social and environmental issues. Teashop and garden. (L2) 01229 581127 www.lanternhouse.org

Laurel & Hardy Museum, 4c Upper Brook St. Large collection of memorabilia, personal items and photos. Continuous film shows in the town where Stan Laurel was born on 16th June 1890. Open daily Feb-Dec 10-4.30. (L2) 01229 582292 www.laurel-and-hardy-museum.co.uk

Swarthmoor Hall. The home of Judge Thomas and Margaret Fell who in 1652 welcomed George Fox (the founder of Quakerism). It later became the powerhouse of Quaker belief. For on the death of her husband, Margaret became the wife of George Fox. Fine example of an Elizabethan manor house built in 1586, and furnished in the early C17 period. B&B and three self catering apartments. Open all year Tu-F for guided tours around the six historic rooms at 2.30 pm. (L2) 01229 583204 www.swarthmoorhall.co.uk

Heritage First, Lower Brook St. From the Romans to the Domesday Book, from the C18 Canal to the present day. Open all year M-Sa 9.30-4.30 (closed W Xmas-whit). (L2) www.rootsweb.com

Short Easy Walks...

Sandscale Dunes & Beach Car Park. (G3) Popular with local dog walkers. You can walk as far as you like and wander about through the dunes or onto the flat beach and look across the estuary to the distant, Lakeland hills.

Isle of Walney. (H7) A flat promontory with nature reserve, bird sanctuary and sand dunes. The beach is popular with kite surfers. Ornithologists like the isolation. For walkers who like a long beach with a distant horizon, none better. Choose your own spot.

For Lake cruises, Country House hotels, Beatrix Potter, sailing and fine cuisine.

The railway has brought millions of visitors to the shores of Lake Windermere. Yet, one wonders how many have ventured beyond Bowness and Windermere to climb the low fells of southern Lakeland, or perhaps to bathe in the solitude of Coniston Water and walk in the steps of the eminent Victorian philosopher, John Ruskin.

This is an area rich in history and literary endeavour. King Edward III brought the Flemish to Kendal to develop the medieval woollen industry. William Wordsworth was educated in Hawkshead, John Ruskin retired to Brantwood overlooking Coniston Water and Beatrix Potter spent much of her life at Near Sawrey, a short distance from Lake Windermere.

The landscape is gentler than its northern neighbours and more temperate with rolling, undulating fells kinder to the less ambitious walker. And, should you chose to celebrate following a day on the fells, the area is rich in hostelries and Country House hotels.

Steam Yacht Gondola

CONISTON, KENDAL, WINDERMERE
84

Coniston
Kendal
Windermere
Hawkshead
Hawkshead Hill
B5285
High Cross
Highfield
Hawkshead Grammar School Museum
Roger Ground
Court House (NT)
Belmount
Beatrix Potter Gallery
Gillbank
Colthouse
Town End
t Gate
Letterbarrow
803
Belle Grange
Long Height
Three Dubs Crags
Red Nab
Millerground Landing
Miller Howe
Jericho at the Waverley
WINDERMERE
ST MARY

Far End
Fells Low Yewdale
Hill Fell
High Water Head
Hollin Bank
CONISTON
ST ANDREW
Ruskin Museum
Steam Yacht Gondola (NT)
Blue Bird Café
Bank Ground
How Head
Esthwaite Lodge
High Man
Wise Een Tarn
Moss Eccles Tarn
Lake Bank
Three Dubs Tarn
Claife Heights
Old Laundry Theatre
Hole in the Wall
BOWNESS-ON-WINDERMERE
Howbeck
The World of Beatrix Potter
ST MARTIN
The Fairfield
Bowness Bay Boating (Explore Windermere)

Bowmanstead
Haws Bank
Thurston
Monk Coniston Moor
Hawkshead Moor
Beechmount Country House Hotel
B26
Near Sawrey
West Vale
Harrowslack
Belle Isle
Low Fell
Low H
Ferney Green

Jumping Jenny
Brantwood
Lawson Park
Grizedale Arts
Matchell Coppice
Grizedale Forest
Tower Bank Arms
Hill Top (NT)
(Beatrix Potter's Cottage)
Far Sawrey
Claiffe
The Ferry
High Cunsey
Linthwaite House Hotel
Lindeth

Coniston Water
Heald Brow Pasture
Grizedale Forest Park & Visitor Centre
Grizedale
Theatre In The Forest
Forest Sculpture
782
Great Intake
Grizedale Tarn
Out Dubs Tarn
Eel House
Cunsey Beck
Storr's
Blackwell
A5074
Bellman Ground
B5360

The Park
High Birk
Scale Green
Parkmoor
1091
798
Satterthwaite
Studio Artist
675
Breasty Haw
High Dale Park
864
Middle Dale Park
Low Cunsey Farm
Holme Well
Ling Holm
Beech Hill Hotel
Rosthwaite
Birket House
Gill Head
Lowhouse Beck
Winster
HO TRIN

Grass Paddocks
Long Crags
Great Knott
Force Mills
Crag
Low Dale Park
Thwaite Head Fell
Graythwaite Hall
Low Graythwaite Hall
Field Head
Burrow House
Long Tongue
Moor How
Ludder Burn
Hart Barrow
Bryan Beck
Barkbo

Bethecar Moor
Cairn
High Bethecar
Low Bethecar
Ickenthwaite
Ash Slacks
Force Forge
Thwaite Head
Thwaite Moss
Roger Ridding
Rawlinson's Intake
Blake Holme Plantation
Strawberry Bank
Bowlan Bridg

Stock
Furness Fells
White Stock Hall
Rusland
Crosslands
745
Great Green Hows
The Brows
High Dam
Windermere
Gummer's How
1054
Light Wood
Heights
Burblethwait Hall
Raven Barrow

Abbot Park
Side House
Hill Park
Hulleter
Skinner Pastures
Rusland Heights
791
Finsthwaite Heights
Finsthwaite
Stott Park Bobbin Mill (EH)
High Stott Park
Town Head
Cartmel Fe
Sow How
Foxfield

Oxen Park
Haybridge Nature Reserve
Yew Barrow
Boretree Tarn
The Knoll
Lake Side
Aquarium of the Lakes
Tower
Fell Foot Park (NT)
Thorphin Hall

559
Colton
Bouth
Croaks
795
Ellerside Spire
Town End
LAKESIDE & HAVERTHWAITE RAILWAY
Line Riggs
Staveley-in-Cartmel
Simpson Ground
High Tarn Head
Low Tarn Green

Spark Bridge
Ridding Side
Elinghearth
Bouth Fall Stile
Abbots Reading
Newby Bridge
Canny Hill
White Stone Enclosure
Hare Hill
Barrow Hollin

Lane Head
Tottlebank
Ireland Moss
Lane End
Causeway End
Backbarrow
Fell Side
Hazel Rigg
Fiddler Hall
Ayside
Newton Fell
A590(T)

Hill Top
Haverthwaite
Lady Syke
Poolfoot
River Leven
Low Wood
Brow Edge
Black Beck
Oak Head
Seatle
Barber Green
High Newton

Penny Bridge
Greenodd
Fish House Moss
Bigland Hall Equestrian
Bigland Tarn
High Cark
Nether Newton
Sun Gre
Buck Crag

Smithy Green
Toppin Rays
Deer Dike Moss
Mearness Farm
B5278
Burn Barrow Wood
Grassgarth
Green Hurst
Sturdys
Field Broughton
Elle How

Arrad Foot
Newland Beck
Mearness Point
Greenodd Sands
Nab Point
Stribers Moss
High Frith
Stribers
Speel Bank
High Gate Side
Wood Broughton
Broughton Lodge
Lindale
Cas Hea

Plumpton Cottage Farm
Hazelhurst Point
Ashes Point
Green Hills
Frith Hall
Low Frith
White Moss
Ellerside
Over Ridge
Burns's Farm
Beck Side
Garret House
Green Bank
Hampsfield
Longlands Farm
Marlewood

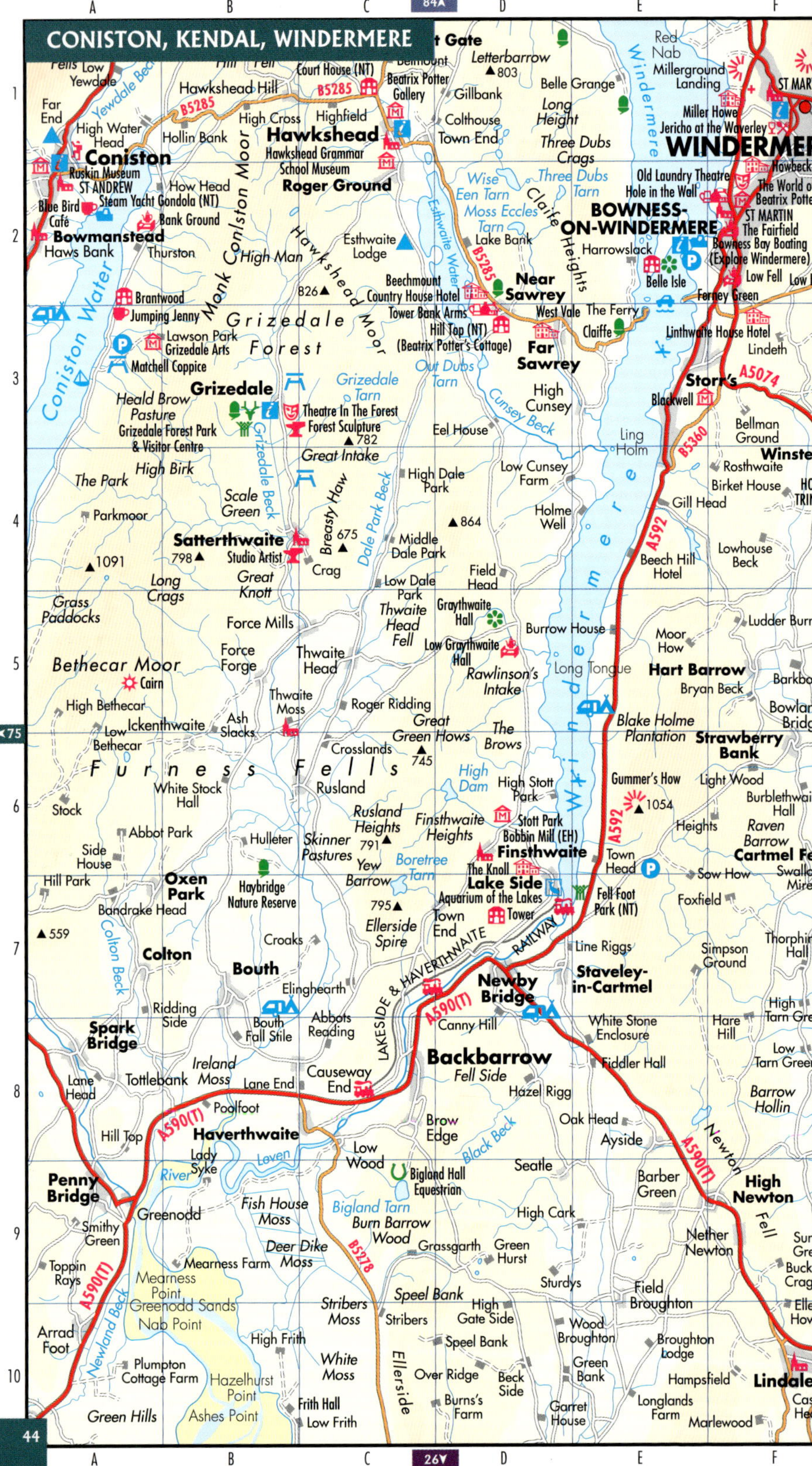

44
26

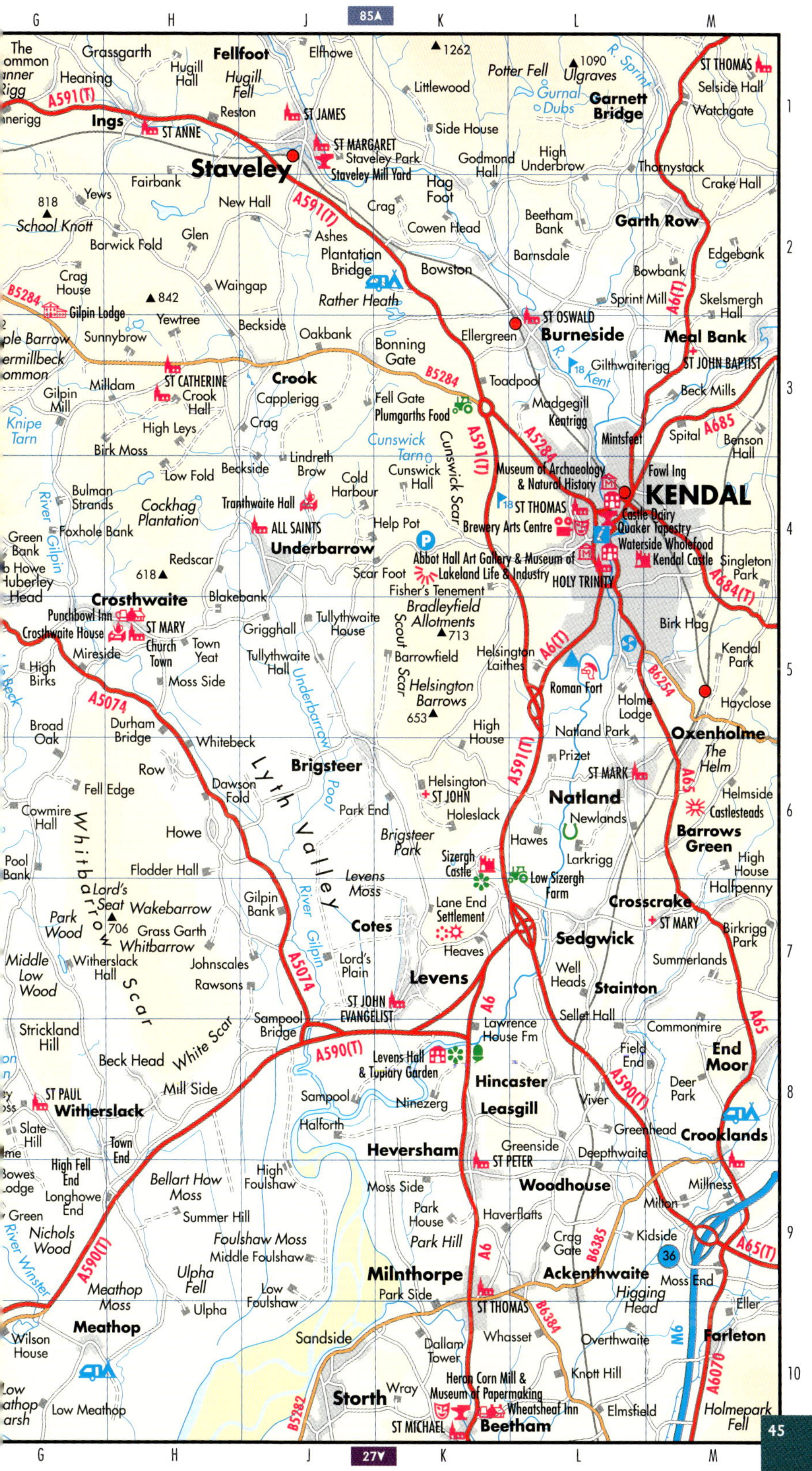
85A
G
H
J
K
L
M

The Common
Inner Rigg
enerigg
Grassgarth
Heaning
A591(T)
Ings
ST ANNE
Staveley
Fairbank
Hugill Hall
Fellfoot
Hugill Fell
Reston
ST JAMES
Elfhowe
1262
ST MARGARET
Staveley Park
Staveley Mill Yard
Side House
Potter Fell
Ulgraves
1090
R. Sprint
Gurnal Dubs
Garnett Bridge
ST THOMAS
Selside Hall
Watchgate
1

Yews
818
School Knott
Borwick Fold
New Hall
Glen
Crag
Hag Foot
Cowen Head
Godmond Hall
High Underbrow
Thornystack
Crake Hall
Garth Row
Beetham Bank
Barnsdale
Bowbank
Edgebank
2

B5284
Crag House
842
Waingap
Yewtree
Plantation Bridge
Ashes
Bowston
Rather Heath
Sprint Mill
A6(T)
Skelsmergh Hall

Gilpin Lodge
ple Barrow
ermillbeck ommon
Sunnybrow
Beckside
Oakbank
Bonning Gate
B5284
Toadpool
ST OSWALD
Ellergreen
Burneside
Gilthwaiterigg
ST JOHN BAPTIST
Meal Bank
Beck Mills
A685
3

Knipe Tarn
Gilpin Mill
Milldam
ST CATHERINE
Crook Hall
Crook
Capplerigg
Crag
Fell Gate
Plumgarths Food
Madgegill
Kentrigg
R. Kent
18
Mintsfeet
Spital
Benson Hall
A6

Green Bank
b Howe
uberley Head
High Leys
Birk Moss
Low Fold
Beckside
Lindreth Brow
Cold Harbour
Cunswick Tarn
Cunswick Hall
Cunswick Scar
Museum of Archaeology & Natural History
Fowl Ing
KENDAL
4

Bulman Strands
Foxhole Bank
Cockhag Plantation
Tranthwaite Hall
ALL SAINTS
Help Pot
18
ST THOMAS
Brewery Arts Centre
Castle Dairy
Quaker Tapestry
Waterside Wholefood

Crosthwaite
Redscar
Blakebank
Underbarrow
Scar Foot
Fisher's Tenement
Abbot Hall Art Gallery & Museum of Lakeland Life & Industry
HOLY TRINITY
Kendal Castle
Singleton Park
A684(T)

618
Punchbowl Inn
Crosthwaite House
ST MARY
Church Town
Town Yeat
Grigghall
Tullythwaite House
Bradleyfield Allotments
713
Scout Scar
Helsington Laithes
Roman Fort
Holme Lodge
Birk Hag
Kendal Park
5

Mireside
High Birks
Church Town
Moss Side
Tullythwaite Hall
Barrowfield
Helsington Barrows
653
Natland Park
B6254
Hayclose
Oxenholme

A5074
Broad Oak
Durham Bridge
Whitebeck
Brigsteer
High House
Prizet
ST MARK
The Helm
Helmside
6

Cowmire Hall
Fell Edge
Row
Dawson Fold
Lyth Valley
Pool
Helsington
ST JOHN
Holeslack
Natland
Newlands
Castlesteads
Barrows Green
High House
Halfpenny

Pool Bank
Lord's Seat
Wakebarrow
Howe
Flodder Hall
Gilpin Bank
River Gilpin
Brigsteer Park
Park End
Hawes
Larkrigg
Sizergh Castle
Low Sizergh Farm
Crosscrake
ST MARY
Birkrigg Park
7

Park Wood
706
Grass Garth
Whitbarrow
Whitbarrow Scar
Johnscales
Rawsons
Levens Moss
Cotes
Lord's Plain
Lane End Settlement
Heaves
Levens
Sedgwick
Well Heads
Stainton
Summerlands
High House

Middle Low Wood
Witherslack Hall
A5074
Sampool Bridge
ST JOHN EVANGELIST
Lawrence House Fm
A6
A590(T)
Sellet Hall
Commonmire
End Moor
A65

Strickland Hill
ST PAUL
Witherslack
Beck Head
White Scar
Mill Side
Sampool
Levens Hall & Topiary Garden
Ninezerg
Hincaster
Field End
Deer Park
8

Slate Hill
me
Bowes odge
Town End
High Fell End
Longhowe End
Halforth
Heversham
Leasgill
Greenside
ST PETER
Viver
Deepthwaite
Greenhead
Crooklands

Green
Nichols Wood
A590(T)
Bellart How Moss
Summer Hill
High Foulshaw
Moss Side
Park House
Woodhouse
Haverflatts
Milton
Millness
9

River Winster
Meathop Moss
Foulshaw Moss
Middle Foulshaw
Ulpha Fell
Low Foulshaw
Milnthorpe
Park Side
Crag Gate
B6385
Ackenthwaite
Higging Head
36
Moss End
Eller
B6384

Meathop
Wilson House
Ulpha
ST THOMAS
Whasset
Overthwaite
M6
Farleton
A6070

Low athop arsh
Sandside
Dallam Tower
Knott Hill
Elmsfield
Holmepark Fell

Low Meathop
Wray
Storth
Heron Corn Mill & Museum of Papermaking
Wheatsheaf Inn
ST MICHAEL
Beetham
B5282
B6384
A65(T)

27
45

Bowness on Windermere

BOWNESS & WINDERMERE

Originally known as Bulness and Birthwaite respectively. These two towns are today considered as one. The town's prosperity gathered pace with the arrival of the railways in 1848. William Wordsworth forecast the multitudes of visitors, but tried and failed to halt the railway. The cotton barons and nouveau riche of Lancashire built enormous Italianate and Gothic mansions besides the shores of Windermere. Today, many are hotels. In summer, the railway delivers thousands of day visitors, and the town takes on a seaside atmosphere. Bowness is where you can hop on a Steamer and view the lake from amidships. You can also hire a rowing boat. It may appear to be bedlam but with a short skip and jump you can be on your own, striking forth across the fells with not a tourist in sight. (F2)

Special Places to Visit...

Blackwell (The Arts & Crafts House). This is considered to be Britain's finest surviving Arts & Crafts house designed by Mackay Hugh Baillie Scott. The elegant interiors are complemented by original features and period furniture, all designed to create a work of harmony. The gardens comprise a series of terraces which look out upon fabulous views. The Arts & Crafts movement was championed by William Morris and John Ruskin, and was largely centred around the Cotswolds. The movement was a reaction against poor design, mechanisation of labour and mass production. It believed the Industrial Revolution had devalued the work of the craftsman and so set about emphasising the importance of hand craftmanship in the production of affordable everyday objects. Blackwell was built for Sir Edward Holt, a wealthy Manchester brewer. Nothing was spared in creating this romantic idyll far from the smog of Victorian industrial life. Tearoom, craft and bookshop. Open daily early Feb to Dec 31, 10.30-5. (E3) 015394 46139 www.blackwell.org.uk

The World Of Beatrix Potter, Crag Brow. After an expensive revamp, it is possible to see, hear, touch and even smell the characters and places from her famous books. Open daily, all year from 10 (closed 28 Jan-8 Feb). (F2) 015394 88444 www.hop-skip-jump.com

Windermere Lake Cruises. Steamers and launches sail daily throughout the year between Ambleside, Bowness and Lakeside with all year round connections for the Aquarium of the Lakes and the World of Beatrix Potter plus main season connections for Brockhole Visitor Centre, Lakeside and Haverthwaite Steam Railway, Fell Foot Country Park, Wray Castle and Ferry House for buses to Hill Top and Hawkshead. Steamers and larger launches have licensed bars and coffee shops. Open daily from 9. (E2) 015394 43360 www.windermere-lakecruises.co.uk

Blackwell, The Arts & Crafts House

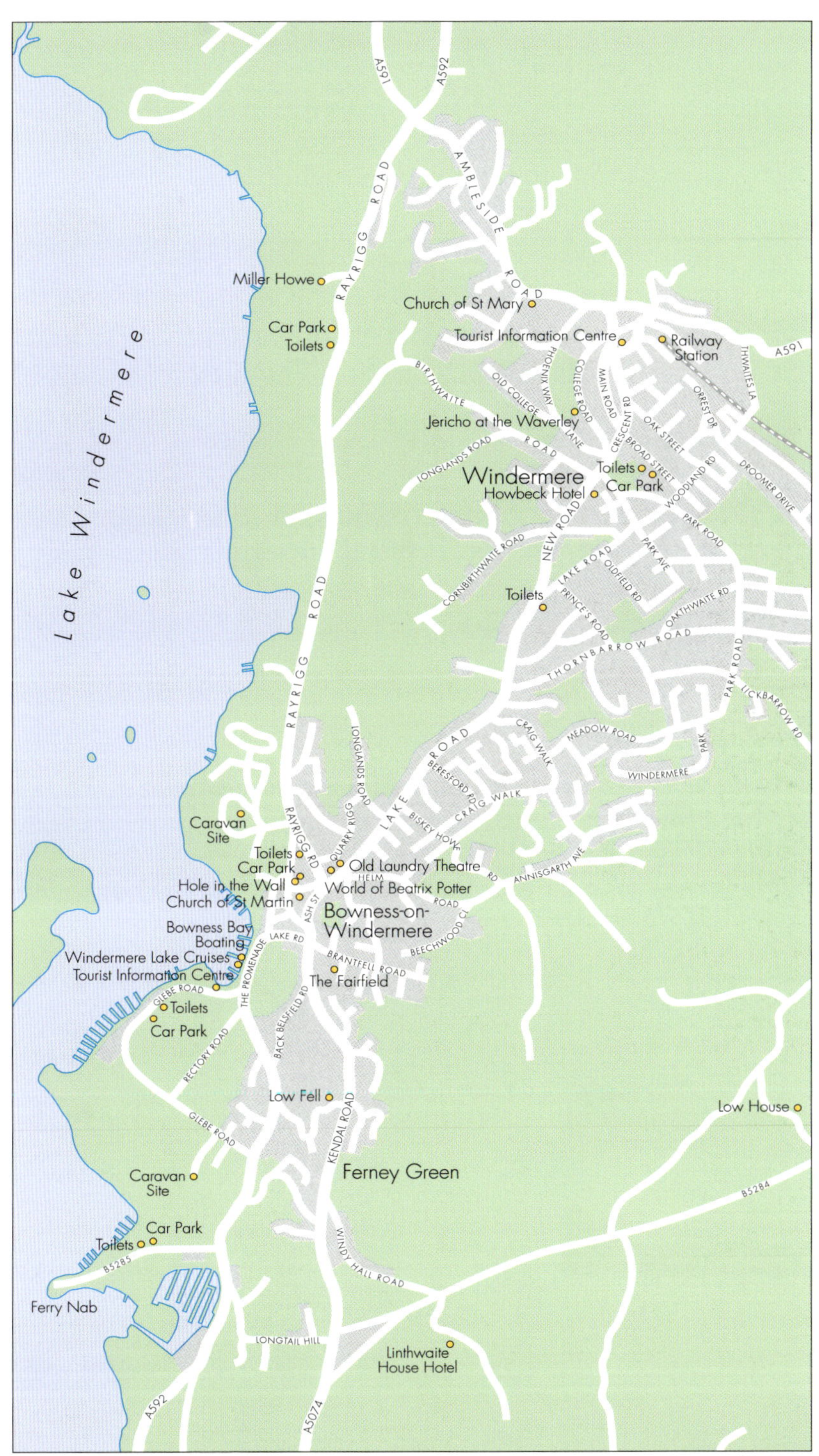

Bowness and Windermere

685	St Cuthbert granted land around Carlisle, where he founds a priory, and Cartmel and establishes a hermitage on Derwent Water's island	875	Danes sack Carlisle
		925	Norse arrive

Windermere is England's largest lake, but perhaps not the most beautiful. The northern skyline is indented with volcanic peaks, the southern shores are heavily wooded with broadleaf trees. There are splendid views from Orrest Head, Claife Heights and Brockhole. The lake can be noisy and congested with traffic although a 10mph speed limit is now in place and this has cut the numbers of craft on the water. (D9)

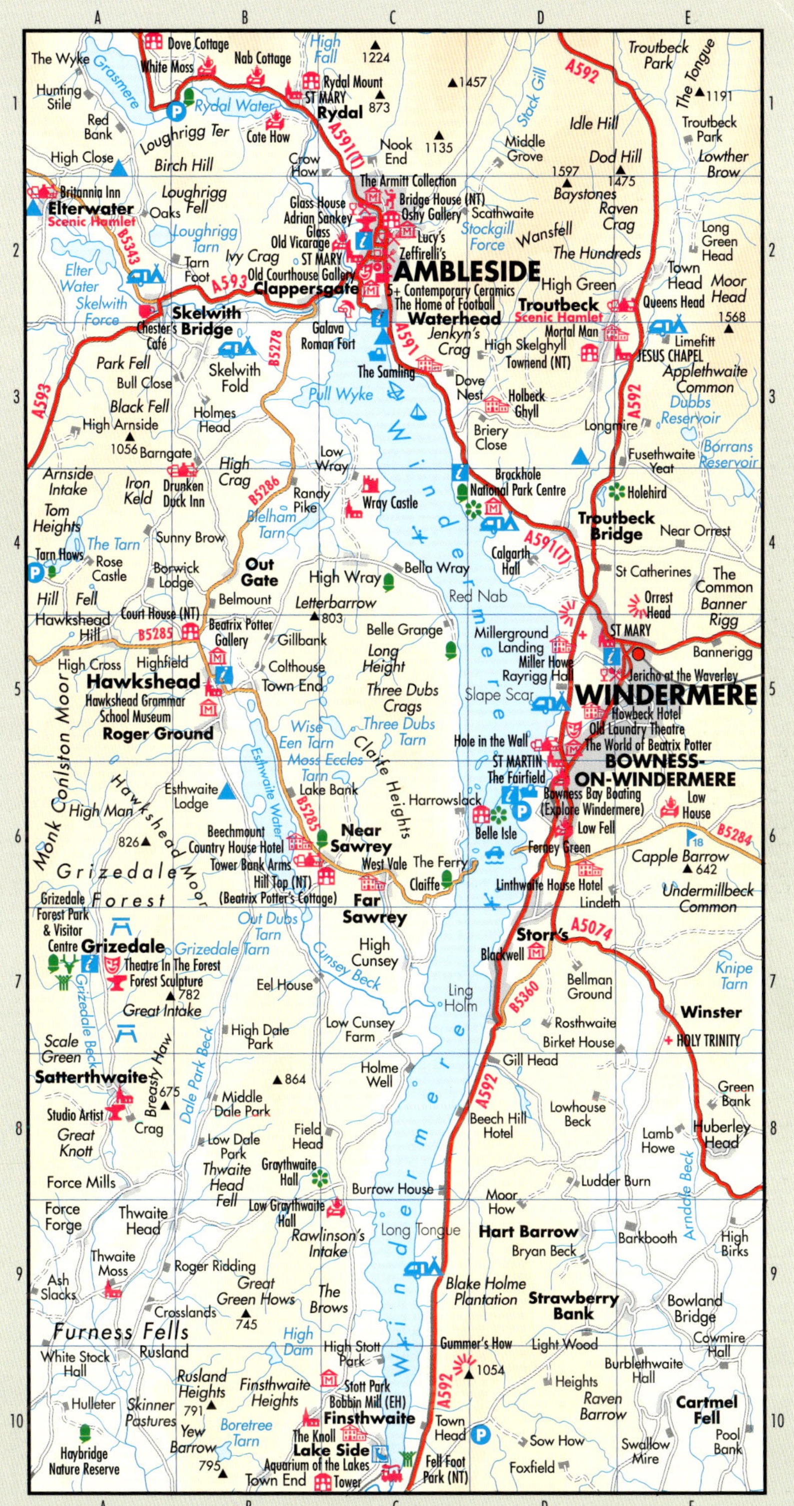

The Wyke
Hunting Stile
Red Bank
High Close
Dove Cottage
White Moss
Grasmere
Rydal Water
Nab Cottage
High Fall
1224
Rydal Mount
ST MARY
Rydal
873
1457
Troutbeck Park
The Tongue
1191
Loughrigg Ter
Birch Hill
Cote How
Crow How
Nook End
1135
Middle Grove
Idle Hill
Dod Hill
Troutbeck Park
Lowther Brow
Elterwater
Scenic Hamlet
Britannia Inn
Loughrigg Fell
Oaks
Loughrigg Tarn
Glass House
Adrian Sankey Glass
Old Vicarage
ST MARY
The Armitt Collection
Bridge House (NT)
Oshy Gallery
Scathwaite
Stockgill Force
1597
Baystones
Wansfell
1475
Raven Crag
The Hundreds
Long Green Head
B5343
Elter Water
Skelwith Force
Ivy Crag
Tarn Foot
Old Courthouse Gallery
Clappersgate
AMBLESIDE
Lucy's
Zeffirelli's
5+ Contemporary Ceramics
The Home of Football
Waterhead
High Green
Troutbeck
Scenic Hamlet
Queens Head
Town Head
1568
Moor Head
B5278
Skelwith Bridge
Chester's Café
Skelwith Fold
Galava Roman Fort
The Samling
Jenkyn's Crag
High Skelghyll
Townend (NT)
Mortal Man
JESUS CHAPEL
Applethwaite Common
A593
Park Fell
Bull Close
Black Fell
High Arnside
1056 Barngate
Holmes Head
High Crag
Pull Wyke
Low Wray
Dove Nest
Holbeck Ghyll
Briery Close
Longmire
Dubbs Reservoir
Borrans Reservoir
Arnside Intake
Tom Heights
The Tarn
Tarn Hows
Rose Castle
Iron Keld
Drunken Duck Inn
B5286
Blelham Tarn
Randy Pike
Wray Castle
Windermere
Brockhole
National Park Centre
Holehird
Troutbeck Bridge
Near Orrest
Fusethwaite Yeat
Hill Fell
Hawkshead Hill
B5285
Borwick Lodge
Sunny Brow
Out Gate
Belmount
High Wray
Letterbarrow
803
Bella Wray
Red Nab
Calgarth Hall
St Catherines
Orrest Head
The Common Banner Rigg
Court House (NT)
Beatrix Potter Gallery
Highfield
Hawkshead
Hawkshead Grammar School Museum
Roger Ground
Gillbank
Colthouse
Town End
Belle Grange
Long Height
Three Dubs Crags
Three Dubs Tarn
Millerground Landing
Miller Howe
Rayrigg Hall
Slape Scar
ST MARY
Jericho at the Waverley
WINDERMERE
Bannerigg
Howbeck Hotel
Old Laundry Theatre
The World of Beatrix Potter
Monk Coniston Moor
Hawkshead Moor
Wise Een Tarn
Moss Eccles Tarn
Esthwaite Water
Lake Bank
Claife Heights
Harrowslack
Hole in the Wall
ST MARTIN
The Fairfield
BOWNESS-ON-WINDERMERE
High Man
826
Esthwaite Lodge
B5285
Beechmount Country House Hotel
Tower Bank Arms
Hill Top (NT)
(Beatrix Potter's Cottage)
Near Sawrey
West Vale
Far Sawrey
Claiffe
The Ferry
Belle Isle
Bowness Bay Boating
(Explore Windermere)
Ferney Green
Low Fell
Linthwaite House Hotel
Lindeth
Low House
Capple Barrow
642
Undermillbeck Common
B5284
Grizedale Forest
Forest Park & Visitor Centre
Grizedale
Theatre In The Forest
Forest Sculpture
782
Great Intake
Out Dubs Tarn
Grizedale Tarn
Cunsey Beck
Eel House
High Cunsey
Low Cunsey Farm
Ling Holm
Storr's
Blackwell
A5074
Bellman Ground
Rosthwaite
Birket House
Knipe Tarn
Winster
HOLY TRINITY
Scale Green
Breasty Haw
Dale Park Beck
High Dale Park
Holme Well
Gill Head
B5360
A592
Lowhouse Beck
Ludder Burn
Green Bank
Huberley Head
Satterthwaite
Studio Artist
Great Knott
675
Crag
864
Middle Dale Park
Low Dale Park
Field Head
Beech Hill Hotel
Moor How
Lamb Howe
High Birks
Force Mills
Force Forge
Thwaite Head
Thwaite Head Fell
Graythwaite Hall
Low Graythwaite Hall
Rawlinson's Intake
Burrow House
Long Tongue
Hart Barrow
Bryan Beck
Barkbooth
Arnside Beck
Bowland Bridge
Cowmire Hall
Ash Slacks
Thwaite Moss
Roger Ridding
Great Green Hows
The Brows
745
Blake Holme Plantation
Strawberry Bank
Light Wood
High Birks
Furness Fells
Rusland
White Stock Hall
Hulleter
Rusland Heights
791
Skinner Pastures
Finsthwaite Heights
High Dam
High Stott Park
Gummer's How
1054
Heights
Raven Barrow
Burblethwaite Hall
Cartmel Fell
Haybridge Nature Reserve
Yew Barrow
795
Boretree Tarn
Finsthwaite
Stott Park Bobbin Mill (EH)
The Knoll
Lake Side
Aquarium of the Lakes
Town End
Tower
A592
Town Head
Fell Foot Park (NT)
Sow How
Foxfield
Swallow Mire
Pool Bank
A591(T)
A592
A593
A5074
49

Country House Hotels in the Windermere area...

Miller Howe Restaurant & Hotel, Rayrigg Road. The stuff of legend: Originally made famous by the colourful TV chef John Tovey (now retired to South Africa) who made such an impression on (and changed for the good) Lakeland eating habits. The new owners have capitalised on a sensational position overlooking Windermere, and the stupendous views are to be seen from the luxurious bedrooms. Contemporary furnishings laced with antiques and bright modern art adorn the walls. Look out for the double-seat in the hall. Wonderful! (F1) 015394 42536 www.millerhowe.com

Linthwaite House Hotel & Restaurant, Crook Road. Caters for a more conservative clientele. Perhaps not as luxurious as some but still good value. Look out for their Special Offers. The Dining Room is a treat. 015394 88600 www.linthwaite.com

Where to Stay Eat, Drink & Be Merry...

Jericho at The Waverley, College Road. This is a new venture run by Chris Blades who has cooked for the rich and famous, and decided to go it alone. The rooms are undergoing refurbishment in a contemporary style. It is a Restaurant With Rooms where dining is considered a serious and delicious business. (F1) 015394 42522 www.jerichos.co.uk

Hole Int Wall, Bowness. This is a locals' pub, and all the better for it. It is busy and comfortable, and noisy when the musicians let rip, as they often do. The ceiling is adorned with chamber pots and jugs, and wood carvings. Mainly local beers and the food is standard pub fare. It's tucked away 100 yards behind the church. (E2) 01539 443488

B&Bs...

The Fairfield Garden Guesthouse, Brantfell Road. Tony Blaney describes his B&B as boutique style. His Edwardian villa is on the Arts & Crafts trail (see Blackwell) and has many fine architectural features. The bedrooms are contemporary with state of the art bathrooms. (F2) 015394 46565 www.the-fairfield.co.uk

Low Fell B&B , Kendal Road. Louise Broughton welcomes you into her charming Edwardian villa with its stunning front arch built by the Pattinson builders of Windermere. A friendly and solid family home with one double, and a family room with fabulous bathroom. No dogs. (F2) 01539 445612 www.low-fell.co.uk

Jericho ss

Where to Stay in Windermere...

Howbeck, New Road. Small hotel provides luxurious B&B with dinner an option. The ten bedrooms are elegant and individually decorated, and all come with spa baths. (F1) 015394 44739 www.howbeck.co.uk

Low House. If you are seeking a luxurious B&B set within a verdant combe but a stone's throw from Windermere, look no further. Low House is a charming C17 country house furnished with family antiques, paintings, books and log fires. The bedrooms are comfortable and tastefully decorated (F2) 015394 43156 www.lowhouse.co.uk

Low House

Traditional meets luxurious chic in this country house hotel of great style. A world of elegant furnishings, antiques and roaring log fires, all made to great effect by effortless service. It is an experience to share with a loved one, to unwind in sumptuous bedrooms, perhaps to lie in a huge bath with champagne. All is possible. For the ultimate in discretion, the secretive or romantic will lean to the separate lodges oozing with sensational luxury, enormous bathrooms, an outdoor Jacuzzi... hedonism gone wild. Once you have savoured an enormous bath your thoughts may turn to food and this is where Gilpin hits the mark. No wonder it has been acclaimed as one of the top three hotels in Britain. (G2) Crook Rd. 015394 88818 www.gilpinlodge.com

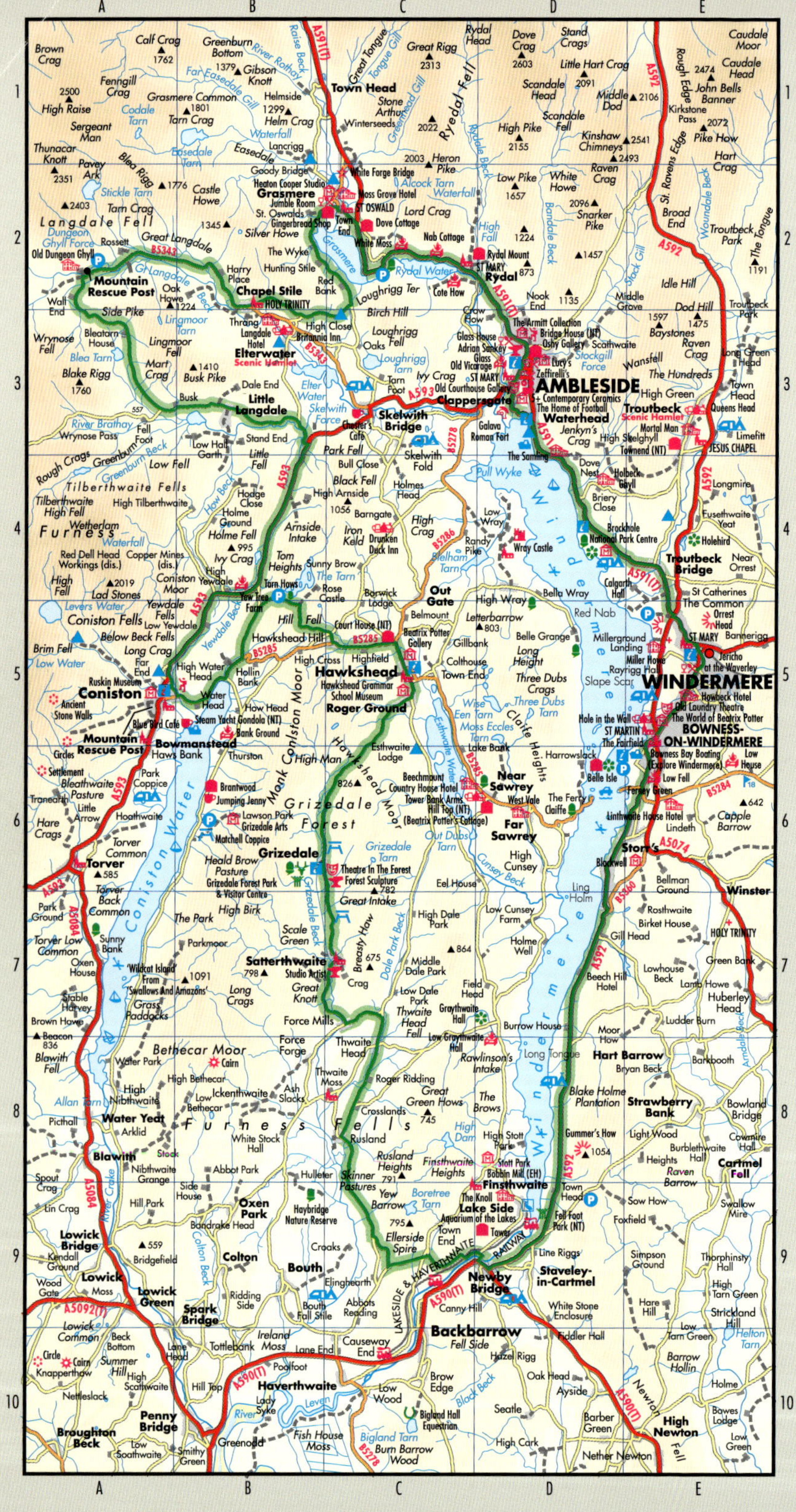

A B C D E
1
Brown Crag
Calf Crag 1762
Greenburn Bottom
Gibson Knott 1379
Great Tongue
Tongue Gill
Great Rigg 2313
Rydal Head
Dove Crag
Stand Crags
Caudale Moor
Caudale Head 2474
Fenngill Crag
Greenburn Bottom
Far Easedale Gill
Raise Beck
River Rothay
Great Rigg
Little Hart Crag 2091
Rough Edge
John Bells Banner
High Raise 2500
Grasmere Common
Helmside
Helm Crag 1299
Stone Arthur
Winterseeds
Town Head
Scandale Head
Scandale Fell
Middle Dod 2106
Kirkstone Pass 2072
Sergeant Man
Tarn Crag 1801
Codale Tarn
Waterfall
2003
Heron Pike
High Pike 2155
Kinshaw Chimneys 2541
Pike How
Thunacar Knott
Pavey Ark 2351
Easedale
Easedale Tarn
Lancrigg
Goody Bridge
White Forge Bridge
Heron Pike
Low Pike 1657
Raven Crag 2493
Snarker Pike 2096
Broad End
Hart Crag
2
Stickle Tarn 1776
Castle Howe
Heaton Cooper Studio
Grasmere
Jumble Room
Gingerbread Shop
St Oswalds
Moss Grove Hotel
ST OSWALD
Town End
Dove Cottage
Nab Cottage
Rydal Mount
ST MARY
Rydal 873
1457
Idle Hill
Troutbeck Park
1191
Langdale Fell
2403
Tarn Crag
Great Langdale 1345
Silver Howe
The Wyke
White Moss
Lord Crag
High Fall 1224
1135
Middle Grove
1597
Dod Hill 1475
Troutbeck Park
Dungeon Ghyll Force
Rossett
Old Dungeon Ghyll
Mountain Rescue Post
Oak Howe 1224
Harry Place
Hunting Stile
Chapel Stile
HOLY TRINITY
Red Bank
Loughrigg Ter
Rydal Water
Cote How
Nook End
Nab Scar
Craw How
Glass House
The Armitt Collection
Bridge House (NT)
Scathwaite
Raven Crag
Long Green Head
The Hundreds
Town Head
Queens Head
3
Wall End
Side Pike
Wrynose Fell
Bleatarn House
Lingmoor Fell
Lingmoor Tarn
Thrang
Langdale Hotel
Britannia Inn
High Close
Loughrigg Fell
Loughrigg
Oaks
Birch Hill
Adrian Sankey
Glass
Old Vicarage
ST MARY
Zeffirelli's
Lucy's
AMBLESIDE
Contemporary Ceramics
The Home of Football
High Green
Mortal Man
High Skelghyll
Troutbeck
Scenic Hamlet
Queens Head
Blake Rigg 1760
Mart Crag
Busk Pike 1410
Busk
Dale End
Little Langdale
557
Elter Water
Skelwith Force
Elterwater
Scenic Village
Skelwith Bridge
Ivy Crag
Tarn Foot
Clappersgate
Galava Roman Fort
Waterhead
Jenkyn's Crag
Townend (NT)
Limefitt
JESUS CHAPEL
4
Furness
Red Dell Head Workings (dis.)
Copper Mines (dis.)
2019
Lad Stones
Rough Crags
Greenburn
Low Fell
Tilberthwaite Fells
Tilberthwaite High Fell
Wetherlam 2019
High Tilberthwaite
Hodge Close
Holme Ground
995
Arnside Intake
Tom Heights
Tarn Hows
Rose Castle
Borwick Lodge
Out Gate
Belmount
High Wray
Letterbarrow 803
Low Wray
Wray Castle
Randy Pike
Bella Wray
Brockhole
National Park Centre
Calgarth Hall
Troutbeck Bridge
Near Orrest
Fusethwaite Yeat
Holehird
St Catherines
The Common
Orrest Head
ST MARY
Bannerigg
5
Coniston Fells
Coniston Moor
Low Yewdale
Below Beck Fells
Brim Fell
Low Water
Long Crag
Far End
Ruskin Museum
Coniston
Blue Bird Cafe
Yew Tree Farm
Hill Fell
Hawkshead Hill
Court House (NT)
Beatrix Potter Gallery
Hawkshead
Hawkshead Grammar School Museum
Roger Ground
Gillbank
Colthouse
Town End
High Wray
Belle Grange
Long Height
Three Dubs Crags
Three Dubs Tarn
Wise Een Tarn
Moss Eccles Tarn
Lake Bank
Millerground Landing
Miller Howe
Rayrigg Hall
Slape Scar
WINDERMERE
Howbeck Hotel
Old Laundry Theatre
The World of Beatrix Potter
ST MARTIN
The Fairfield
Hole in the Wall
BOWNESS-ON-WINDERMERE
Bowness Bay Boating
Low Fell
Low House
6
Mountain Rescue Post
Bowmanstead
Haws Bank
Thurston
Brantwood
Jumping Jenny
Lawson Park
Matchell Coppice
Grizedale Arts
Grizedale Forest
High Man
826
Esthwaite Lodge
Esthwaite Water
Beechmount
Country House Hotel
Tower Bank Arms (NT)
(Beatrix Potter's Cottage)
Near Sawrey
West Vale
Far Sawrey
Claife
The Ferry
Belle Isle
Harrowslack
Linthwaite House Hotel
Ferney Green
642
Capple Barrow
7
Torver
585
Torver Back Common
Sunny Bank
Parkmoor
High Birk
Scale Green
Great Intake
Grizedale
Heald Brow Pasture
Grizedale Forest Park & Visitor Centre
Theatre In The Forest
Forest Sculpture 782
Out Dubs Tarn
Cunsey Beck
Eel House
High Cunsey
Low Cunsey Farm
Holme Well
Ling Holm
Rosthwaite
Birket House
Gill Head
Winster
Bellman Ground
Beech Hill Hotel
Lowhouse Beck
Lamb Howe
Huberley Head
Green Bank
8
Beacon 836
Blawith Fell
Bethecar Moor
Cairn
High Betthwaite
Satterthwaite 798
Great Knott
Long Crags
675
Force Mills
Thwaite Head
Breasty Haw
Middle Dale Park
Low Dale Park
Thwaite Head Fell
Graythwaite Hall
Burrow House
Rawlinson's Intake
Moor Fen
Ludder Burn
Long Tongue
Hart Barrow
Bryan Beck
Barkbooth
Blake Holme Plantation
Strawberry Bank
Bowland Bridge
Cowmire Hall
9
Water Park
High Nibthwaite
Ickenthwaite
Low Bethecar
Ash Slacks
Thwaite Moss
Roger Ridding
Crosslands
Rusland
Great Green Hows 745
The Brows
High Dam
High Stott Park
Stott Park
Bobbin Mill (EH)
Gummer's How 1054
Light Wood
Burblethwaite Heights
Raven Barrow
Cartmel Fell
Water Yeat
Arklid
Blawith
Nibthwaite Grange
White Stock Hall
Abbot Park
Hulleter
Skinner Pastures
Rusland Heights 791
Finsthwaite Heights
Finsthwaite
Lake Side
Aquarium of the Lakes
Town End
Fell Foot Park (NT)
Sow How
Foxfield
Swallow Mire
10
Lowick Bridge
Kendall Ground
Lowick
Wood Gate
Lowick Green
Oxen Park
Haybridge Nature Reserve
Bandrake Head
Side House
Colton
Ridding Side
Booth
Elinghearth
Abbots Reading
Yew Barrow 795
Boretree Tarn
Ellerside Spire
Town End
HAVERTHWAITE
The Knoll
Lake Side
Newby Bridge
Canny Hill
Backbarrow
Fell Side
Staveley-in-Cartmel
Line Riggs
White Stone Enclosure
Fiddler Hall
Simpson Ground
Hare Hill
Thorphinsty Hall
High Tarn Green
Strickland Hill
Barrow Hollin
Holme
Bowes Lodge
Lowick Common
Circle
Cairn
Knapperthaw
Summer Hill
Lane Head
Tottlebank Moss
Lane End
Causeway End
Brow Edge
Hazel Rigg
Oak Head
Ayside
Barrow Green
Low Green
High Newton
Broughton Beck
Penny Bridge
Greenodd
Fish House Moss
Bigland Tarn
Burn Barrow Wood
Seatle
High Cark
Barber Green
Nether Newton

Overlooking Langdale

Windermere to Ambleside to Grasmere to Dungeon Ghyll to Coniston to Hawkshead to Newby Bridge to Windermere (43 miles)

The route starts from Windermere and runs close to the shore of the lake through the attractive tourist centre of Ambleside and on past the smaller lakes of Rydal Water and Grasmere, to Grasmere village. From here a steep, twisty road crosses into Great Langdale, revealing stupendous views of the high mountains of Lakeland. Penetrating deep into the Dale, the road reaches the climbing centre of Dungeon Ghyll, and makes a difficult but rewarding climb over to Little Langdale. From Coniston the route skirts the upper end of Coniston Water and makes a diversion to the beautiful Tarn Hows. Thence, to the picturesque village of Hawkshead and through Grizedale Forest Park, finally reaching the foot of Windermere at Newby Bridge and returning by the main road along the eastern shore of the lake.

From **Windermere**. Leave by Church Street SP Ambleside.

2.5 miles to **Brockhole National Park Centre**.

2 miles to **Ambleside**. Keep to L fork on entry, and follow signs to **Keswick**.

2 miles to **Rydal**.

2 miles to **Grasmere**. Turn L SP **Grasmere Village**. Go into village and turn L at church. In just under **2** miles fork R up hill SP **Langdale**. At foot of hill keep straight on SP **Dungeon Ghyll**.

2 miles to **Dungeon Ghyll** (Newish hotel). Continue past Old Hotel and shortly bear L up twisting road. In about 3 miles merge L with road from Wrynose Pass.

4.5 miles to **Little Langdale (not signed)**. In 1 mile keep R SP **Coniston**, and R again at top of hill, SP **Coniston**.

5.5 miles to **Coniston**. Turn L SP **Hawkshead**. In 1 mile keep L with road, then shortly turn L SP **Tarn Hows**.

2.5 miles to **Tarn Hows**. In 1 mile turn L back into main road.1 mile further on turn R SP **Hawkshead**.

2.5 miles to **Hawkshead**. Keep to main road to R round village. Turn R at T-junction and shortly L SP **Newby Bridge**. In a quarter mile turn R SP **Grizedale**.

2.5 miles to **Grizedale Forest Visitor Centre**.

1.5 miles to **Satterthwaite**. In 1 mile turn L at T-junction, and R in a further half mile - then follow signs to **Newby Bridge**.

4.5 miles to **Newby Bridge**. Keep R over bridge, then L into main road. Shortly turn L SP **Windermere**.

7.5 miles to **Bowness**. Keep R SP **Windermere**.

1 mile to **Windermere**.

CONISTON

A former C18 mining community built from the dark slate cut from the surrounding hills. Coniston is set in a magnificent situation with 'The Old Man of Coniston' rising behind. The nearby rocks and crags have turned this village into a popular centre for rock climbers and more recently walkers. Not as busy a centre as Ambleside or Keswick, it does however have a loyal following who use it as their base. Brantwood was the home of John Ruskin and his elaborately carved tomb lies in the C16 Church of St Andrew. The mirror-like waters of Coniston attracted the Campbell family to attempt their World Water Speed records. The Campbells drew a loyal and devoted following and their tale is told in the local Ruskin Museum and down by the lake in the Bluebird Café. (G6)

Yew Tree Farm, Coniston

Special Places of Interest...

Ruskin Museum, Yewdale Rd.
A super little museum often described as 'the most thought-provoking in the Lakes,' which promotes its themes as Pure Inspiration: the radical artist and thinker, John Ruskin. Pure Courage: the World Water Speed ace, Donald Campbell. Pure Lakeland: The Story of Coniston. Open daily early Mar to early Nov 10-5.30, Nov to Feb 10.30-3.30 (A1) 015394 41164 www.ruskinmuseum.com

Where to Eat, Drink & Be Merry...

Bluebird Café, Lake Road.
Just the place to enjoy a coffee or toasted sandwich while you wait to board the Steam Yacht Gondola or Coniston Cruise. With fine views over the lake there can be few better spots to relax and admire the collection of Campbell memorabilia. Open daily. 015394 41649 www.thebluebirdcafe.com

Jumping Jenny, Brantwood.
One of Cumbria's great eating-out institutions. It's a Med-Style bistro set in the "Old Stables". All is prepared and made on the premises and you can be guaranteed fresh food. It does, however, mean having to queue up at busy times, but be patient. You can lunch outside and taken in Ruskin's view. Open daily 11-5 (closed M & Tu in winter). (A3) 01539 441715 www.jumpingjenny.com

Where to Stay...

Bank Ground Farm. Former farmhouse now offering B&B in an elevated position on the eastern shores of Coniston. The setting for many of Arthur Ransome's Swallows & Amazon stories. Self-catering. (A2) 015394 41264 www.bankground.com

John Ruskin's Tomb, Coniston

Yew Tree Farm. Featured in the movie "Miss Potter" as Beatrix Potter's home. A special little piece of Lakeland dedicated to the rearing of Herdwick sheep and the Belted Galloway cattle. Grade 11 listed, it's a traditional C17 Cruck-frame house. The luxurious accommodation is festooned with antiques and oak panels. Set amidst a maze of footpaths which all appear to descend on the Walkers Tearoom, open daily June-Oct, rest of year W/Es, 11-4. 015394 41433 www.yewtree-farm.co.uk

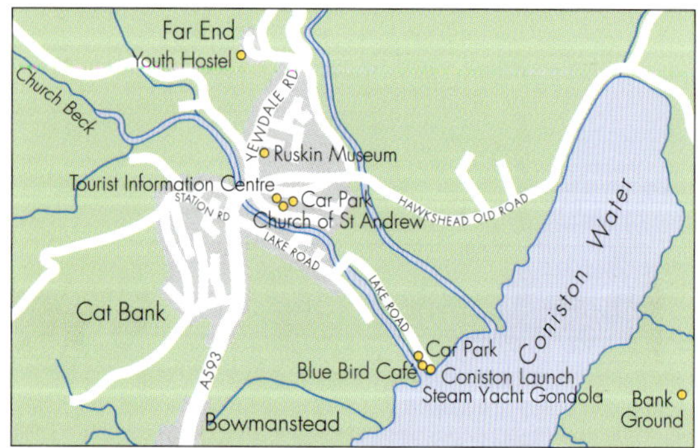

Coniston

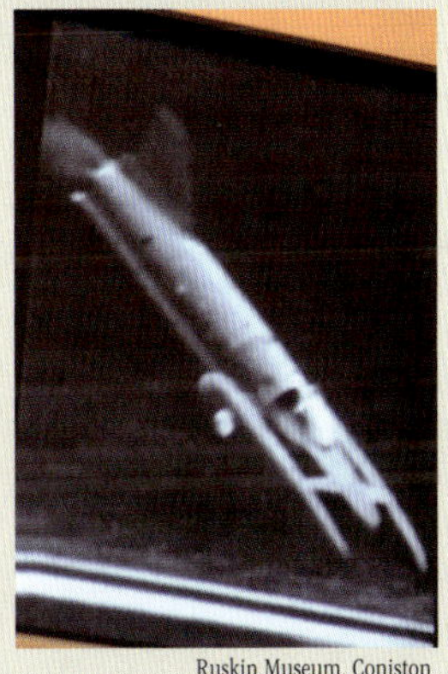

Ruskin Museum, Coniston

Hird Wood
Old Yoke Quarry
Yoke ▲ 2163
Hartrigg
Overend
Troutbeck Park
Lowther Brow
Quarry (disused)
Scale Knotts
Scales
od Hill ▲ 1475
Raven Crag
Ing Bridge
▲ 584
Buck Crag ▲ 1727
Saletarn Knotts
Cowsty Knotts
▲ 1300
Piked Howes
Garburn
Ewe Crags
Garburn Pass
Green Head
6
7
Nook Ho.
Kentmere Hall
St Cuthbert's
G
Long Green Head
Maggs h
GARBURN ROAD
Town Head
Moor Head
Sallows ▲ 1691
Kentmere
5
Kentmere Park
Quarry (disused)
Wardless
8
Quarry (disused)
Limefitt
▲ 1568
Sour Howes
Whiteside End
909 ▲
Long Houses
Applethwaite Common
Bank Ho.
Kentmere Hall Plantn.
Millrigg
The Howe 754 ▲
Ancient Settlemen
DUBBS ROAD
Longmire
Park Beck
Dubbs Reservoir
Fusethwaite Yeat ▲ 896
4
Park Beck
Sawmill Cottage
Reservoir
▲ 968
Croft Head
Millrigg Knott
Millgate
▲ 9
Ancient Settlement
High Borrans
▲ 839
Browfoot
Far Orrest
3
High House Fm
9
▲ 901
Williamson's Monument
Crosses
Near Orrest
Fellfoot
Causeway
1
Heights
St Catherines
Grassgarth
Mislet
Broadgate
Hugill Hall
Common
Banner Rigg
▲ 871
2
Orrest Head
Heaning
Hugill Fell
Elleray
Grove
Low Ho.
Rawgill
A591
A591
Bannerigg
Ings
A591
Reston
Sta
NDERMERE
Heathwaite
Blackmoss
Fairbank
N
W E
S
Whasdike
New Hall
500   1000 metres
500   1000 yards
Yews
Reservoir
▲ 818
Hag End
Borwick Fold
to Crook
to Crook

Windermere to **Kentmere** and the **Garburn Pass**

12.5 miles (20km)8 off-road, 4.5 road. (Starting from Kentmere, 9.5 miles, 8 off-road).

Grade 2 to 3.
Riding Time 2.5 to 3 hours.

A challenging route with all its difficulties concentrated in the 2 km Garburn Pass, a steep push from the Kentmere side, followed by a rough, technical downhill. Equally good in reverse, but the grassy (often muddy) bridleways north from Mislet are easier to navigate when climbing, and the numerous gates less frustrating.

(0) Start from the Information Centre car park opposite Windermere Railway Station. From Windermere take the A591 towards Kendal, climbing steeply. Just after the brow of the hill, turn left up narrow lane, signposted Common Farm on tree. Follow this to X-roads in 500m.

(1) Turn right for Mislet, bearing right again at fork to second fork on edge of Mislet.

(2) Straight ahead for 100m to iron gate and bridleway signpost on left. Turn left into tarmac farm drive for 700m to High House Farm. Through the iron gate and immediately right through second gate to pass between white farmhouse and barn into stony lane.

(3) Follow lane north. Straight on at wall junction with double gates to follow wall on right. Turn right (east) as indicated at next gateway, then back left at another gate, signpost bridleway Kentmere, to continue north along wall. Track becomes boggy for next 1km to the Park Beck, watch for peat hollows.

(4) Ford the stream & go straight on through gate to follow wall ahead. Track becomes firmer for smooth 500m downhill from Whiteside End, then rougher and steeper to a gate and fortified Kentmere Hall farmhouse.

(5) Right along farm lane to junction with tarmac rd opposite St Cuthbert's Church. Turn left up the lane for 200m to junction. Ignore gate ahead and turn left to follow signpost Garburn Track.

(6) Tarmac ends at a cottage, bear right onto stony track, signposted Garburn Pass. Up this rideable track, then rougher and steeper for 1km then through a gate below the top of the pass. Mostly easier to push, giving opportunities to enjoy views.

(7) Descent is steep, rocky and relentlessly rough for next km, and most walk the worst, rocky steps. Becomes easier and faster to gate warning of a fork.

(8) Fork left onto Dubbs Road, the smoother track slightly uphill away from the valley. Soon descends again for a fast 2km past the reservoir to the road.

(9) Turn left for 200m, then right to rejoin outward route at the x-roads. Straight on to the A591.

"Every increased possession loads us with new weariness."

"Labour without joy is base. Labour without sorrow is base. Sorrow without labour is base. Joy without labour is base."

"Let us reform our schools, and we shall find little reform needed in our prisons."

"Sunshine is delicious, rain is refreshing, wind braces up, snow is exhilarating; there is no such thing as bad weather, only different kinds of good weather."

"There are many religions, but there is only one morality."

"Without mountains the air could not be purified, nor the flowing of the rivers sustained."

The Ruskin Museum

Brantwood was the home of John Ruskin, the eminent Victorian writer, philosopher and critic from 1872 for the last 28 years of his life. Ruskin's pictures, furniture and books are on view. His stature, together with William Morris, among the "Arts & Crafts Movement" was immense. Yet, despite this, his profile in the Lakes tends to hide behind the two colossi, William Wordsworth and Alf Wainwright. This is a pity because his influence during his lifetime probably had a more far-reaching effect on the general populace than these other two men. In Spring the azaleas, rhododendrons and daffodils bloom. The house's elevated position provides superb views across Coniston Water, and to the 'Old Man'. Look out for Ruskin's little boat, a real gem. Bookshop, excellent coffee/tea shop and nature trail. Open daily mid-Mar to mid-Nov 11-5.30, mid-Nov to mid-Mar W-Su 11-4.30. (A2) 015394 41396 www.brantwood.org.uk

The eastern side of Coniston Water provides the finest views, with the 'Old Man of Coniston' in the background. Follow the road down past Brantwood, John Ruskin's home. Further down is Machel Coppice, a fine spot for picnics and nature trails. Further picnic spots beside the A5084. In 1967, Coniston witnessed the tragic scene of Donald Campbell's death, when Bluebird somersaulted during his attempt to further his own world water speed record of 260.35mph. At a more sedate pace, a very satisfying experience is to take a trip on the Steam Yacht Gondola, or with Coniston Launch Services. (A4)

Coniston Launch. Traditional craft sailing from Coniston boat landings (from 10.30am) and various jetties around the Lake, throughout the year. For private charter, Swallows & Amazons and Campbells on Coniston cruises. (A2) 01768 775753 www.conistonlaunch.co.uk

Steam Yacht Gondola (NT).
First launched in 1859, and
now renovated by the Trust. The
saloons are opulently furnished
and cater for 86 passengers. Gondola
sails to a daily timetable in season,
starting at 11, except Sa from 12.
1 Apr-31 Oct. Piers at Coniston,
Park-A-Moor (SE end of lake),
Monk Coniston (for walks to
Tarn Hows) and Brantwood.
Parties from Coniston Pier.
(A2) 015394 41288
www.nationaltrust.org.uk

Langdale Fell
Thunacar Knott
Pavey Ark
Stake Pass
Langdale Pikes
2351
Blea Rigg
2403
Castle Howe
Goody Bridge
Easedale Tarn
Easedale
Lancrigg
Heaton Cooper Studio
White Forge Bridge
2003
Heron Pike
Low Pike
1657
White Howe
Raven Crag
2493
St. Ravens Edge
Broad End
Tarn Crag
Great Langdale
Grasmere
Jumble Room
St. Oswalds
Gingerbread Shop
ST OSWALD
Alcock Tarn Waterfall
Lord Crag
High Fall
1224
Snarker Pike
2096
1457
A592
Mickleden
Dungeon Ghyll Force
Rossett
1345
Silver Howe
The Wyke
Hunting Stile
Moss Grove Hotel
Town
Dove Cottage
White Moss
Nab Cottage
Rydal Mount
ST MARY
Rydal
873
Nook End
Idle Hill
Raven Crag
B5343
Harry Place
Red Bank
Grasmere
Rydal Water
A591
1135
Middle Grove
1475
Old Dungeon Ghyll
Middlefell
Mountain Rescue Post
Oak Howe
1224
Chapel Stile
HOLY TRINITY
Loughrigg Ter
Cote How
Crow How
The Armitt Collection
Bridge House (NT)
Osby Gallery
1597
Baystones
Raven Crag
Stool End
Oxendale
Wall End
Side Pike
Thrang
Langdale Hotel
Birch Hill
Loughrigg Fell
Glass House
Adrian Sankey Glass
Old Vicarage
Scathwaite
Stockghyll Force
Wansfell
Kettle Crag
Bleatarn House
Lingmoor Tarn
High Close
Loughrigg Oaks
ST MARY
Zeffirelli's
AMBLESIDE
High Green
Wrynose House
Elterwater
Scenic Hamlet
Busk Pike
1410
Mart Crag
Elter Water Skelwith Force
Ivy Crag
Tarn Foot
A593
Old Courthouse Gallery
Contemporary Ceramics
The Home of Football
Waterhead
Queens Head
Mortal Man
Pike of Blisco
2304
Blake Rigg
1760
Busk
Little Langdale
Dale End
Chesters Café
Skelwith Bridge
Galava Roman Fort
Clappersgate
Jenkyn's Crag
High Skelghyll
Townend (NT)
Red Tarn
Black Crag
Three Shire Stone
River Brathay
Fool Foot
Stand End
Park Fell
Bull Close
Skelwith Fold
Holmes Head
The Samling
Dove Nest
Holbeck Ghyll
Gaitkins
Wrynose Breast
Wrynose Pass
Little Fell
High Arnside
Black Fell
Low Wray
B5286
Pull Wyke
Briery Close
Brockhole National Park Centre
Holehird
Wet Side Edge
Rough Crags
Greenburn Beck
Low Fell
Hodge Close
Holme Fell
1056
Barngate
High Crag
Randy Pike
Wray Castle
Troutbeck Bridge
Furness
Tilberthwaite Fells
High Tilberthwaite
Holme Fell
995
Arnside Intake
Iron Keld
Drunken Duck Inn
Elterwater
Calgarth Hall
Little Carrs
2250
Tilberthwaite High Fell
Wetherlam
Waterfall
Tom Heights
Sunny Brow
High Cross
Out Gate
High Wray
Bella Wray
Red Nab
ST MARY
Swirl How
Red Dell Head Workings (dis.)
Copper Mines (dis.)
Ivy Crag
Tarn Hows
Rose Castle
Borwick Lodge
Belmount
Letterbarrow
803
Belle Grange
Long Height
Millerground Landing
Miller How
Jericho at the Waverley
Hookrigg
2019
Lad Stones
Coniston Moor
Yew Tree Farm
Hill Fell
Court House (NT)
Beatrix Potter Gallery
Gillbank
Three Dubs Crags
WINDERMERE
Howbeck Hotel
Levers Water
High Fell
Yewdale Moor
Low Yewdale
Hawkshead Hill
B5285
High Cross
Highfield
Hawkshead
Colthouse
Town End
Wise Een Tarn
Three Dubs Tarn
Old Laundry Theatre
Hole in the Wall
Raven Tor
Coniston Fells
Below Beck Fells
Far End
High Water Head
Hollin Bank
Hawkshead Grammar School Museum
Roger Ground
Moss Eccles Tarn
Lake Bank
BOWNESS-ON-WINDERMERE
The World of Beatrix Potter
Brim Fell
Long Crag
Ruskin Museum
Coniston
Water Head
How Head
Cloife Heights
Harrowslack
Cove Quarries (dis.)
2635
The Old Man of Coniston
Ancient Stone Walls
Blue Bird Café
Steam Yacht Gondola
Bank Ground
High Man
826
Esthwaite Water
Beechmount Country House Hotel
Tower Bank Arms
Hill Top (NT)
Near Sawrey
West Vale
The Ferry
Claiffe
Belle Isle
Bowness Bay Boating
Low Fell
Little Arrow Moor
Blind Tarn
Mountain Rescue Post
Bowmanstead
Haws Bank
Thurston
Grizedale Forest
Lawson Park
Grizedale Arts
Matchell Coppice
Far Sawrey
High Cunsey
Linthwaite House Hotel
Lindeth
Old Coal Pike
Settlement
Bleathwaite Pasture
Jumping Jenny
Brantwood
Beatrix Potter's Cottage
Out Dubs Tarn
Ferny Green
Store's
A5074
Blackwell
Torver High Common
Hare Crags
Little Arrow
Hoathwaite
Grizedale
Theatre In The Forest
Forest Sculpture
782
Ling Holm
Bellman Ground
Bull Haw Moss
Torver Common
Heald Brow Pasture
Grizedale Forest Park & Visitor Centre
Great Intake
Eel House
Low Cunsey Farm
Holme Well
Rosthwaite
Birket House
Lowhouse Beck
Brocklebank Ground
Torver
585
Torver Back Common
High Birk
Scale Green
Breasty Haw
675
High Dale Park
864
Beech Hill Hotel
Southerstead
Park Ground
A5084
Sunny Bank
Parkmoor
Satterthwaite
Studio Artist
Long Crags
Great Knott
Middle Dale Park
Field Head
Gill Head
Ludder Burn
Green Rigg
Torver Low Common
The Park
798
1091
Low Dale Park
Thwaite Head Fell
Graythwaite Hall
Burrow House
Moor How
Greaves Ground
Oxen House
'Wildcat Island' From Swallows And Amazons
Grass Paddocks
Force Mills
Thwaite Head
Roger Ridding
Great Green Hows
745
Low Graythwaite Hall
Rawlinson's Intake
Long Tongue
Hart Barrow
Bryan Beck
Pool Scar
Stable Harvey Moss
Stable Harvey
Bethecar Moor
Cairn
Force Forge
Thwaite Moss
Crosslands
Rusland
The Brows
Blake Holme Plantation
Strawberry Bank
678
836
Brown Howe
Beacon
Blawith Fell
Water Park
High Bethecar
Ash Slacks
High Dam
Stott Park
Gummer's How
1054
Light Wood
Woodland Fell
Beacon Tarn
High Nibthwaite
Low Ickenthwaite
Bethecar
Rusland Heights
791
Finsthwaite Heights
Bobbin Mill (EH)
Town End
Sow How
Heights
Raven Barrow
Wool Knott
Cockenshell
Allan Tarn
Water Yeat
Arklid
White Stock Hall
Hulleter
Skinner Pastures
Yew Barrow
Finsthwaite
Lake Side
Aquarium of the Lakes
Fell Foot Park (NT)
Foxfield
Picthall
Cockenshell Farm
Stock
Nibthwaite Grange
Side House
Abbot Park
Hill Park
Boretree Tarn
795
Ellerside Spire
Town End
Tower
LAKESIDE & HAVERTHWAITE RAILWAY
Heights
Simpson Ground
Cairn
Tottlebank
Blawith
Lowick Bridge
559
Bridgefield
Oxen Park
Bandrake Head
Colton
Croaks
Booth
Elinghearth
Abbots Reading
Newby Bridge
Staveley-in-Cartmel
Line Riggs
Crake Birk
Lin Crag
Kendall Ground
Lowick
Lowick Green
Moss
Ridding Side
Bouth Fell Stile
Canny Hill
White Stone Enclosure
Fiddler Hall
Hare Hill
Subberthwaite Common
Cairn
High Stennerley
Low Stennerley
A5092 (T)
Spark Bridge
Wood Gate
Lowick Common
Beck Bottom
Lane Bottom
Tottlebank
Ireland Moss
Lane End
Causeway End
Backbarrow
Fell Side
Hazel Rigg
Brow Edge
Oak Head
Ayside
Barrow Hollin
Quarry (dis.)
Gawthwaite
Circle
Cairn
Summer Hill
High Scathwaite
Hill Top
Haverthwaite
Lady Syke
Low Wood
Black Beck
Seatle
Barber Ground
High Newton
Groffa Crag
Hawkswell
Nettleslack
Penny Bridge
Greenodd
River Leven
Fish House Moss
Bigland Hall Equestrian
Bigland Tarn
High Cark
Nether Newton
Buck Crag
Eller Howe
Broughton Beck
Well House
Low Southwaite
Smithy Green
Deer Dike Moss
Burn Barrow Wood
Grassgarth
Green Bank
Lindale
Moor House
Rake
Bencragg
Stony Crag
Higher Lath
B5281
Bowstead Gates
Mansrigg
The Alps
536
Arrad Foot
Toppin Rays
Newland Bottom
Plumpton Cottage Farm
Hazelhurst Point
Mearness Point
Greenodd Sands
Nab Point
Mearness Farm
High Frith
Frith Hall
White Moss
Ellerside
Stribers Moss
Speel Bank
Stribers
High Gate Side
Wood Broughton
Speel Bank
Green Bank
Broughton Lodge
Longlands
Hampsfield
Bortree Stile
Beck Side
Newland
Green Hills
Newland Beck
A590 (T)
Burns's Farm
Field Broughton
Sturdys

Coniston Water

Coniston to Greenodd to Newby Bridge to Near Sawrey to Hawkshead to Skelwith Bridge to Elterwater to Coniston (40 miles)

A short drive from Coniston, exploring the country between Coniston Water and Windermere. The route follows the east side of Coniston Water, with magnificent views across to the village and the "Old Man" towering above. At Greenodd it reaches the point where the waters from the two lakes unite to form an estuary lowing into Morecombe Bay. A fast highway runs to Newby Bridge, whence the route follows the west side of Windermere and through the Sawreys (of Beatrix Potter fame) to the attractive village of Hawkshead. Return can be made direct to Coniston but the suggested route makes a detour through Skelwith Bridge and the charmingly situated village of Elterwater.

From **Coniston**. Leave by the **B5285** SP **Hawkshead**. In 1 mile turn R along lakeside SP **Brantwood**.

2.5 miles to **Brantwood**.

7 miles to **Lowick Bridge (unsigned)**. Turn L SP **Spark Bridge**.

2 miles to **Spark Bridge**. Turn L SP **Newby Bridge**. In about half a mile turn R SP **Greenodd** and a little further on turn L into main road.

1.5 miles to **Greenodd**. Keep L with road, then shortly L again SP **Kendal**.

3 miles to **Haverthwaite Station**.

2 miles to **Newby Bridge**. Turn L over bridge, keep round to L, then turn R SP **Lakeside**.

1 mile to **Lakeside Quay**. In half a mile keep R SP **Sawrey**.

0.5 mile to **Graythwaite Hall**. Shortly fork R SP **Cunsey**.

5 miles to **Far Sawrey**. Keep L SP **Near Sawrey**.

0.5 mile to **Near Sawrey**.

2 miles to **Hawkshead**. Bear R on entry and follow main road round SP **Coniston**. In half a mile keep straight on SP **Ambleside**.

1 mile to **Outgate**. Turn L.

2 miles to **Drunken Duck Inn**. Straight on. In 1 mile turn L and in just under a mile turn R into main road.

3 miles to **Skelwith Bridge**. Turn sharp L after crossing bridge.

1.5 miles to **Elterwater**. Turn L SP **Coniston**. In under 2 miles turn R at T-junction into main road SP **Coniston**.

6 miles to **Coniston**.

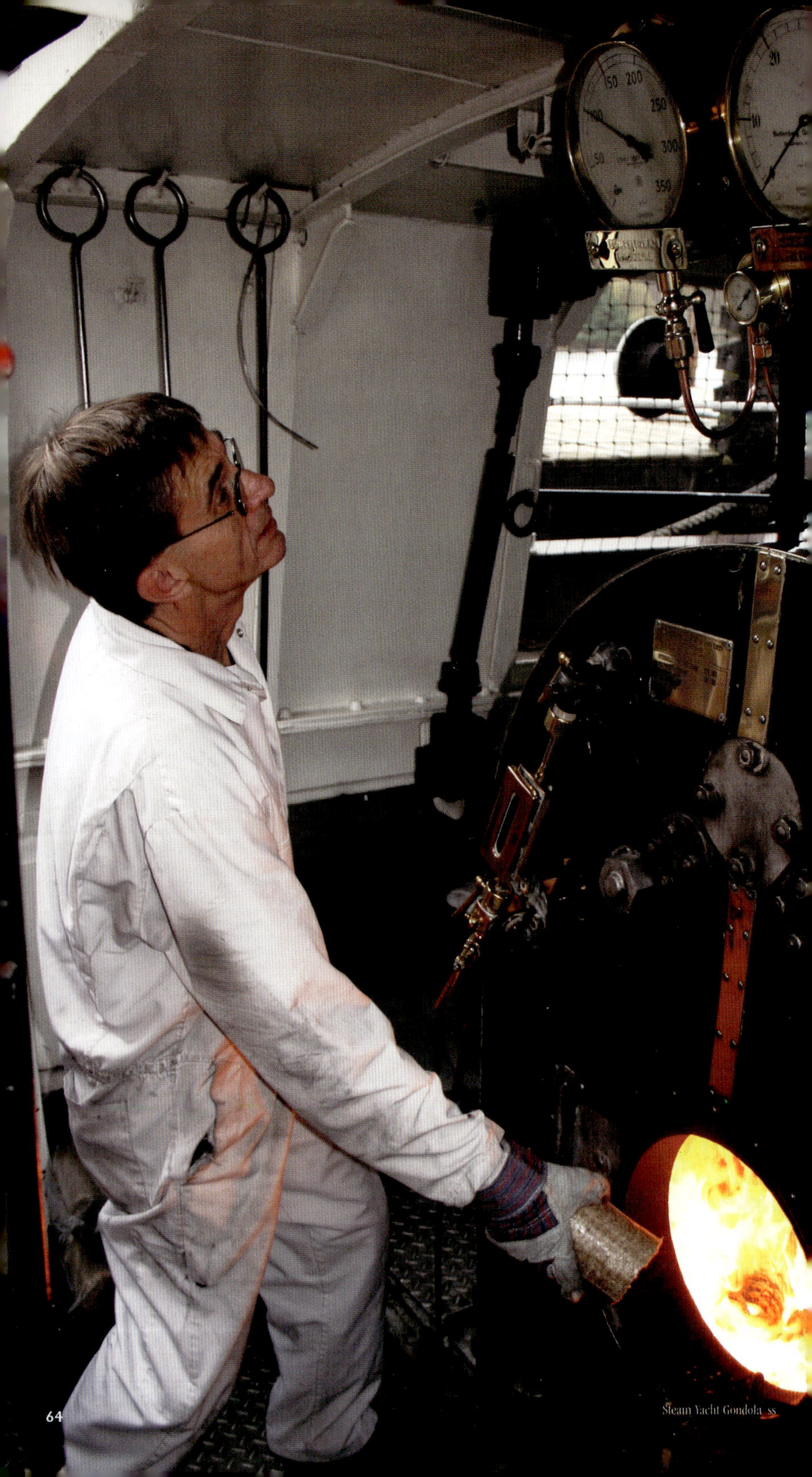

Steam Yacht Gondola ss

HAWKSHEAD

If you arrive by car or coach you are ushered into the large car park. This has enjoyed its fair share of criticism, for some argue the village is more theme park than Cumbrian vernacular. You choose. Whatever, it's a busy, pedestrianised village with many C17 timber-framed buildings hovering around little squares and cobbled streets. There are inns and tearooms aplenty. Should you be energetic you may decide you have had enough of the Stepford Wives syndrome and take the rewarding four-mile walk, beloved of Willie Wordsworth, back to Windermere. (C1)

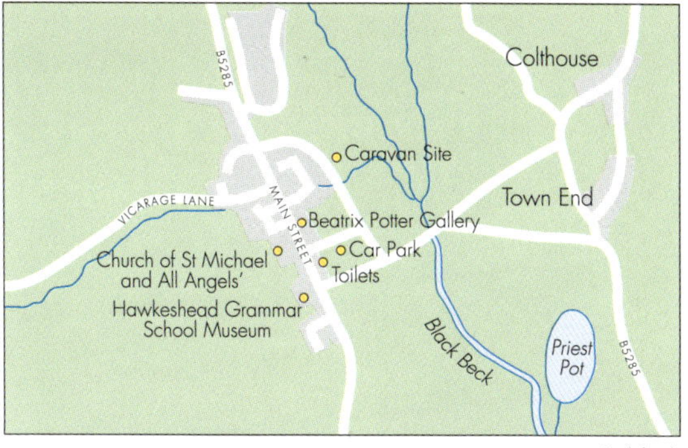

Hawkshead

Special Places to Visit...

Beatrix Potter Gallery, Main St. (NT) Annually changing exhibition of Beatrix Potter's original illustrations from her 'little tales'. Information and artefacts from her later career as a farmer, conservationist and political activist. Atmospheric old building. Trails for children. Open Mar W/Es, Apr-Oct Sa-W, June-Aug & Oct Th 10.30-4.30. (C1) 015394 36355. www.nationaltrust.org.uk

Esthwaite Water. A pretty little lake, surrounded by fields and woodland, and well stocked with fish. Fishing permits from the Esthwaite Estate. On the west side, the Hawkshead Trout Farm. A footpath, loved by Wordsworth who wrote of this lake in The Prelude, leads to the north west shore from Hawkshead. (D2)

Hawkshead Grammar School Museum. Founded in 1585, and attended by William Wordsworth, 1779-87. Contains his desk, on which he carved his name. Open East-Oct M-Sa 10-12.30, 1.30-5. Su 1-5. (C1) 015394 36735 www.hawksheadgrammar.org.uk

Sawrey. Far Sawrey and Near Sawrey are two little villages set in wooded and hilly country very much associated with Beatrix Potter who lived and farmed here. (D2)

Hill Top. (NT) C17 farmhouse owned by Beatrix Potter, used in illustrations for some of her 'Tales'. Treasured objects and furniture. Traditional cottage garden. Themed shop. Timed tickets. BP Gallery nearby. Open Mar W/Es, then Apr-Oct Sa-W, also Th June-Aug & Oct, 10.30-4.30. (H&) 015394 36269 www.nationaltrust.org.uk

Where to Eat, Drink & Be Merry...

Sawrey Hotel, Far Sawrey. A pleasant enough spot to rest and have a drink whilst sitting in the sunshine. The bar's layout is interesting. It was once the stables but how the horses entered is a mystery to me. The bedrooms are basic. 015394 43425 www.sawrey-hotel.co.uk

Tower Bank Arms, Near Sawrey. A small country inn featured in the "Tales of Jemima Puddleduck". The simple décor is pleasing to the eye, the food is nourishing and sourced locally and the bedrooms are comfortable. 015394 36334 www.towerbankarms.com

Hill Top ss

1220	Cockermouth granted a charter	1267	Founding of the Egremont Crab (apple) Fair
1239	Sir Walter Strickland moves into Sizergh Castle as part of marriage settlement	1275	First recording of hamlet known as Ambleside
		1315	Robert the Bruce raids and destroys much of Cockermouth

Kendal Museum ss

KENDAL

The former Roman fort of Alauna and a flourishing wool town in the C14 largely established by John Kemp of Flanders who was granted special dispensation by Edward III to establish a woollen industry. The heavy cloth, Kendal Green, became nationally famous and was mentioned in Shakespeare's plays. The town's coat of arms reads, as translated from the Latin, 'Wool is my Bread'. The Castle was the birthplace of Katherine Parr, Henry VIII's last and surviving wife. It is often called "The Auld Grey Town", however, today, Kendal is a busy market town and administrative centre. If you can park or find your way out of the one-way system, bravo, for you did well. Your persistence will be richly rewarded. Kendal is a town not to be overlooked. It has some fine museums and the riverside walk is a delight. A fine parish church next to Abbot Hall and the castle ruins. Kendal is the major shopping outlet for the Lakes. (L4)

Special Places to Visit...

Abbot Hall Art Gallery. A fine collection of paintings (Romneys and English Watercolours), furniture and Objets d'Arts in an elegant Georgian villa. Changing exhibitions of contemporary painters, having hosted ones for Lucian Freud, Bridget Riley, Stanley Spencer and Walter R Sickert. Open mid-Jan to Xmas, M-Sa 10.30-5. (L4) 01539 722464 www.abbothall.org.uk

Brewery Arts Centre, Highgate. A lively modern arts complex, with a continuous programme of theatre, folk, jazz, mime and two-screen cinema. Restaurant. Open all year M-Sa 9.30am to 11.00pm., Su 11-midnight. (L4) 01539 725133 www.breweryarts.co.uk

Museum Of Lakeland Life, Abbot Hall. Everyday life in Lakeland from the C17 to the present day. Crafts (the Arts & Craft movement), costume, furniture and farming and local industries. It has something for everyone. Open early Jan to Xmas M-Sa 10.30-5 (-4 Jan-Mar & Nov-Dec). (L4) 01539 722464. www.lakelandmuseum.org.uk

Kendal Museum, Station Road. Documents the archaeology and natural history of the Lake District and thus not to be missed by anyone studying Lakeland life. There are Roman and Egyptian artefacts, a world wildlife exhibition and a gallery devoted to the colossus, Alfred Wainwright. Open Th, F, Sa 12-5. (L4) 01539 721374. www.kendalmuseum.org.uk

Castle Dairy, 26 Wildman St. Formerly the castle's dairy used during Katherine Parr's stay. Hand-carved four-poster bed. Now a restaurant, open Tu-Sa for lunch and dinner. (L4) 01539 730334

Kendal Castle. These C13 ruins of Kendal Castle, once home to the Parr family, stand on Castle Hill and provide wonderful views over the market town of Kendal. (L4)

Kendal, Holy Trinity. Nave and aisle enlarged to Early English style. (L4)

The Quaker Tapestry Exhibition Centre. Stramongate. 77 panels of embroidery explore the Quaker journey from the C17 to today. This extraordinary achievement was undertaken by 4,000 men, women and children from 15 countries between 1981 and 1996. Café. Open Apr-Dec M-F 10-5. (L4) 01539 722975 www.quaker-tapestry.co.uk

Where to Eat, Drink & Be Merry...

Waterside Wholefood & Vegetarian Café, Waterside. Well established café serving vegan and vegetarian meals, all cooked on the premises. Open M-Sa 8.30-4.30. (L4) 01539 729743 www.watersidewholefood.co.uk

Museum of Lakeland Life, Abbot Hall ss

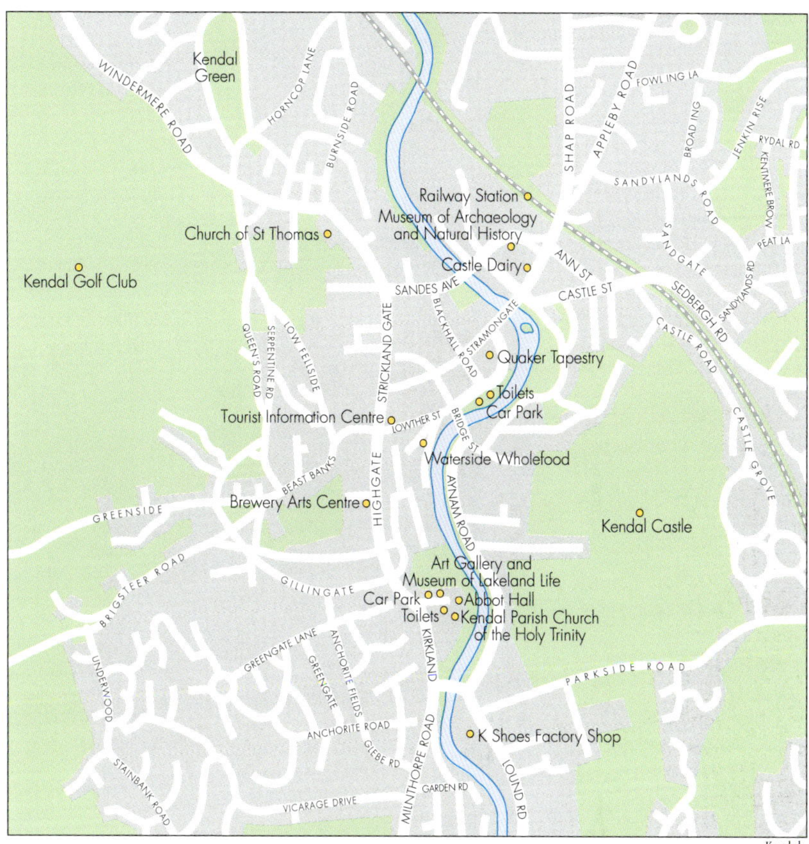

Kendal

Just Outside Kendal...

Low Sizergh Farm, Sizergh.
Dairy farm of long standing, in fact, 'Sizergh' is the Norse word for summer pasture. You may stroll around the farm, sit in their tearoom, or delight in the farm shop or craft gallery. Open daily. (L6) 015395 60426
www.lowsizerghbarn.co.uk

Plumgarths Food Shop, Crook Road. Set in a 55-acre farm they sell a range of high quality food sourced from local farmers and small scale suppliers located throughout Cumbria. Open daily 9-5. (K3) 01539 736300
www.plumgarths.co.uk

Punchbowl Inn & Restaurant, Crosthwaite. A stylish and modern inn that epitomises the expectations of our Age. The bedrooms are lavish and luxurious, the restaurant serves fine cuisine and the bar is relaxed and carefree. You won't wish to leave. (H5) 015395 68237
www.the-punchbowl.co.uk

Where to Stay...

Crosthwaite House. Robin and Marnie have been hosting B&B for the past 40 years in their C18 Georgian home. The house looks out across the beautiful Lyth Valley and is within walking distance of the foodie inn, The Punchbowl. The bedrooms are spacious and comfortable. Robin is from Keswick and is a musician, former climber and caver, and a mine of long tales. His father worked for the famous Abraham Brothers of Keswick. Self-catering cottages, next door. Opens from mid-March. (H5) 015395 68264
www.crosthwaitehouse.co.uk

Low Jock Scar, Selside.
You'll know you are in good hands the moment you meet Rosalyn, a natural hostess. Full of exuberance, enthusiasm and friendliness, backed up by John hovering in the background who tends their glorious garden beside an idyllic river. Dinner is available. Five double/twin rooms. (M10) 01539 823259
www.lowjockscar.co.uk

Tranthwaite Hall. A working dairy and sheep farm in an isolated position at the end of a long drive. The house is as old as the hills and dates from 1174 and is full of character with oak doors and beams, a black iron grange and family antiques. All the bedrooms have bathrooms. (J4) 015395 68285
www.tranthwaitehall.co.uk

Country Pursuits...

Bigland Hall Equestrian. Full range of equine activities and trail riding over spectacular scenery for all abilities, as well as quad biking, archery, fishing and clay shooting available. They will arrange accommodation for you. (C9) 015395 30333 www.biglandhall.com

Esthwaite Water Trout Fishing. Fish for Brown and Rainbow trout whether you're an expert or beginner. Fly only from boats in 200 acres of water. Tuition and rod hire available. Permits from boathouse on south shore. (D2) 015394 36541 www.hawksheadtrout.com

Fell Foot Park & Garden, Nr Newby Bridge. (NT) An 18-acre country park with gardens now restored to their former glory, plus bathing, fishing, rowing boats for hire (East-Oct). Information Centre, shop & tearoom (11-5), caravanning (Mar-Oct), Park Open daily 9-5. (E7) 015395 31273 www.nationaltrust.org.uk

Grizedale Forest Park. An example of integrated land use with farming and forestry working side by side. There are coded waymarked trails highlighted by garish banners which remind me of promotional material more at home in a supermarket, all I suppose for the benefit of the urban walker. You can also take part in an orienteering course and follow their mountain bike routes (better to buy a map and strike out on your own), woodland sculptures - they will charge you to photograph, car parks (charge), picnic sites, play area, shop, exhibition and cafe. Visitor Centre open daily from 10. One can't help feeling that they are trying to empty your pockets at every turn. The Forestry Commission was set up by the government at the time of the World War I to make sure the country had enough trees. Supposedly to fill the trenches with hardy and lasting timber. They then covered every conceivable piece of land with pine. This was in the 50s and 60s, luckily they saw sense and now have a more diverse policy. The exorbitant parking charge still grates! (B3) 01229 860010 www.forestry.gov.uk

Esthwaite Water

MY Workshop and Gallery, Staveley

Special Places to Visit...

Aquarium Of The Lakes. Britain's leading fresh water aquarium featuring the UK's largest collection of fresh water fish. Coffee/gift shop. Open daily from 9. (D7) 015395 30153 www.aquariumofthelakes.co.uk

Finsthwaite Tower. Derelict building set in 65 acres of woodland. Built in honour of the Royal Navy's servicemen who defeated the fleets of the French, Spanish and Dutch in 1799. Footpath to tower, but closed for interior viewing. (D6)

Graythwaite Hall. Spring flowering shrubs, azaleas and rhododendrons in a woodland setting of 12 acres, landscaped by Thomas Mawson in 1896. Dutch and Rose Gardens, typical of the late C19 and early C20. Open daily Apr-Aug 10-6. (D5) 015395 31333 www.graythwaitehall.co.uk

Grizedale Arts, Lawson Park Farm. This organisation organizes a mixed programme of events, projects and activities. A new site is being renovated as a home for contemporary and traditional artists, farmers, gardeners, and performing artists. (B3) 01539 441050 www.grizedale.org

1512   Katherine Parr (Henry VIII's sixth wife) was born in Kendal Castle

1564   Elizabeth I permits iron ore to be mined in Borrowdale. The Society of Mines Royal is formed, an Anglo-German enterprise managed by Haug, Langnauer & Co of Augsburg

Grizedale Sculpture

Lakeside & Haverthwaite Railway Co Ltd

Halecat Garden. Unusual plants a speciality (hydrangeas), biennials, perennials and shrubs - many on sale in Nursery. Open M-F 8-5 (& W/Es after Easter). (G8) 01539 552229

Lakeside & Haverthwaite Railway Co Ltd. Standard gauge steam locomotives running through 3 1/2 miles of contrasting lake and river scenery. Connections at Lakeside with Windermere. Cruises to Bowness and Ambleside. Open East, then May-Oct 10.35 to 16.15. (C8) 015395 31594 www.lakesiderailway.co.uk

Staveley Mill Yard. This small enterprise park has become (almost by accident) one of Lakeland's great attractions. It is set neatly between Kendal and Windermere, and has something to interest all the family, be it an art gallery, baker, bike shop, brewery, café or furniture workshops. (J1)

Hawkshead Brewery. This tailor-made brewery built beside the River Kent produces 4 cask ales and seasonal beers. Its mission is to revitalise and to be at the heart of the revolution to revive our national drink - beer. You can visit the Beer Hall, Brewery Tap, Sampling Room and the Visitor Centre. Tours are arranged at 1, 2 & 3 pm on weekends (for the over 12s). (J1) 01539 822644 www.hawksheadbrewery.co.uk

Lucy Cooks. The successful deli-bistro business from Ambleside have opened this cookery school with a range of individual one-day courses suitable for all ages. They tackle children's courses, pudding nights, aga sagas, barbecue delights, fab fish, perfect pasta. Whatever you choose, it will switch on your taste buds. (J1) 015394 32288 www.lucycooks.co.uk

MY Workshop & Gallery, 22-25 Mill Yard. Fine pieces of intricate and sweetly shaped furniture are made in the workshop. Upstairs, the gallery displays ceramics, glass and paintings. Open daily. (J1) 01539 822852 www.millyardgallery.com

Out of the Woods Workshop. Rustic-style furniture made on the premises. Open M-F 8-5, Sa 11-3. (J1) 01539 822033 www.outofthewoodsinteriors.co.uk

Wilf's Café. If you are driving up the M6 and don't fancy the service station and need to gear up before a morning or afternoon on the fells, there's no better place to tank up then here. It could become a habit that you start the day with Wilf's Rarebit. A great place to have a late breakfast, coffee, lunch, veggie meals, salads, puds. Special Evenings of French, Mexican. (J1) 01539 822329 www.wilfs-cafe.co.uk

Graythwaite Hall

| 1566 | World's first pencil factory opens in Keswick using "wad" black lead/graphite from mines at Seathwaite | 1580 | Levens Hall built |
| 1578 | First recorded evidence of work at Eskdale Corn Mill | 1585 | Hawkshead Grammar School founded by Edwin Sandys, Archbishop of York |

Levens Hall

Levens Hall & Topiary Garden.
Elizabethan house with world
famous topiary garden laid out in
1694. Built around a C13 Pele tower.
Jacobean furniture, fine paintings
and earliest English patchwork.
Woodland play area. Steam
Collection. Tea room and gift shop.
Open Apr to mid-Oct Su-Th, House
12-4.30, Garden and tea room 10-5.
(K6) 015395 60321
www.levenshall.co.uk

Lyth Valley. The orchards in
Spring bask in the glory of damson
blossom. The first is harvested
in the autumn. (J6)

**Peter Hall & Son, Danes Rd.
Staveley.** Family-run firm creating
exquisite hand crafted furniture
and gifts. The showroom displays
furniture and interior accessories.
Visit the Viewing Gallery to watch
craftsmen and restorers at work.
Open M-F 9-5, Sa showroom only
10-1. (J1) 01539 821633
www.peter-hall.co.uk

**Robert Fletcher Wildlife Artist,
Satterthwaite.** Robert Fletcher
draws wildlife and landscape scenes
in pencils and crushed pastels.
Originals and prints for sales.
His studio is open most days.
01229 860234
www.robertfletcherwildlifeartist.co.uk

Sizergh Castle (NT).
The Strickland family home for
750 years. Impressive C14 Pele
Tower. Much altered in Tudor times,
with the finest Elizabethan carved

Stott Park Bobbin Mill

overmantles in the county. English
and French furniture. Family
portraits. Stuart relics. The Trust's
largest Rock Garden. Rose and Dutch
gardens. Tea room. NT shop. Open
mid Mar to Oct Su-Th 1-5, garden
from 11am. (K6) 015395 60951
www.nationaltrust.org.uk

Stott Park Bobbin Mill (EH).
Built in 1835 to supply wooden
bobbins and cotton reels to the
Lancashire textile industry. Open
Apr-Oct M-F 10-5. (D6) 01539 531087

Peter Hall & Son, Staveley ss

1620	Cartmel Church restored by George Preston of Holker Hall
1626	Townend Farm, Troutbeck built by George Browne (High Constable in 1667)

1635 Windermere ferry capsizes and 47 in wedding party
are drowned

Greenod

Where to Stay...

Beechmount Country House.
Near Sawrey. This is an Arts & Crafts movement house that has recently been transformed from a ghastly mess into a charming home with many fine features. The bedrooms are luxurious and decorated with understated taste and no surprise the Schofields proclaim this as a luxurious B&B. 015394 36356 www.beechmountcountryhouse.co.uk

Buckle Yeat, Near Sawrey.
A quintessential Lakeland cottage B&B and home to Mr McGregor which will delight many of Potter's fans. Cosy, comfy and traditional, and a stone's throw from Hilltop. 015394 36446 www.buckle-yeat.co.uk

Low Graythwaite Hall.
Superior B&B in a beautiful C16 house. There are five double bedrooms with bathroom, and Dairy Cottage for self-catering. Indoor swimming pool, private boathouse on Windermere and four acres of gardens and woodland in which to roam. 015395 31676 www.lowgraythwaitehall.co.uk

West Vale Country House,
Far Sawrey. A small hotel managed with great enthusiasm and flair. I note "nothing was left out, everything was taken care of'. Recently decorated in a colourful contemporary style. 015394 42817 www.westvalecountryhouse.co.uk

Villages of Interest...

Cartmel Fell. Unique parish church built in 1504 by local farmers who didn't wish to make the long journey into Cartmel. C17 three-decker pulpit, C16 east window and C16-17 box pews. Arthur Ransome lived nearby at Low Ludderburn from1925-35 where he wrote Swallows & Amazon. (G6)

Greenodd. Former port used for the shipment of iron ore and slate. Not much to show for it today but in the late C19 one of the busiest shipbuilding yards in England. Just imagine the tall ships tied up at the head of the estuary. The picnic area beside the busy A590 is a showcase for birdlife: waders, wildfowl, terns, gulls, oyster-catchers, curlews and mallard - all to be seen enjoying the expansive estuary flats. (A9)

Short, Easy Walks...

Brantwood Garden Walks. (A2) You have a choice of various guided garden walks (with maps) and a childrens trail through the extensive estate with knowledgeable guides on hand from Easter to October every Wednesday, Thursday, Friday and alternate Sundays at 2.15pm. No pre-booking required. Or, you can follow the trail of your choice, alone. Some paths are quite steep in places. Reception provides a charming little booklet detailing each walk.

Grizedale Forest Paths. (B3) A full Information Pack is available from the Visitor Centre detailing the various graded routes from 1 to 9.5 miles along forest roads, tracks and bridleways. If you enjoy walking around Tescos or Sainsburys you'll feel at home here. The waymarked signs resemble supermarket billboards. There are easy paths and there are more challenging routes, and these pass beside ancient beech trees, sculptures and disused smelting works.

Gummer's How Viewpoint. (E6) It's a gentle ascent of 1 mile/1.3km from the Forestry Commission car park to this fine viewpoint overlooking the southern stretch of Windermere, the Coniston Fells, Coniston Old Man, Scafell Pike and Wetherlam.

Greenodd to Low Wood
(or vice versa). (A9) A linear route that takes in part of the Cumbria Coastal Way. It crosses the estuary then enters woodland before following the River Leven into Low Wood. Easier to park in Greenodd. The distance is about 3.5 miles/5 km and follows a bridlepath and farm tracks.

Orrest Head Viewpoint from Windermere. (F1) 1 mile/1.6 km. This is an easy ascent up a track that starts on the A591 on the opposite side of the road to the Railway Station. It's a short walk rising to 784 feet above sea level and provides fine views of the fells, Windermere, Morecambe Bay and the Pennines. Average time taken to reach the top is twenty minutes. Worth the effort if you have a free hour to spend.

Scout Scar Viewpoint from Car Park. (K4) This is an easy stroll of half-a-mile along a well-worn path from the car park on the Underbarrow Road to a fine panoramic viewpoint.

Patterson Boatworks, Hawkshead ss

The coastal towns of Barrow-In-Furness, Maryport and Whitehaven have long been known as centres of shipbuilding but it was not until the wealthy Manchester industrialists settled on the shores of Windermere for their weekends and holidays that Lakeland boatbuilding came into its own. The combination of ambition and ostentation created the "Golden Age of Steamboating on the Lake". Each industrialist tried to out do his neighbour by building the grandest steam yacht. Many of these fine boats are to be found now in the Windermere Steamboat Museum which is currently closed and undergoing a colossal refurbishment programme under the direction of the Lakeland Arts Trust.

But, it was not just steam yachts that came to be built in the Lake District. The great shipyards of Barrow and Whitehaven turned out apprentices who moved on to practice their trade in the small boatyards of Bowness, Windermere and Hawkshead; Shepherds and Patterson Boatworks or with the National Trust's Steam Yacht Gondola.

At the beginning of the twentieth century, The Royal Windermere Yacht Club asked the designer Herbert Crossley to design a yacht that was small, easy to handle and able to be sailed by amateur crews of two. It had to be cheap to maintain, be easily rigged and suitable as a cruising yacht. In 1904 he came up with the 17ft Class. The first five were built by Shepherds of Windermere. The specifications for this class were exacting. A 17ft waterline, and overall length of 25ft 6 inches, a minimum beam of 5ft 10 inches, and a 4 ft

Merlin, Type 17, James Nield's Yard, Windermere

Patterson Boatworks ss

Patterson Boatworks ss

Patterson Boatworks ss

draft. A lead ballast of 16 hundredweight, and sail area not to exceed 300 square feet. The result was a most beautifully proportioned yacht. Still very much in evidence today on Lake Windermere. The original ruling of becoming a member of this august sailing club was that every new member had to have a new yacht built. This in turn created a thriving boat building community. This ruling has since been overturned due to the fabrication costs. However, these yachts can be seen racing each other at weekends, and are a site to behold!

Patterson Boatworks ss

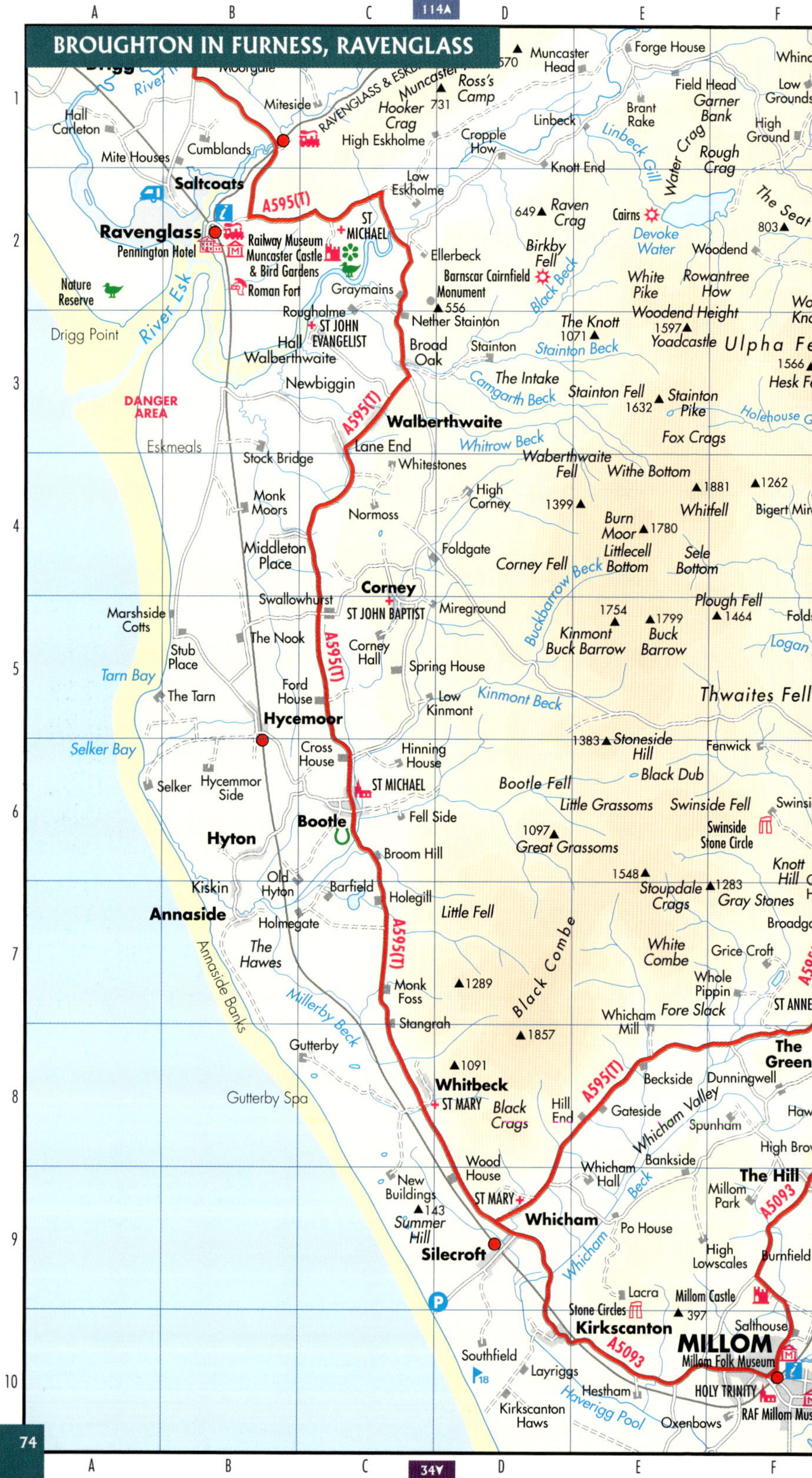

BROUGHTON IN FURNESS, RAVENGLASS
Drigg
River
Moorgate
Miteside
RAVENGLASS & ESKDALE
Muncaster Head
Forge House
Whinc
Hall Carleton
Hooker Crag
731
Ross's Camp
Field Head
Garner Bank
Low Grounds
Mite Houses
Cumblands
High Eskholme
Cropple How
Linbeck
Brant Rake
Water Crag
High Ground
Saltcoats
Low Eskholme
Knott End
Linbeck Gill
Rough Crag
The Seat
A595(T)
ST MICHAEL
649
Raven Crag
Cairns
803
Ravenglass
Pennington Hotel
Railway Museum
Muncaster Castle & Bird Gardens
Ellerbeck
Birkby Fell
Devoke Water
Woodend
Nature Reserve
Barnscar Cairnfield Monument
Black Beck
White Pike
Rowantree How
Woodend Height
Wo Kno
Roman Fort
Graymains
556
Roughholme
ST JOHN EVANGELIST
Nether Stainton
The Knott
1071
1597
Yoadcastle
Ulpha Fe
Drigg Point
River Esk
Hall Walberthwaite
Broad Oak
Stainton
Stainton Beck
1566
Hesk Fe
Newbiggin
A595(T)
Camgarth Beck
The Intake
Stainton Fell
1632
Stainton Pike
Holehouse G
DANGER AREA
Walberthwaite
Whitrow Beck
Waberthwaite Fell
Fox Crags
Eskmeals
Lane End
Whitestones
High Corney
Withe Bottom
1881
1262
Stock Bridge
1399
Whitfell
Bigert Min
Monk Moors
Normoss
Burn Moor
1780
Littlecell Bottom
Sele Bottom
Middleton Place
Foldgate
Corney Fell
Beck
Marshside Cotts
Swallowhurst
Corney
ST JOHN BAPTIST
Mireground
1754
Plough Fell
1464
Fold
The Nook
Corney Hall
Buckbarrow Beck
Kinmont Buck Barrow
1799
Buck Barrow
Logan
Stub Place
Spring House
Tarn Bay
Ford House
Low Kinmont
Kinmont Beck
Thwaites Fell
The Tarn
Hycemoor
1383
Stoneside Hill
Fenwick
Selker Bay
Cross House
Hinning House
Black Dub
Selker
Hycemmor Side
ST MICHAEL
Bootle Fell
Little Grassoms
Swinside Fell
Swinsi
Hyton
Bootle
Fell Side
1097
Great Grassoms
Swinside Stone Circle
Broom Hill
1548
Stoupdale Crags
1283
Knott Hill
Gray Stones
Kiskin
Old Hyton
Barfield
Holegill
Little Fell
Broadga
Annaside
Holmegate
The Hawes
1289
Black Combe
White Combe
Grice Croft
Whole Pippin
A50
ST ANNE
Annaside Banks
Millerby Beck
Monk Foss
Fore Slack
Stangrah
1857
Whicham Mill
A595(T)
The Green
Gutterby
1091
Whitbeck
ST MARY
Black Crags
Hill End
Beckside
Dunningwell
Gutterby Spa
Gateside
Whicham Valley
Spunham
Haw
Wood House
Whicham Hall
Bankside
High Brov
New Buildings
ST MARY
Beck
The Hill
Millom Park
A5093
143
Summer Hill
Whicham
Po House
High Lowscales
Silecroft
Whicham
Burnfield
Lacra
Millom Castle
Stone Circles
397
Salthouse
Kirkscanton
MILLOM
Millom Folk Museum
Southfield
A5093
Layriggs
HOLY TRINITY
18
Hestham
Hoverigg Pool
Oxenbows
RAF Millom Mus
Kirkscanton Haws

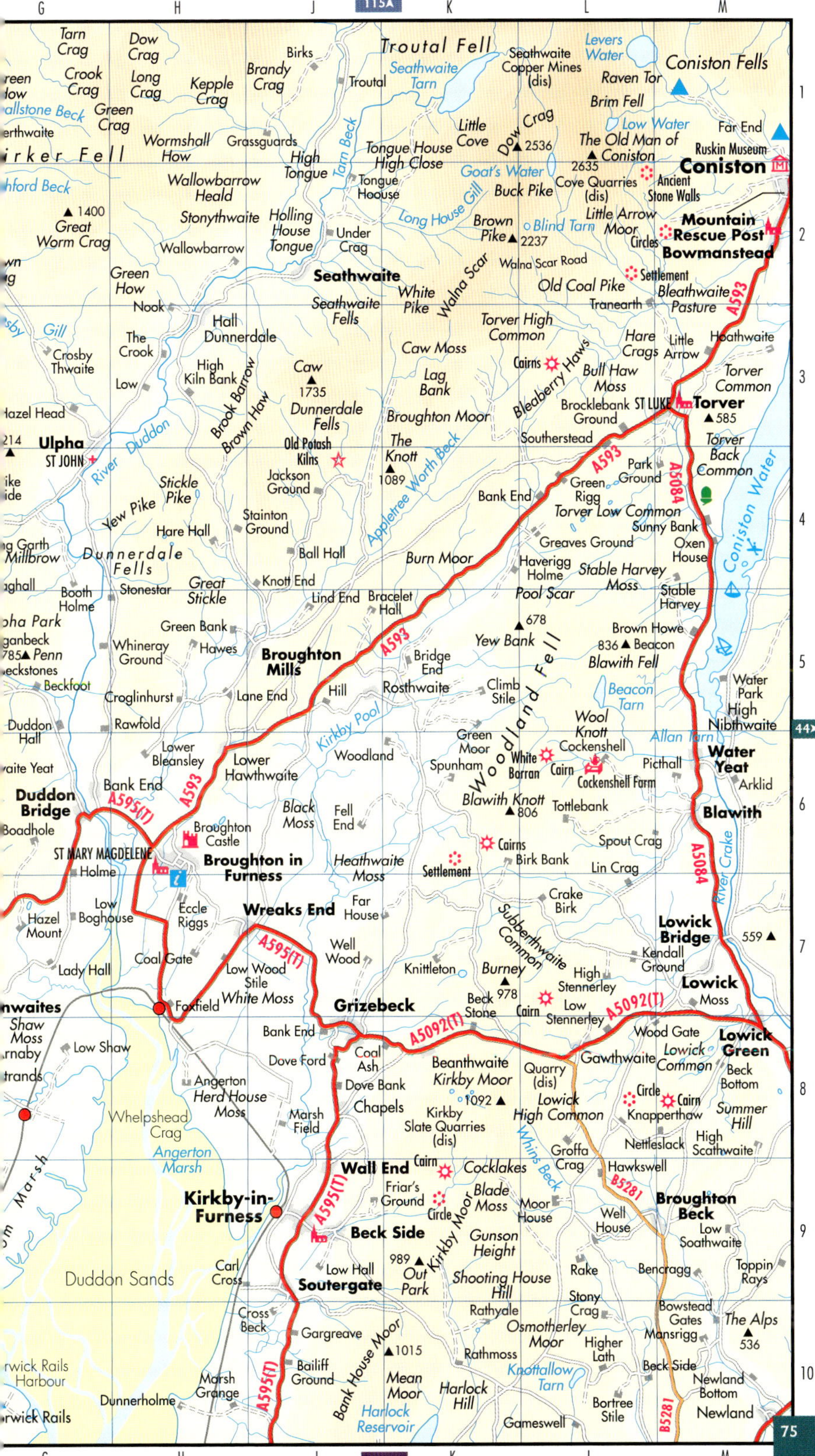
115
Coniston Fells
Tarn Crag
Crook Crag
Dow Crag
Long Crag
Kepple Crag
Brandy Crag
Birks
Troutal Fell
Seathwaite Tarn
Levers Water
Raven Tor
Brim Fell
Far End
Green How
allstone Beck
erthwaite
irker Fell
Green Crag
Wormshall How
Grassguards
High Tongue
Troutal
Tongue House
High Close
Seathwaite Copper Mines (dis)
Little Cove
Dow Crag
2536
Low Water
The Old Man of Coniston
2635
Ruskin Museum
Coniston
nford Beck
Wallowbarrow Heald
Stonythwaite
Holling House Tongue
Under Crag
Tongue Hoouse
Long House Gill
Goat's Water
Buck Pike
Brown Pike
2237
Blind Tarn
Cove Quarries (dis)
Little Arrow Moor
Ancient Stone Walls
Mountain Rescue Post
Bowmanstead
1400
Great Worm Crag
Wallowbarrow
White Pike
Walna Scar
Walna Scar Road
Old Coal Pike
Circles
Settlement
Tranearth
Bleathwaite Pasture
wn g
Green How
Nook
Hall Dunnerdale
Seathwaite
Seathwaite Fells
Caw Moss
Torver High Common
Hare Crags
Little Arrow
Hoathwaite
Torver Common
sby Gill
The Crook
High Kiln Bank
Caw
1735
Lag Bank
Cairns
Bull Haw Moss
Crosby Thwaite
Low
Brook Barrow
Brown Haw
Dunnerdale Fells
Broughton Moor
Bleaberry Haws
Brocklebank Ground
Southerstead
ST LUKE
Torver
585
azel Head
214
Ulpha
ST JOHN
River Duddon
Old Potash Kilns
The Knott
1089
Appletree Worth Beck
Bank End
Green Rigg
Park Ground
Torver Back Common
ike de
Yew Pike
Stickle Pike
Jackson Ground
Stainton Ground
Bank End
Torver Low Common
Sunny Bank
Coniston Water
A5084
ga Garth Millbrow
Dunnerdale Fells
Hare Hall
Ball Hall
Burn Moor
Greaves Ground
Haverigg Holme
Stable Harvey Moss
Oxen House
ghall
Booth Holme
Stonestar
Great Stickle
Knott End
Lind End
Bracelet Hall
Pool Scar
Stable Harvey
ha Park
ganbeck
785
Penn
eckstones
Beckfoot
Whineray Ground
Hawes
Green Bank
Broughton Mills
Hill
Rosthwaite
Bridge End
Yew Bank
678
Blawith Fell
836
Beacon
Brown Howe
Water Park High Nibthwaite
Duddon Hall
Croglinhurst
Lane End
Climb Stile
Beacon Tarn
aite Yeat
Rawfold
Lower Bleansley
Lower Hawthwaite
Woodland
Green Moor
Wool Knott
Cockenshell
Allan Tarn
Water Yeat
Duddon Bridge
Bank End
A595(T)
A593
Spunham
White Barran
Cairn
Cockenshell Farm
Picthall
Arklid
oadhole
Broughton Castle
Black Moss
Fell End
Blawith Knott
806
Tottlebank
Blawith
ST MARY MAGDELENE
Holme
Broughton in Furness
Heathwaite Moss
Settlement
Birk Bank
Lin Crag
Spout Crag
River Crake
A5084
Hazel Mount
Low Boghouse
Eccle Riggs
Wreaks End
Far House
Crake Birk
Lowick Bridge
559
Lady Hall
Coal Gate
A595(T)
Low Wood Stile
White Moss
Well Wood
Knittleton
Burney
978
Subberthwaite Common
High Stennerley
Kendall Ground
Lowick
Moss
nwaites
Shaw Moss
rnaby
Foxfield
Grizebeck
Beck Stone
Cairn
Low Stennerley
A5092(T)
Lowick Green
Low Shaw
Bank End
Dove Ford
Coal Ash
A5092(T)
Wood Gate
Gawthwaite
Lowick Common
Beck Bottom
rands
Angerton Herd House Moss
Dove Bank
Chapels
Beanthwaite
Kirkby Moor
1092
Quarry (dis)
Lowick High Common
Circle
Knapperthaw
Cairn
Summer Hill
Whelpshead Crag
Marsh Field
Kirkby Slate Quarries (dis)
Groffa Crag
Nettleslack
High Scathwaite
Angerton Marsh
Wall End
Cairn
Cocklakes
Whins Beck
Hawkswell
B5281
Broughton Beck
m Marsh
Kirkby-in-Furness
A595(T)
Friar's Ground
Circle
Blade Moss
Moor House
Well House
Low Soathwaite
Beck Side
Gunson Height
Bencragg
Toppin Rays
Duddon Sands
Carl Cross
Low Hall
Soutergate
989
Out Park
Shooting House Hill
Rake
Bowstead Gates
Mansrigg
The Alps
536
Cross Beck
Gargreave
Rathyale
Osmotherley Moor
Stony Crag
Higher Lath
Beck Side
Newland Bottom
rwick Rails Harbour
Marsh Grange
A595(T)
Bailiff Ground
Bank House Moor
1015
Mean Moor
Rathmoss
Harlock Hill
Knottallow Tarn
Gameswell
Bortree Stile
B5281
Newland
rwick Rails
Dunnerholme
Harlock Reservoir

Ravenglass & Eskdale Railway

Blue Flea, RAF Millom Museum ss

BROUGHTON IN FURNESS

Translated from the Saxon, Broughton means 'The hamlet by the stream', and is a friendly old market town, untarnished by its many visitors, and one of the gems of Southern Lakeland. There are a number of fine C18 houses and the original clock designed in 1768 still works in the Market Hall. A number of inns are positioned on corners of the shaded village square. The Pele Tower is all that remains of the former castle, or Brocton, as first mentioned in the Domesday Book. A search around the churchyard reveals endless tombs of persons well into their hundredth year. It must be the air, dodgy memories and energetic slant of the hill. (H6)

MILLOM

Former coal and iron ore centre overlooking Duddon Sands and the sheltered beach at Haverigg. (F10)

Special Places to Visit...

Millom Castle. A few remaining ruins surround farm buildings. (F9)

Millom Folk Museum.

An enthusiastic little museum exhibits local Hodbarrow Iron Ore mine, agriculture, the local poet Norman Nicholson, shipping and natural history. TIC. Open Good F-Oct Tu-Sa 10-5. (F10) 01229 772555 www.millomfolkmuseum.co.uk

RAF Millom Museum.

Aero engines, cockpits, helicopter, photographs and more. Open W/Es all year 10.30-5, also East-Sept M, W & F. (F10) 01229 777446 www.rafmillom.co.uk

RAVENGLASS

This romantic village looks out across the Esk estuary which teems with birdlife. It is, and has been, a start-off point for Roman adventures, climbing adventures and romantic adventures for the railway station has been the stop-off point for many couples heading out to beautiful Eskdale and the mountains beyond. (B2)

Ravenglass & Eskdale Railway

('Tall Ratty'). Legendary narrow gauge railway line opened in 1875 to transport iron ore, and later passengers. The oldest engine in use was built in 1894, the newest at Ravenglass in 1976. The 7 mile line runs from the coast to picturesque Eskdale. Railway Museum. Ratty Arms. Open daily mid-Mar to 31 Oct. 26 Dec-2 Jan plus limited winter W/E services Nov-Mar. (B2) 01229 717171 www.ravenglass-railway.co.uk

Walls Castle. The bath house is all that survives of the Roman fort Glannaventa. Well preserved, with red sandstone, and rendered inside with pink mortar. (B2)

Where to Stay...

The Pennington Hotel. This is just what was required in Ravenglass. A place to stay and eat, if visiting the neighbouring sites. The Penningtons of Muncaster Castle have designed a contemporary style hotel which overlooks the brooding estuary. Much of the food originates from their estate; fell bred lamb, rare breed pork and vegetables from their kitchen garden. (B2) 01229 717222 www.thepennington.co.uk

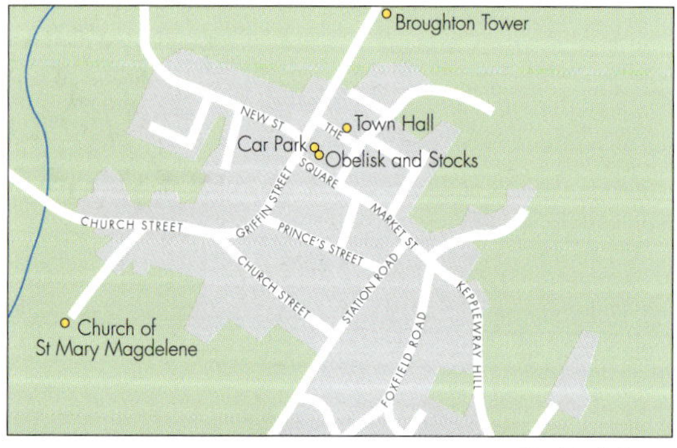

Broughton-In-Furness

This historic castle has been home to the Penningtons for 800 years, and is a treasure trove of art and antiques, surrounded by breathtaking gardens and the World Owl Centre with displays Mar-Nov. Wild herons fed daily 4.30pm. Interactive MeadowVole Maze. Darkest Muncaster events most winter weekends. Café and gift shops. Garden. Owl centre and maze open daily 10.30-6. Castle open mid-Feb to 4 Nov Su-F 12-5. (C2) 01229 717614. www.muncaster.co.uk

Muncaster Church. Saxon and Viking stones in churchyard. Pennington monuments. (C2)

River Duddon

MOUNTAINS

The Old Man of Coniston,
2635ft/803m. Provides a shapely
backdrop to Coniston Water. (L1)
Route 1. Set out from Coniston
village and cross the old railway
bridge. Follow the steepish road to
Walna Scar road. The path bears
right, and up to Goat's Water, and
onto the summit. Return via Low
Water, through the mess of stones
and coppermines into Coppermine
Valley. (M2)

Special Places to Visit...

Birks Bridge Rapids. Several
cascades have punished the
rocks to create lovely clear pools,
ideal for bathing. (G4)

Duddon Valley. The river Duddon's
source is high on Pike O Blisco and
Wyrnose Pass, and is a meandering
stream until it meets Cockley Beck
Bridge where its mood and tempo
change to a thrilling rush. The
ravine at Birks (Burks) Bridge is a
dark and narrow gorge whence the
river follows a natural course to flow
eventually into the expanse
of Duddon Sands. This valley
inspired William Wordsworth to
write 35 sonnets. (H3-H8)

Swinside Stone Circle.
Its other name is Sunkenkirk possibly
indicating a former place of worship,
rites or sacrifice. An isolated and
impressive site of 55 stones at the top
of a rough track. (F6)

Where to Stay...

Cockenskell Farm, Blawith.
This is a typical C17 Cumbrian
farmhouse or Longhouse in an
isolated position at the end of a long
and winding track. Your hostess is
wonderfully straight talking. Her
home is beautifully decorated, awash
with lime plaster, beams and family
antiques. Luxurious B&B at its
very best. (L6) 01229 885217
www.cockenskell.co.uk

1692	Levens Hall topiary built by Monsieur Beaumont, the King's gardener	1738	Founding of the Backbarrow iron furnance
1717	Fire destroys much of Lowther Castle	1745	Battle of Clifton, last military battle fought on English soil
		1750	Hill farmers begin the construction of stone wall enclosures

**For climbing and fell walking, sailing, mountaineering,
Lakeland poets.**

This is the heart and soul of the Lake District. It was this landscape that so
bewitched and beguiled the C19 lakeland poets: Wordsworth, Southey and Coleridge.
A landscape so achingly beautiful that these men of great articulation were stunned
into silent awe.

The Central Fells has it all. The enchanting valleys of Borrowdale, Eskdale,
Ennerdale, Langdale and Wasdale overlooked by the towering peaks of Fairfield,
Great Gable, Helvellyn and England's highest mountain, Scafell.

Ancient history can be felt throughout the Lakes. Langdale is known to be the source
of a particular type of Neolithic polished stone axe head, created on the slopes of the
Pike of Stickle and traded all over prehistoric Great Britain and Europe. Neolithic
cup and ring marks are found on the Langdale Boulders and the remains of Hard
Knott Pass Fort (a Roman fort) can be seen at the top of Hard Knott Pass.

The magnificent lakes and tarns: Buttermere, Grasmere, Rydal Water – one of the
smallest, Tarn Hows, Wastwater and (northern) Windermere. Some are linked by
treacherous (and unforgettable) passes: Honister, Hardknott and Wrynose.
Wastwater is one of the finest examples of a glacially 'over-deepened' valley. The
surface of the lake is about 200 feet above sea level, while its bottom is over 50 feet
below sea level.

Ascending Great Gable

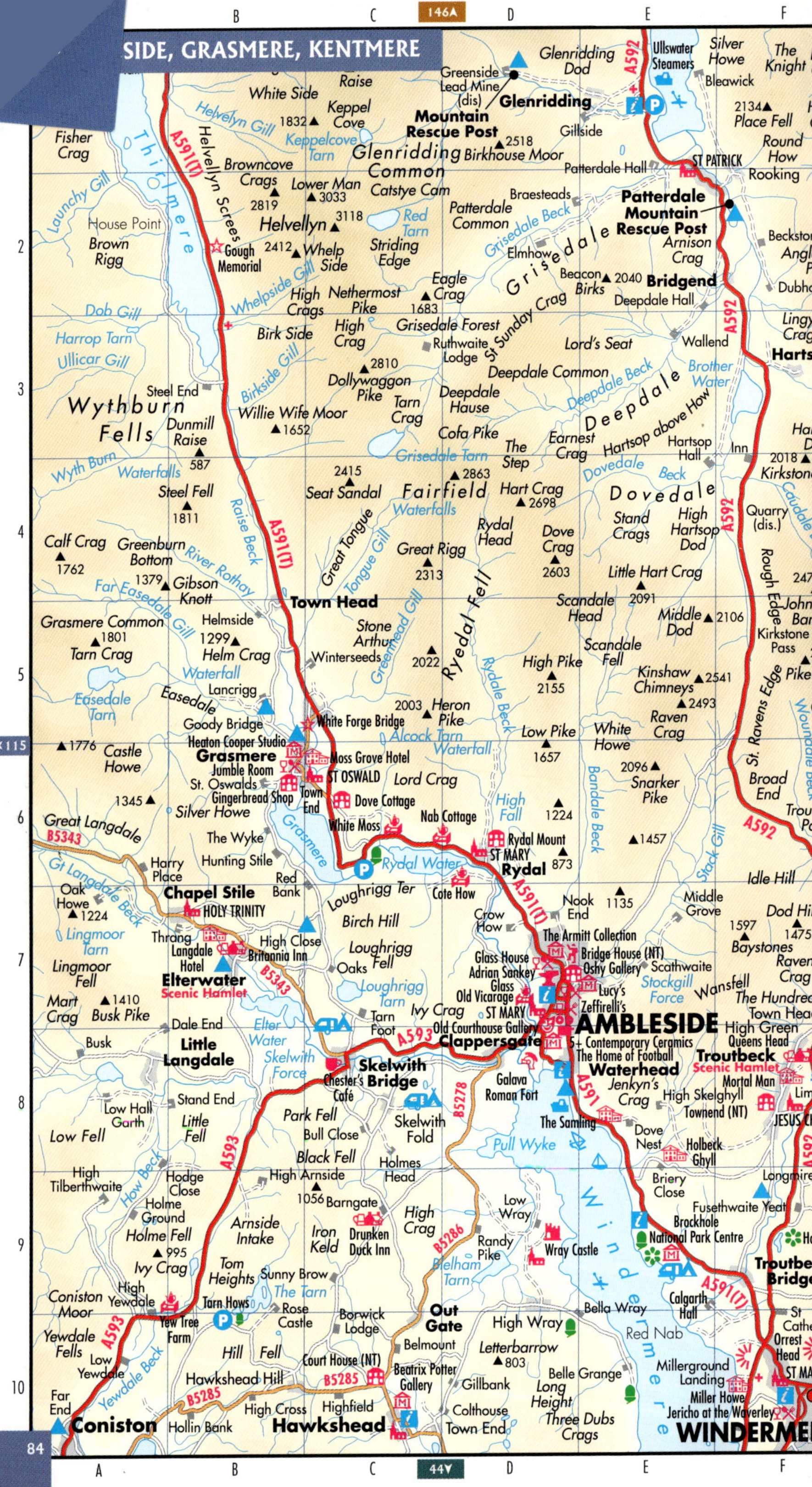

SIDE, GRASMERE, KENTMERE
146A
Fisher Crag
Launchy Gill
House Point
Brown Rigg
Dob Gill
Harrop Tarn
Ullicar Gill
Thirlmere
A591(T)
Helvellyn Gill
Keppelcove Tarn
White Side
Raise
Keppel Cove
1832
Helvellyn Screes
Browncove Crags
2819
Lower Man 3033
Catstye Cam
Red Tarn
Helvellyn
3118
Wythburn Fells
Steel End
Dunmill Raise
587
Whelpside Gill
Gough Memorial
2412
Whelp Side
Striding Edge
High Crags
Nethermost Pike
1683
High Crag
Birk Side
Birkside Gill
2810
Dollywaggon Pike
Tarn Crag
Willie Wife Moor
1652
Grisedale Tarn
Wyth Burn
Waterfalls
Steel Fell
1811
Raise Beck
A591(T)
2415
Seat Sandal
Great Tongue
Tongue Gill
Fairfield
2863
Waterfalls
Hart Crag
2698
Greenside Lead Mine (dis)
Mountain Rescue Post
Glenridding Dod
Glenridding
Gillside
2518
Birkhouse Moor
Glenridding Common
Patterdale Hall
A592
Ullswater Steamers
Silver Howe
The Knight
Bleawick
2134
Place Fell
Round How
Rooking
ST PATRICK
Patterdale Common
Braesteads
Grisedale Beck
Elmhow
Grisedale
Patterdale Mountain Rescue Post
Beacon 2040
Deepdale Hall
Arnison Crag
Bridgend
Beckstones
Angle
Dubho
Eagle Crag
Patterdale
St Sunday Crag
Grisedale Forest
Ruthwaite Lodge
Lord's Seat
Deepdale Common
Deepdale Beck
Wallend
Brother Water
Harts
Lingy Crag
Deepdale Hause
Cofa Pike
The Step
Earnest Crag
Hartsop above How
Hartsop Hall
Inn
Deepdale
Dovedale Beck
Ha De
2018
Kirkstone
Dove Crag
2603
Rydal Head
Dovedale
Stand Crags
High Hartsop Dod
Quarry (dis.)
247
Rough Edge
Great Rigg
2313
Rydal Fell
Scandale Head
Little Hart Crag
2091
Middle Dod 2106
Kirkstone Pass
John Ban
Pike
Calf Crag
1762
Greenburn Bottom
1379
Gibson Knott
River Rothay
Far Easedale Gill
Town Head
Stone Arthur
Winterseeds
Greenhead Gill
2022
Heron Pike
Scandale Fell
High Pike
2155
Scandale
Kinshaw Chimneys 2541
2493
Raven Crag
St. Ravens Edge
Woundale Beck
Pike
Grasmere Common
1801
Tarn Crag
Helmside
1299
Helm Crag
Waterfall
Lancrigg
Easedale Tarn
Easedale
Goody Bridge
White Forge Bridge
Heaton Cooper Studio
Grasmere
Jumble Room
St. Oswalds
Gingerbread Shop
Silver Howe
1345
1776
Castle Howe
Great Langdale
B5343
Gt Langdale Beck
Lingmoor Tarn
Oak Howe
1224
Moss Grove Hotel
ST OSWALD
Town End
White Moss
Lord Crag
Dove Cottage
Nab Cottage
2003
Alcock Tarn Waterfall
High Fall
Grasmere
Nab Cottage
1224
Low Pike
1657
White Howe
2096
Snarker Pike
Broad End
Trout Pa
Raven Crag
Bandale Beck
1457
A592
Idle Hill
The Wyke
Hunting Stile
Harry Place
Red Bank
Rydal Mount
ST MARY
Rydal
873
Rydal Water
Loughrigg Ter
Cote How
Crow How
Nook End
1135
Middle Grove
Dod Hil
1597
1475
Baystones
Chapel Stile
HOLY TRINITY
Thrang
Langdale Hotel
High Close
Britannia Inn
Birch Hill
Loughrigg Fell
Oaks
The Armitt Collection
Bridge House (NT)
Glass House
Adrian Sankey Glass
Old Vicarage
ST MARY
Oshy Gallery
Scathwaite
Stockgill Force
Wansfell
Raven Crag
The Hundred
Lingmoor Fell
Elterwater
Scenic Hamlet
Mart Crag
1410
Busk Pike
Busk
Dale End
B5343
Loughrigg
Tarn Foot
Ivy Crag
Old Courthouse Gallery
Clappersgate
Lucy's
Zeffirelli's
AMBLESIDE
5+ Contemporary Ceramics
The Home of Football
High Green
Town Head
Queens Head
Troutbeck
Scenic Hamlet
Mortal Man
Lim
Little Langdale
Elter Water
Skelwith Force
Chester's Café
Skelwith Bridge
A593
B5278
Galava Roman Fort
Waterhead
Jenkyn's Crag
High Skelghyll Townend (NT)
JESUS CH
Low Hall Garth
Low Fell
Stand End
Little Fell
Park Fell
Bull Close
Skelwith Fold
Black Fell
Holmes Head
B5286
The Samling
Pull Wyke
Dove Nest
Holbeck Ghyll
High Tilberthwaite
Hodge Close
Holme Ground
Holme Fell
A593
How Beck
High Arnside
1056 Barngate
High Crag
Low Wray
Briery Close
Fusethwaite Yeat
Brockhole National Park Centre
Ho
Troutbe
Bridge
Arnside Intake
995
Ivy Crag
Tom Heights
Drunken Duck Inn
Iron Keld
B5286
Bleham Tarn
Randy Pike
Wray Castle
Windermere
Coniston Moor
High Yewdale
Tarn Hows
Sunny Brow
The Tarn
Rose Castle
Borwick Lodge
Out Gate
High Wray
Bella Wray
Calgarth Hall
Red Nab
St Cathe Orrest Head
ST MA
Yewdale Fells
Yew Tree Farm
Low Yewdale
Yewdale Beck
A593
Hill Fell
Court House (NT)
Belmont
Belle Grange
Long Height
Millerground Landing
Miller Howe
Jericho at the Waverley
Far End
Coniston
B5285
Hollin Bank
Hawkshead Hill
High Cross
Highfield
Hawkshead
B5285
Beatrix Potter Gallery
Gillbank
Colthouse Town End
Three Dubs Crags
WINDERMER
A591(T)
A592
84
44
A B C D E F

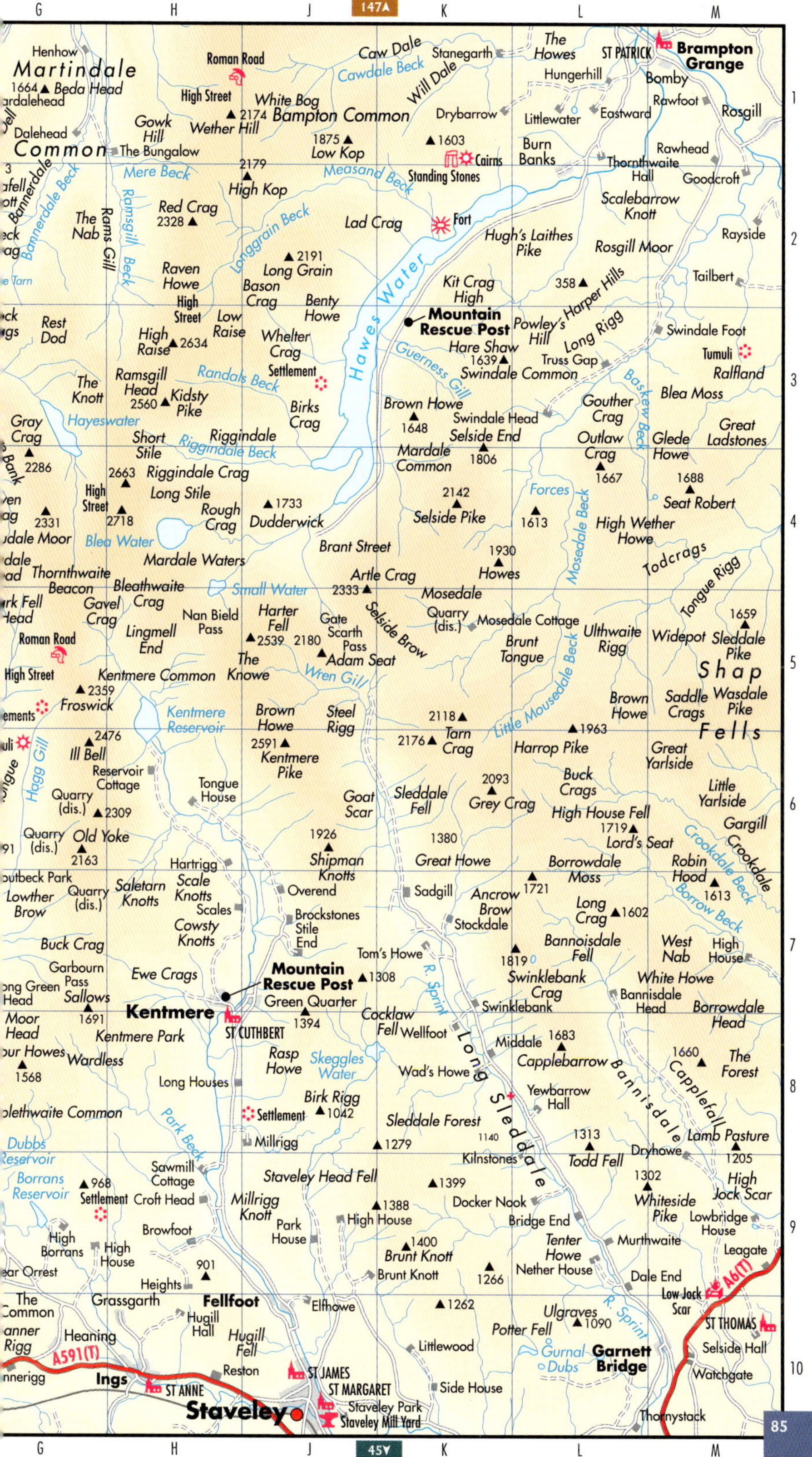

G H J K L M
147▲
Martindale
Henhow
Roman Road
Caw Dale
Cawdale Beck
Stanegarth
The Howes
ST PATRICK
Brampton Grange
1664 ▲ Beda Head
ardalehead
Will Dale
Hungerhill
Bomby
ell
High Street
White Bog
▲ 2174 Bampton Common
Drybarrow
Littlewater
Rawfoot
Rosgill
Dalehead
Gowk Hill
Wether Hill
Eastward
Rawhead
Common
The Bungalow
1875 ▲
Low Kop
▲ 1603
Burn Banks
Thornthwaite Hall
Goodcroft
3
afell
2179
Measand Beck
Standing Stones
Scalebarrow Knott
ott
Mere Beck
High Kop
eck
The Nab
Red Crag
2328 ▲
Lad Crag
Fort
Hugh's Laithes Pike
Rosgill Moor
Rayside
Bannerdale Beck
Rams Gill
Ramsgill Beck
Longgrain Beck
Tailbert
Tarn
Raven Howe
▲ 2191
Long Grain
Kit Crag High
358 ▲
Harper Hills
Swindale Foot
ck
Rest Dod
High Street
Bason Crag
Benty Howe
Mountain Rescue Post
Powley's Hill
Long Rigg
Tumuli
Ralfland
ags
High Raise
▲ 2634
Low Raise
Whelter Crag
Hare Shaw
1639 ▲
Truss Gap
Swindale Common
Blea Moss
The Knott
Ramsgill Head
2560 ▲
Kidsty Pike
Randals Beck
Settlement
Brown Howe
1648 ▲
Swindale Head
Selside End
Gouther Crag
Glede Howe
Great Ladstones
Gray Crag
Hayeswater
Short Stile
Riggindale
Birks Crag
Mardale Common
1806 ▲
Outlaw Crag
1667 ▲
1688 ▲
Seat Robert
2286 ▲
Riggindale Beck
2142 ▲
Forces
High Wether Howe
en ag
2663 ▲
Riggindale Crag
Selside Pike
1613 ▲
Mosedale Beck
dale Moor
High Street
Long Stile
Rough Crag
▲ 1733
Dudderwick
1930 ▲
Howes
Todcrags
Tongue Rigg
2331 ▲
2718 ▲
Blea Water
Brant Street
Artle Crag
2333 ▲
Mosedale
1659 ▲
dale ad
Thornthwaite Beacon
Bleathwaite Crag
Small Water
Selside Brow
Quarry (dis.)
Mosedale Cottage
Ulthwaite Rigg
Widepot
Sleddale Pike
rk Fell ead
Gavel Crag
Harter Fell
Gate Scarth Pass
Brunt Tongue
Shap
Roman Road
Lingmell End
Nan Bield Pass
▲ 2539
2180 ▲
Adam Seat
High Street
Kentmere Common
The Knowe
Wren Gill
Brown Howe
Saddle Crags
Wasdale Pike
ements
▲ 2359
Froswick
Steel Rigg
2118 ▲
Little Mousedale Beck
Brown Howe
Fells
uli
Ill Bell
2476 ▲
Kentmere Reservoir
2591 ▲
Kentmere Pike
2176 ▲
Tarn Crag
1963 ▲
Great Yarlside
Quarry (dis.)
Reservoir Cottage
▲ 2309
Tongue House
Goat Scar
Sleddale Fell
Grey Crag
2093 ▲
Harrop Pike
Buck Crags
High House Fell
Little Yarlside
Gargill
91
Quarry (dis.)
2163 ▲
Old Yoke
1926 ▲
Shipman Knotts
1380
Great Howe
1719 ▲
Lord's Seat
Robin Hood
Crookdale
utbeck Park
Hartrigg
Scale Knotts
Overend
Sadgill
Borrowdale Moss
1613 ▲
Lowther Brow
Quarry (dis.)
Saletarn Knotts
Scales
Brockstones Stile End
Ancrow Brow
1721 ▲
Long Crag
1602 ▲
Borrow Beck
Buck Crag
Cowsty Knotts
Tom's Howe
1819
Bannoisdale Fell
West Nab
High House
Garbourn Pass
Ewe Crags
▲ 1308
Swinklebank Crag
White Howe
ong Green Head
Sallows
Mountain Rescue Post
Green Quarter
Cocklaw Fell
Swinklebank
Bannisdale Head
Borrowdale Head
Moor Head
1691
Kentmere
ST CUTHBERT
1394
Wellfoot
Middale
1683 ▲
Capplebarrow
1660 ▲
The Forest
Capplefall
ur Howes
Kentmere Park
Wardless
Rasp Howe
Skeggles Water
Wad's Howe
Yewbarrow Hall
Lamb Pasture
1568
Long Houses
Birk Rigg
Sleddale Forest
1313
Todd Fell
Dryhowe
1205
lethwaite Common
Park Beck
Settlement
▲ 1042
1140
Kilnstones
1302
Whiteside Pike
High Jock Scar
Dubbs Reservoir
Millrigg
Sawmill Cottage
Staveley Head Fell
1279 ▲
▲ 1399
Docker Nook
Bridge End
Lowbridge House
Borrans Reservoir
▲ 968
Settlement
Croft Head
Millrigg Knott
Park House
1388 ▲
High House
Tenter Howe
Nether House
Murthwaite
Dale End
Leagate
High Borrans
High House
901
Heights
1400 ▲
Brunt Knott
Brunt Knott
1266 ▲
Low Jock Scar
A6(T)
ear Orrest
The Common
Grassgarth
Fellfoot
Elfhowe
▲ 1262
Ulgraves
1090 ▲
ST THOMAS
Selside Hall
anner Rigg
Heaning
A591(T)
Hugill Hall
Hugill Fell
Reston
Littlewood
Potter Fell
Gurnal Dubs
Garnett Bridge
Watchgate
Ings
ST ANNE
Staveley
ST JAMES
ST MARGARET
Side House
Staveley Park
Staveley Mill Yard
Thornystack
nnerigg
45▼
85

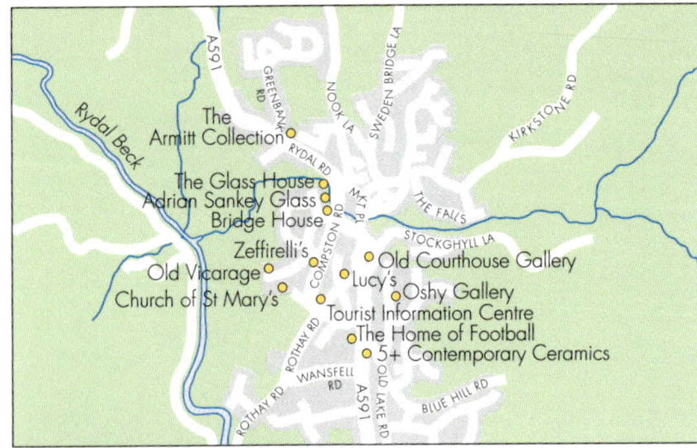

Ambleside

AMBLESIDE

The busiest of the walking and climbing centres in the Lake District due no doubt to its sheltered position in the Rothay Valley at the head of Windermere. It also has easy access to the Langdales and Western Fells, Helvellyn and the North Eastern Fells and, to the south, the lakes of Windermere and Coniston. The town is hilly with alleys, cobbled streets, hotels and inns, a mass of B&Bs, and a bevy of outdoor shops. A holiday mood greets the visitor, for the streets are teeming with folk, most with a common purpose (to shop and window shop), or perhaps to strike out across the surrounding hills.

The mild climate encourages vegetation and the roads leading out of Ambleside are alive with azaleas, copper beeches and laburnum, and the rhododendrons grow wild. The cottage walls are covered with clematis, roses and honeysuckle. It is a marvellous spectacle but is only the Starter, the Main Course is yet to come. Drive north at dawn towards Rydal and Grasmere and you will be astounded at this Lakeland landscape. The sheer symetry of the rolling hills, the perfectly positioned trees and stonewalls, the mirror-like waters of

River Rothay, Ambleside

Rydal and Grasmere, all have left poets dumbfounded and lost for words. It is one of the most beautiful and captivating roads in England. But, drive on this road during the peak period and keen concentration is required or you will miss seeing this gentle landscape. Better still, park your car and walk. Take the footpath on the east side of the A591 opposite Scandale Bridge and this will lead you through Rydal Park to Rydal Hall and village. The old town, dating back to the C15, lies on the Kirkstone side. Ambleside Sports in August. International Sheepdog Trials in Rydal Park. (E7)

Where to Eat, Drink & Be Merry...

Glass House, Rydal Road.
Just the venue for a relaxed meal out with family and friends. This former C15 fulling (cloth) mill has been sympathetically converted into a modern and bright restaurant. Yards of wood and old machinery to view. Open for lunch, early supper and dinner. (D7) 01539 432137 www.theglasshouserestaurant.co.uk

Lucy's On A Plate. The eating habits of Ambleside changed for the good when Lucy opened her specialist grocery and deli in 1989. Such was her success that she moved into catering and bravo for that. This is a delightful café/bistro that serves breakfast and good, wholesome food for families, couples and one and all. Evening meals from 6pm. (D7) 015394 32288 www.lucysofambleside.co.uk

Zeffirelli's, Compston Road.
A clever and successful combination of cinema, restaurant and jazz bar. You can either sit outside, downstairs in the cafe or restaurant, or upstairs in the Jazz bar. Food is simple Italian; pasta, pizzas and salads. Bright artworks line the walls. Open all day. (D7) 015394 33845 www.zeffirellis.com

Where to Stay...

Old Vicarage B&B, Vicarage Road. A Victorian house of great girth and character, and populated by families who want comfort and fun at a reasonable price. It's a bit like a grand youth hostel and is wonderfully unpretentious and immune to our crazy designer-led world. Swimming Pool. Dogs rush about in the Entrance Hall. Go for the more modern rooms. Kids love it. (D7) 015394 33364 www.oldvicarageambleside.co.uk

Just Outside Ambleside...

Chesters Café by the River, Skelwith Bridge.
Smart café serves fabulous cakes, coffees and hearty casseroles prepared from an open kitchen. Open daily 10-5. Next door, an interior design outlet. (C8) 015394 32553 www.chesters-cafebytheriver.co.uk

Lucy's of Ambleside ss

1774   Belle Isle, Windermere built by Nottingham merchant, Thomas English

1775   Gray's guidebook publshed

1778   The Jesuit, Thomas West's Guide to the Lakes is the first of many guidebooks selling ten editions by 1812

Special Places to Visit...

Adrian Sankey Glass, Rydal Rd.
Small workshop producing a range of contemporary, lead crystal glass designs, inspired by the natural world with skills developed over hundreds of years. Open daily 9-5.30. (D7) 01539 433039
www.glassmakers.co.uk

The Armitt, Rydal Rd.
Interactive exhibition of Lakeland life. The former home of artists, pioneers and writers. Open daily 10-5. (D7) 015394 31212
www.thearmittcollection.com

5+ Contemporary Ceramics, 101 Lake Road. Small co-operative of craftsmen and artists displays ceramics, photography, paintings and jewellery. Open daily from 10. (D7) 01539 433821

The Home Of Football, 100 Lake Rd. Stuart Clarke's photographic gallery records the changing face of football since the Hillsborough tragedy. With over 60,000 images from the game's grass roots in the park with jumpers for goalposts, to the World Cup. Open daily 10-4. (D7) 015394 34440
www.homesoffootball.co.uk

Old Courthouse Gallery, Market Place. The largest and most comprehensive contemporary art gallery in the Lakes exhibits ceramics, clocks and mirrors, furniture, glass, lighting, paintings, sculpture, wood and jewellery. Open M-Sa 10-5, Su 10-4. (D7) 015394 32022 www.ocg-arts.com

Oshy Gallery, Old Stamp House Yard. A poppet of a gallery displaying art and ceramics with the emphasis on decorating your home with contemporary objects. (D7) 015394 32641

Just Outside Ambleside...

Holehird. A fine collection of rhododendrons, azaleas, conifers, ornamental and flowering shrubs and trees. Three National Collections; Astilbe, Hydrangea and Polystichum. Open daily, all year, dawn to dusk. (F9) 015394 46008
www.holehirdgardens.org.uk

River Brathay, Ambleside

Kirkstone Galleries, Skelwith Bridge. Contemporary design-led interiors. Hand painted crockery, beautiful glassware, unusual furniture, mirrors and lamps. Open daily. (C8) 01539 43082

Lake District Visitor Centre, At Brockhole. Situated on the shores of Windermere amid 30 acres of gardens and grounds. Two floors of new interactive exhibitions telling the story of the Lake District. Shop, café, adventure playground, events and lake cruises. Open daily Apr to Oct, Grounds and gardens all year. (E9) 015394 46601
www.lake-district.gov.co.uk

Stagshaw Garden (NT). Woodland garden with a fine collection of rhododendrons, azaleas, camellias and shrubs. The adjacent Skelghyll Woods offer walks and access to the distant fells. Open daily Apr-June 10-6.30, July-Oct by appointment. (E8) 01539 446027
www.nationaltrust.org.uk

Townend (NT).
A classic stone and slate Cumbrian farmhouse built in 1626 for George Brown, Statesman (wealthy yeoman farmer) and his bride, Susannah Rawlinson. It remained in the Brown family until 1943. The interior displays custom made furnishings, family papers and books. Open mid March to 2 November, W-Su 1-4(5 in summer months). (F8) 015394 32628
www.nationaltrust.org.uk.

Townend Farm Barn. A bank barn built on a grand scale in the 1660s. Slits in the upper walls are to ventilate the hay.

Holehird Gardens ss-bk

| 1780 | Hunting Mayor ceremony introduced at the Queen's Head Inn, Troutbeck | 1783 | William Wordsworth's father dies leaving him as a penniless orphan |
| 1780 | Building of Lyulph's Tower, Ullswater | 1785 | William Wordsworth's first known poem written |

Holbeck Ghyll ss

Drunken Duck Inn. This is a clever combination of an inn that brews its own beers (taglag, catnap, cracker ale), serves bar and restaurant cuisine of the highest calibre, has excessive demands for its luxurious accommodation and sits well within a network of footpaths. A winning combination, Yes Sir! Book well in advance. (C9) 015394 36347 www.drunkenduckinn.co.uk

Holbeck Ghyll, Holbeck Lane. One of the three Michelin Star restaurants in the Lakes, and another hotel in an unsurpassed, elevated position overlooking the lake and mountains. A family run business made successful by David and Patricia Nicholson's professionalism and bloody-minded hard work over the past twenty years. You will be pampered and looked after. The rooms are luxurious and the health spa will relax you into dreamy Neverland. Private suites. (E8) 015394 32375 www.holbeckghyll.com

Langdale Hotel & Country Club, Great Langdale. A modern hotel plush with contemporarily designed bedrooms and a spa offering health and hedonist style treatments. Self-catering apartments. Time Share. Bars and restaurants. (A7) 015394 37302 www.langdale.co.uk

The Samling ss

The Samling. This takes the boutique hotel onto another level of hedonism with sheer, unadulterated luxury coupled with service of discretion and understanding rarely equalled. A hotel famed for attracting celebrities, media tycoons and the affluent City broker. The bathrooms are quite exceptional (with marble surrounds over the baths!), and the five individual suites have hot tubs with views looking out across the fells. Each of the eleven bedrooms is quite different and breakfast in bed is encouraged. Service is impeccable, as is discretion, and you can wander aimlessly across the sixty-seven acres overlooking Windermere fondly believing they are yours, and yours alone. (E8) 015394 31922 www.thesamling.com

Blue Bedroom, The Samling ss

Junior Suite, The Samling ss

Red Bedroom, The Samling ss

The Samling ss

The Terrace, Holbeck Ghyll ss

1785	Broad Water renamed Brothers Water after two brothers are drowned while ice-skating	1780	Thomas West's Guide to the Lakes published
1786	Gilpin's guidebook published	1793	William Wordsworth's first book of poems are published, An Evening Walk, but are poorly reviewed by the critics

GRASMERE

Grasmere means 'The lake with the grassy shore'. Quite magical at dawn with the early dew and rising mist. A popular picnic spot with Dorothy and William Wordsworth. Home of mute swans, coot and moorhen. Rowing boats can be hired from Allonby's and a trip to the island for a picnic is not to be missed. Loughrigg Terrace provides excellent views of the lake, the Fairfield Horseshoe and Helvellyn. (B6)

Dorothy Wordsworth, Rydal Mount

William Wordsworth, Rydal Mount

William Wordsworth lived here, with his family and friends, from 20 December 1799 to 1808, where he was to write some of his best poetry. Dorothy wrote her Grasmere Journal here from 1800-1803. A fascinating guided tour offers an insight into C19 life as experienced by this literary giant. The cottage was formerly an inn called the Dove and Olive Branch. Next door, the Wordsworth Museum & Art Gallery. Bookshop.

Tea Rooms & Italian Restaurant. Award-winning Jerwood Centre is the research centre for Wordsworth studies. Open daily 9.30-5.30, closed 5-30 January & 24-26 Dec. (B6) www.wordsworth.org.uk

The Rainbow

My heart leaps up when I behold
A rainbow in the sky:
So was it when my life began;
So is it now I am a man;
So be it when I shall grow old,
Or let me die!
The Child is father of the Man;
I could wish my days to be
Bound each to each by
natural piety.

This poem was written in 1802 and first published in 1807. In 1815 Wordsworth used the last three lines as an epigraph to Ode: Intimations of Immortality.

The home of William Wordsworth from 1813-1850. The house contains many family possessions (portraits and first editions). The 4 1/2 acre garden has two terraces designed by Wordsworth, and is considered by some to be of great interest. Open daily Mar-Oct 9.30-5, Nov-Feb 11-4 (closed M & Tu in winter & 8 Jan-1 Feb). (D6) 015394 33002 www.rydalmount.co.uk

The best portion of a good man's life is his little, nameless, unremembered acts of kindness and of love.

My heart leaps up when I behold A rainbow in the sky: So was it when my life began; So is it now I am a man

I travelled among unknown me In lands beyond the sea; Nor, England! did I know till then. What love I bore to thee. Tis past, that melancholy dream!

She was a phantom of delight
When first she gleam'd upon my sight;
A lovely apparition, sent
To be a moment's ornament.

The world is too much with us; late and soon,
Getting and spending, we lay waste our powers:
Little we see in Nature that is ours;
We have given our hearts away, a sordid boon!

William Wordsworth, 1770-1850

Romantic Poet. Born in Cockermouth, the second of five children. Educated at Hawkshead Grammar School and St John's College, Cambridge. Nowadays, Wordsworth is considered to be a fundamental part of the Literary Establishment. However, in his youth, he was anything but. Orphaned at a young age, Wordsworth felt isolated and rebelled against the establishment. He travelled widely in Europe ending up in France in 1792 at the onset of the French Revolution (The Reign of Terror). There he was originally enthused with the Revolution, and fell in love with Annette Vallon who gave birth to their child Caroline after he had returned to safety in England. He did, however, later manage to provide them with financial support. The later events of the Revolution left him disillusioned with radical politics and he thereafter devoted his life to literature. With a small inheritance he was able to gain independence and pursue his vocation. In 1793 his first poems were published. He was renting Alfoxton Park in the Quantocks, and fortuitously for both of them, Coleridge was also living in nearby Nether Stowey. They met up, became great friends and changed the style of poetry, forever. During their discussions on life and poetry they took long walks along the Somerset coast so much so that the locals thought them to be foreign spies. However, in 1798 they jointly published The Lyrical Ballads (although Coleridge had only four poems featured). The book ended with one of his finest poems, Tintern Abbey, dedicated to his sister Dorothy. The Lyrical Ballads has been described as the most revolutionary and new book of poetry ever written. The poems were written in a style for the Everyman in a language that could be understood by the lower and middle classes. This was to be the beginning of the Romantic Movement. But, before this style became acceptable, the two poets were criticised on all fronts by the literary establishment and considered as outcasts. They stood by each other and soon moved up to the Lake District, Wordsworth's spiritual and familial home. He married Mary Hutchinson, a childhood sweetheart, and had five children with her. He moved to Dove Cottage in 1799 and it is here that some scholars believe he achieved his finest work before 1807. Life was not easy and two of his children died at Allan Bank, a damp and dismal place. He hated the house, so moved to the Old Rectory in Grasmere in 1811. It was not until 1813 that he moved to Rydal Mount where he spent his remaining years. He was made Distributor of Stamps for Westmorland and this gave him a stipend of £400 per year, an income that made him financially secure. These were probably the most comfortable and happiest years of his life (although not the most interesting for scholars). It was here that he continued to write The Prelude, considered his masterpiece but which was published posthumously. This long autobiographical poem stems from his childhood and adolescence and tackles youth, memory, imagination but, above all, nature in all its intensity and purity. In 1843 he was appointed Poet Laureate. His poetry may be too long for everyone's taste but the following are a useful introduction: The Rainbow, I Wandered Lonely As a Cloud, Tintern Abbey and The Pedlar. The Prelude has some brilliant passages. It is a long piece of prose. Wordsworth was the leading figure of the group of poets within the Romantic Movement known as the Lakeland Poets. Their greatest achievement was to provide a conduit for the Everyman to experience the emotional pull of nature and the natural world in a physical and metaphysical way. In his old age he was sought out by men of learning and politicians for advice. He became the Sage of Rydal, available for every man to visit and meet and learn.

William and Mary Wordsworth, Rydal Mount

Dorothy Wordsworth

Dorothy Wordsworth, 1771-1855

Diarist, English Poet, Letter Writer, Spinster. Famous sister and lifelong companion to her brother William Wordsworth. She was the third of the five children born to her parents but was sent away from home to live with various relatives on the early death of her parents. She later rejoined William in 1798 whilst he was living at Alfoxton House, Somerset. Thereafter they were inseparable. Much has been made of a possible incestuous relationship but there is little or no evidence of this. Just surmise. She was an inspiration to her brother and his friends Coleridge and Southey, and later Thomas De Quincey. It was her grasp of nature and humanity that awoke new levels in William's consciousness and developed his intuition with the natural world. She wrote her Grasmere Journals and a travel account in 1803 of a Scottish journey but with no intent for publication. William dedicated his poem Tintern Abbey to her. She was by all accounts (and we have De Quincey's word on this) of a gypsy complexion:-"rarely in a woman of English birth, had I seen a most determined gypsy tan. Her eyes were not soft as Mrs Wordsworth nor were they fierce or bold, but they were wild and startling, and hurried in their motion." The portrait illustrated hangs at Rydal Mount and is the only known record of her. She never married and, due to a thyroid deficiency and arteriosclerosis, spent the last twenty years of her life struggling with a physical and mental illness. We have much to thank her for. Did she hold the key that opened the vault of her brother's talent?

Samuel Taylor Coleridge, 1771-1834

Critic, Drug Addict, Journalist, Poet, Philosopher, Walker, Womaniser. Born in Ottery St Mary, Devon and educated at Christ's Hospital, Sussex and Jesus College, Cambridge. He is considered one of the great Romantic poets (and philosophers). His poetry is arguably more accessible than his contemporary Wordsworth. While at Cambridge he befriended Robert Southey and they shared the same radical theological and political ideals. In 1795 the two friends married the Fricker sisters of Clevedon. He later fell out with his wife in 1808, quarrelled with Wordsworth in 1810 and moved to Malta for his health - the damp Lakeland climate didn't agree with him. However, earlier he had become a great friend of the Wordsworths and in 1798 published with William Wordsworth the Lyrical Ballads. This they considered to be a groundbreaking and epic event. It was an experimental book of prose written for, and to be understood by, the lower and middle classes - it was poetry for the Everyman. It looked at nature in fresh and appealing ways and was later considered to have heralded the beginning of the Romantic Movement in literature. He was the first mountaineer to record a 100 mile walk across the Lakeland peaks in 1802, and by the description in his journal one would have thought no one else had climbed these mountains. They tended to forget that the illiterate shepherds and miners had done so for years. He was a respected Shakespeare scholar who lectured widely and was a friend of Lord Byron. His poem The Rhyme of the Ancient Mariner (which features in the Lyrical Ballads) is listed in many school syllabi. In his later years he suffered from neuralgia and rheumatic pains becoming dependent on laudanum (opium). His last years were spent as a recluse in Highgate, North London. There he was idolized and visited by many seeking to bathe in the light of a great poet.

A man's as old as he's feeling. A woman as old as she looks.

A man's desire is for the woman, but the woman's desire is rarely other than for the desire of the man.

Common sense in an uncommon degree is what the world calls wisdom.

Friendship is a sheltering tree.

Advice is like snow - the softer it falls, the longer it dwells upon, and the deeper in sinks into the mind.

In politics, what begins in fear usually ends in failure.

S T Coleridge

Robert Southey

Robert Southey, 1774-1843

Biographer, Children's Author, Historian, Poet Laureate 1813-43, Romantic Poet. Educated at Westminster School and Balliol College, Oxford. He was refused entry to Christ Church, Oxford due to adolescent indiscretions. He had written an article condemning flogging! His time at Oxford was ill spent, and by his own admission spent his time boating and swimming, and little else. He became great friends with Coleridge and they set up the Pantisocratic Society with a view to starting a Utopian society in Pennsylvania, US. However, it came to nothing. He was sent to Portugal, returned and tried his hand at law, unsuccessfully. His first poem was published in 1794. In 1797 he received a stipend of £160 per annum from a family friend so he could pursue his writing career. In 1803 he moved to Greta Hall, Keswick with his wife Edith, elder sister of Sara Fricker, Coleridge's wife, where he lived thereafter. Lord Byron dedicated his poem Don Juan to him but later mocked him for his loss of political principles claiming his only interest lay in money and status. By this time he was financing three separate families, all living under one roof at Greta Hall. He wrote the children's classic The Story of Three Bears (original Goldilocks story), countless novels, the poems The Inchcape Rock, The Battle of Blenheim and The Holy Tree and a lengthy History of the Peninsula War 1823-32. His Magnum Opus (which he never finished) was a history of Brazil. He introduced various words into the English language, one being autobiography. His later years were clouded by mental illness and frailty. He is buried in St Kentigern's church, Crosthwaite.

Live as long as you may, the first twenty years are the longest half of your life.

How little do they see what is, who frame their hasty judgments upon that which seems.

No distance of place or lapse of time can lessen the friendship of those who are thoroughly persuaded of each other's worth.

Not where I breathe, but where I love, I live; Not where I love, but where I am, I die.

The loss of a friend is like that of a limb; time may heal the anguish of the wound, but the loss cannot be repaired.

What will not woman, gentle woman dare; when strong affection stirs her spirit.

Thomas de Quincey, 1785-1859

Author, Classicist, Essayist, Intellectual, Opium Addict. Born in Manchester, the son of textile merchant. At an early age he was considered a brilliant classicist. He was forever playing truant and changing schools, and was thus educated (partly) at Bath Grammar School, Winkfield School, Wiltshire, Manchester Grammar School, Brasenose, then Worcester College, Oxford. He was in awe of Wordsworth and travelled to the Lakes on many occasions to visit the great man but each time he lost his nerve. A chance meeting with Coleridge changed all this, when he took him in 1807 to Grasmere, and Dove Cottage. He became great friends with the Wordsworth family and was persuaded to settle down and study. In 1812 he read for the Bar at the Middle Temple but this was short-lived on account of the tragic death of Wordsworth's three year old daughter, Catherine, whom de Quincey adored. This terrible event pushed him over the edge into despair and by 1813 he was addicted to opium. He slid into debt and joined the Blackwoods Edinburgh Magazine. His Confessions of An Opium Eater became a bestseller. All in all, he wrote over 200 articles for various magazines on subjects ranging from philosophy to aesthetics to literary criticism. On his death the Westminster Review praised his writings thus: "filled with passages of power and beauty which have never been surpassed by any prose writer of the Age."

Even imperfection itself may have its ideal or perfect state.

Nobody will laugh long who deals much with opium: its pleasures even are of a grave and solemn complexion.

Solitude, though it may be silent as light, is like light, the mightiest of agencies; for solitude is essential to man. All men come into this world alone and leave it alone.

Tea, though ridiculed by those who are naturally coarse in their nervous sensibilities will always be the favorite beverage of the intellectual.

Nab Cottage, Rydal

GRASMERE

'The lake of the wild boar' is the Viking name for this picturesque Lakeland village. Forever associated with Dorothy and William Wordsworth who lie buried beside each other in St Oswald's Church. It is well situated for trekking around the surrounding fells and crags with many fine B&Bs and tearooms in the close vicinity. The Grasmere Sports Day is in August, the English equivalent of the Highland Games. (B6)

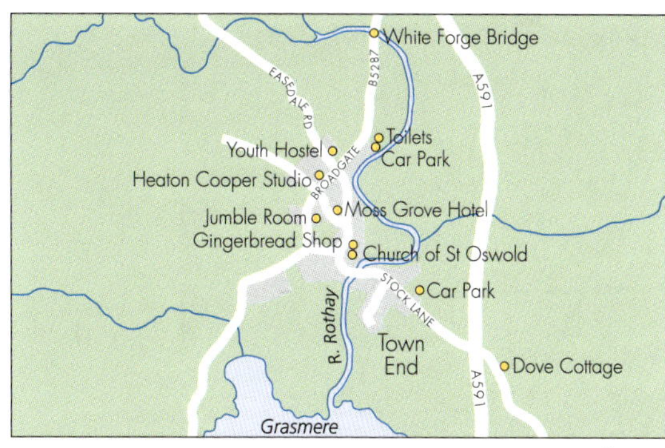

Grasmere

Special Places to Visit...

Heaton Cooper Studio.
An ever-changing exhibition of original watercolours by W. Heaton Cooper R.I. (1903-1995), and his father, A. Heaton Cooper (1863-1929). Specialist art materials and prints on sale. Open daily 9-5. Su 11-5 (C6) 015394 35280. www.heatoncooper.co.uk

Gingerbread Shop, Church Cottage.
Shop built in 1630 as the village school. World famous gingerbread, freshly baked daily to a secret recipe. Open daily. (B6) 015394 35428. www.grasmeregingerbread.co.uk

Slapestones Gallery, Pye Lane.
Open Th-Tu 9.30-5. Specialises in watercolours and oils, predominantly of Lakeland scenes by local artists many of whose forebears have lived here for centuries. 01539 435068 www.slapestonesgallery.co.uk

Where to Eat, Drink & Be Merry...

Jumble Room, Langdale Road.
One of Cumbria's great eating-out institutions, having been run by the same family for 50+ years. They like to describe the restaurant as up - market Bohemia. It is cosy and friendly and the walls are adorned with art. The food is Med-style, bistro-like and veggies are well catered for. Open W-Su 11.30-3.30 and from 6 pm until the food is all eaten! (B6) 015394 35188 www.thejumbleroom.co.uk

Where to Stay...

Cote How Country Guest House & Tea Room. The conservation and protection of the environment drives this business for the food is organic, the passion is for sustainability. The house dates from 1535 and its situation is perfect for short-easy walks. The three bedrooms are luxurious. (D7) 015394 32765 www.cotehow.co.uk

Moss Grove Hotel, Grasmere. Organic is the byword at this 'hotel with a mission' where they provide a sustainable and environmentally friendly approach to hospitality. The beds are made from great beams of pine and the bathrooms are spacious and plush. (B7) 015394 35251 www.mossgrove.com

Nab Cottage, Rydal.
C16 cottage overlooks the dreamy Rydal Water and was once the home of the infamous writer and opium smoker, Thomas De Quincey. It is quaint and traditional with flagstone floors, creaky landings and log fires. Licensed. Light suppers. Residential courses throughout late summer. (C6) 015394 35311 www.rydalwater.com

White Moss House B&B.
What a splendid position! Rooms with a view overlooking Rydal Water. No wonder a great favourite of Wordsworth, for he bought the house for his son, Willie. The Dixons provide professional care and attention that includes award winning cuisine and comfortable bedrooms with all the necessary mod cons. (C6) 01539 435295 www.whitemoss.com

St Oswald's Church

'Rothaymere' or 'Routhermere' meaning "the lake in the valley where the rye is grown". This reedy little lake is one of the prettiest and was another great favourite with the Wordsworths. Gulls roost along the shoreline. Best appreciated on a summer's dawn or winter twilight. Easy circular walk. (C6)

TROUTBECK

A beautiful valley and landscape that according to the National Trust has changed very little since the Middle Ages. The vernacular architecture of stone built farmhouses, cottages and barns is probably unmatched elsewhere in the Lakes, and as you wander along the many footpaths that criss-cross this valley you could believe you had entered an earlier time. And, if your exploration conjures up a thirst, you will be well served by the two village hostelries. (F8)

Where to Eat, Drink & Be Merry and Stay...

The Queens Head. Home of the original 4-poster bed (now makes up the bar) and popular with locals and a favourite of the Coniston Tigers, the legendary band of old climbers. The food is impressive (you could call it a gastro-pub), as are the bedrooms, some with 4-posters but all decorated with colourful fabrics. A convenient spot from where to walk the web of footpaths within the Troutbeck Valley. (F8) 015394 32174 www.queensheadhotel.com

The Mortal Man. An inn since 1689 with a long and chequered history fondly remembered in verse and song. The panoramic view across the Troutbeck Valley is stunning. The inn is undergoing a renaissance under the new manager formerly at The Samling. So expect great things. (F8) 015394 33193 www.themortalman.com

Townend

1802   Samuel Taylor Coleridge embarks on a nine-day
        walking tour of the Lakes
1802   William Wordsworth marries Mary Hutchinson

1805   William Wordsworth's beloved brother John is drowned
        off Portland Bill in the Earl of Abergavenny

Where to Stay...

Fellside Studios. These are private and stylish with separate entrances so you have discretion and great service to hand with breakfast provided. The views are achingly beautiful, the freedom is yours, the time is now. (F8) 015394 34000
www.fellsidestudios.co.uk

Villages of interest...

Chapel Stile. Set at the entrance to Great Langdale where the slate and stone houses were built for the quarrymen and employees of the gunpowder works in nearby Elterwater. (B7)

Elterwater. Small, picturesque village at the foot of the Langdales. Former mining community. Britannia Inn, a popular hostelry. (B7)

Patterdale. 'Patrick's Valley' This pretty village is a convenient centre for hikes out to Helvellyn, Kidsty Pike and High Street. (E2)

Hartsop. A fine collection of traditional C17 Cumbrian farm buildings, and some of them still retain their own spinning galleries. Remains of an C18 corn mill. Nearby, Brother Water, so named because two brothers drowned here. (F3)

Hartsop

Kentmere. You must make a serious detour if you wish to visit this village, and you will be glad you did. Take a mountain bike for there's a fine, circular route starting from the village - see Goldeneye's Mountain Bike Guide. However, the higher up the valley you go, the more spectacular it becomes and as you enter the Kentmere Horseshoe you find yourself within an amphitheatre of mountains. Quite a spectacle. (H8)

Kentmere

Elterwater in winter

Windermere at dusk

Lakes...

Elterwater. Known as the 'Swan Lake'. In winter, the elusive Whooper Swan flies in from Siberia - listen for its trumpeting cry. This tranquil and reedy lake lies secluded in a lush green valley. There are fine views from the eastern side, and the northern banks looking across to the Langdales and Wetherlam. Nearby, the waterfall Skelwith Force. (B7)

Haweswater. This was the second reservoir to be created out of converting natural lakes, rivers and valleys into a man-made reservoir. The decision by the Manchester Corporation to second this land was

Tarn Hows

a matter of great controversy in the 1930s. The village of Mardale was submerged and we are reminded of our loss, for in dry weather its remains are clearly visible. The landscape is wild, remote and free of traffic congestion. From Mardale Head there's a splendid view up to High Street, returning via Riggindale Beck. Another way to discover Haweswater is from Kentmere with a trek up the valley to the Nan Bield Pass. (J3)

Windermere. England's largest lake and without doubt the most famous in Lakeland though perhaps not the most dramatic or beautiful. The northern skyline is indented with volcanic peaks and the southern shore heavily wooded with broadleaf trees. There are splendid views from Orrest Head, Claife Heights and Brockhole. You can also achieve some memorable views from the comforts of a hotel or two overlooking the lake. These are in no order of charm: Miller Howe, The Samling, The Holbeck Ghyll, The Langdale Chase and the Storrs Hall Hotel. These buildings and their like were built by wealthy industrialists of the Victorian and Edwardian

Tarn Hows

era, mostly to impress their wives and mistresses. Today the lake is bounded on the east side by a plethora of state-of-the-art homes owned by wealthy footballers and successful businessmen. The lake can be noisy and congested with traffic although a 10mph speed limit is now in place and this has cut the numbers of craft on the water. No visit to Windermere would be complete without a visit to the Steamboat Museum. Here you will see an array of boat design that originated on Windermere. (D9)

Water Activities...

Lake-Lander, Waterhead Marine. Canoe and kayak hire for all the family. One or two hour rates, half and full day too. Life jackets provided. Take a change of clothes. (D8) 015394 34604

Tarn Hows

Tarn Hows

Windermere Lake Cruises.
Steamers and Launches sail daily throughout the year between Ambleside, Bowness and Lakeside. With all year round connections for the Aquarium of the Lakes and the World of Beatrix Potter plus main season connections for Brockhole Visitor Centre, Lakeside and Haverthwaite Steam Railway, Fell Foot Country Park, Wray Castle and Ferry House for buses to Hill Top and Hawkshead. Steamers and larger launches have licensed bars and coffee shops. Open daily from 9. (D8) 015394 43360 www.windermere-lakecruises.co.uk

Tarn Hows. Probably the most popular tarn, it's very pretty and picturesque; especially in autumn and winter, when it is possible to skate. Two car parks cater for the thousands of visitors. Circular walk. (G6)

Tarn Hows

Tarn Hows

Striding Edge, Helvellyn

Mountains...

Fairfield, 2863ft/873m.
Route 1. Set out from Patterdale. Pass close to Patterdale Hall, bear left onto path leading to St Sunday Crag, and straight up to summit. Return via Hart Crag, and back down Hoggill Brown to Deepdale Bridge with a short roadside walk to car.
Route 2. From Grasmere, a path leads from the Swan Hotel up to Stone Arthur, and on to Great Rigg, and the summmit.
Route 3. Leave Ambleside for Low Sweden Bridge. Path leads to High Pike and Dove Crag. Turn left here for Hart Crag, and the summit of Fairfield. Return via Great Rigg, Heron Pike and Nab Scar. Passing close to Rydal Hall, and Rydal Park to Ambleside. (D4)

Helvellyn, 3113ft/950m. Known as 'The Sunrise Mountain' - because so many climb to see the sunrise on Midsummer's Day. Superb views from the summit. Red Tarn nestles between Swirral Edge and Striding Edge, an exposed serrated ridge popular with mountaineers, and dangerous and slippery in wet or wintry conditions, and scene of a number of fatalities. (C2)
Route 1. Set out from either Glenridding or Patterdale. The paths join up near Lanty's Tarn. From here the path follows a direct route to Striding Edge, a bit of a scramble at times. (D1)
Route 2. From Grasmere the old packhorse road leads towards Great Tongue. Path follows up right side of Grisedale Tarn to Dollywaggon Pike, then continues zig-zagging to the ridge across Nethermost Pike to summit. (B6)
Route 3. A direct and steep route leads from Wythburn Church. A clear zig-zag path, though the least exciting of the three routes but the one to climb if you (like me) need to get up there quickly to photograph the dawn light. (B3)

High Street, 2718ft/829m.
Route 1. Park at the southern tip of Haweswater Reservoir. Follow Gatesgarth Beck up and onto Harter Fell. Cross Nan Bield Pass to Mardale III Bell with Lea Water on the right. Return along Riggindale Crag to Heron Crag, and reservoir.
Route 2. Park at Hartsop. Follow path beside Hayeswater Gill to Hayeswater. Up steep incline to The Knott, and along ridge to cairn. To return, continue a little way along the ridge into Threshwaite Cove. A steep walk down beside Pasture Beck to Hartsop. (H4)

Kirkstone Pass, (454m/1489ft). A good wide road from Ullswater to Windermere passes across here. The Ambleside road leading down from the Inn is steep and narrow and fully justifies its nickname, 'The Struggle'. (F5)

High Street. Roman road which crosses the fells, giving fine panoramic, lakeland views and a superb, long mountain bike traverse. (H2)

Summit by Jon Trotman, Blencathra Arts

Short easy walks...

Ambleside to Rydal Mount. (D7)
A short linear walk of 1 mile/1.6 km
through glorious parkland. Start
from Scandale Bridge 1/2 mile north
of Ambleside on the A591. Turn R
with lodge on your left hand side and
follow broad path which gently rises
through Rydal Park. The trees and
undulating landscape are a marvel.

**Tarn Hows Circuit from
National Trust car park.** (B10)
Get here early before the crowds. It is
an easy 1.5 miles/2.5 km circular
route suitable for prams and
wheelchairs. This well known beauty
spot offers dramatic views of the
surrounding fells and is a fine
introduction to the Lakeland fells.

**Stock Ghyll Force (Waterfall)
from Ambleside.** (E7)
A 2 miles/3.5 km easy walk, slippery
at times (sensible shoes advised) that
starts behind Barclays Bank. Note the
waymarked signs that follows the
river, Stock Ghyll, up to this
spectacular 70 ft waterfall. Spring
conjures up a carpet of daffodils. In
former times 12 watermills were
driven by the power of Stock Ghyll.

1821	John Keats visit Stock Ghyll Force, Ambleside and is moved to write "more than ever"	1825	William Wordsworth buys field next to Rydal Mount now known as Dora's Field
		1826	Pillar Rock's first ascent by the shepherd John Atkinson

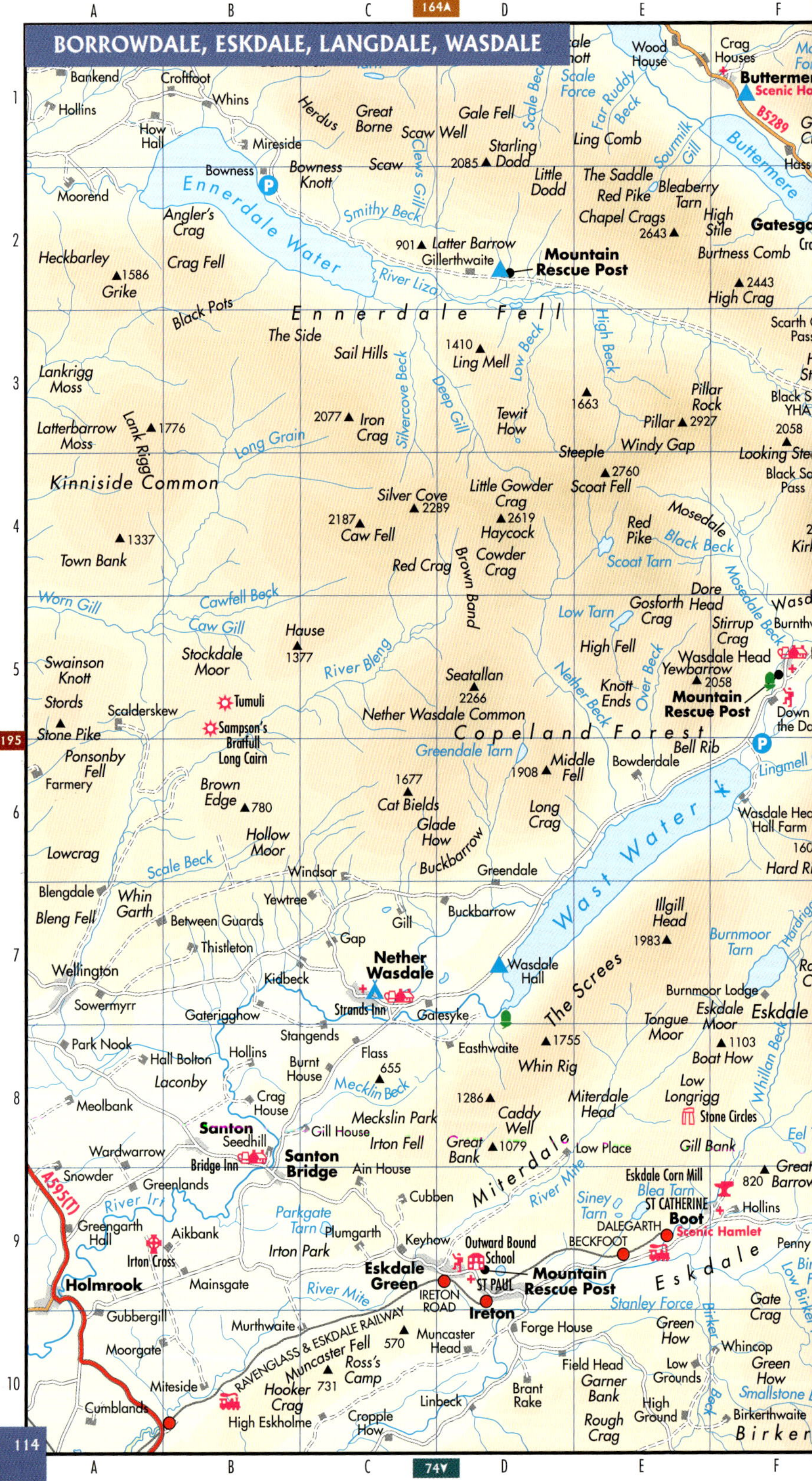
BORROWDALE, ESKDALE, LANGDALE, WASDALE
Bankend
Crofftoot
Whins
Hollins
How Hall
Moorend
Heckbarley
▲1586
Grike
Crag Fell
Angler's Crag
Bowness
Bowness Knott
Crag Fell
Mireside
Scaw
Herdus
Great Borne
Scaw Well
Clews Gill
Smithy Beck
Ennerdale Water
River Liza
Black Pots
The Side
Sail Hills
Silvercove Beck
Deep Gill
Gale Fell
Starling Dodd
2085 ▲
Ling Comb
Scale Beck
Scale Force
Little Dodd
The Saddle
Red Pike
Chapel Crags
2643 ▲
Far Ruddy Beck
Wood House
Crag Houses
Buttermere
Scenic Ho
B5289
Bleaberry Tarn
High Stile
Gatesga
Burtness Comb
▲ 2443
High Crag
Scarth
Pass
Latter Barrow
901 ▲
Gillerthwaite
Mountain Rescue Post
Ennerdale Fell
1410 ▲
Ling Mell
Low Beck
High Beck
1663 ▲
Tewit How
Pillar Rock
Pillar ▲ 2927
Black S
YHA
2058
Looking Ste
Lankrigg Moss
Lank Rigg
▲ 1776
Latterbarrow Moss
Long Grain
2077 ▲
Iron Crag
Steeple
Windy Gap
Black So
Pass
Kinniside Common
▲ 1337
Town Bank
Silver Cove
▲ 2289
2187 ▲
Caw Fell
Red Crag
Little Gowder Crag
▲ 2619
Haycock
Cowder Crag
Brown Band
Scoat Fell
▲ 2760
Red Pike
Scoat Tarn
Mosedale
Black Beck
Kirk
Worn Gill
Cawfell Beck
Caw Gill
Hause
▲ 1377
River Bleng
Low Tarn
Dore Head
Gosforth Head Crag
High Fell
Mosedale Beck
Wasd
Burnthv
Swainson Knott
Stockdale Moor
Seatallan
2266 ▲
Nether Beck
Knott Ends
Over Beck
Stirrup Crag
Wasdale Head
Yewbarrow
▲ 2058
Mountain Rescue Post
Down the Da
Stords
Scalderskew
Tumuli
Sampson's Bratfull
Long Cairn
Nether Wasdale Common
Copeland Forest
Bell Rib
Lingmell
Stone Pike
Ponsonby Fell
Farmery
Brown Edge ▲780
1677 ▲
Cat Bields
Glade How
Greendale Tarn
1908 ▲
Middle Fell
Bowderdale
Long Crag
Wast Water
Wasdale Hea
Hall Farm
160
Hard R
Lowcrag
Scale Beck
Hollow Moor
Buckbarrow
Greendale
Windsor
Blengdale
Bleng Fell
Whin Garth
Between Guards
Yewtree
Gill
Buckbarrow
Illgill Head
1983 ▲
Burnmoor Tarn
Hardri
Rc
C
Thistleton
Gap
Nether Wasdale
Wasdale Hall
The Screes
Wellington
Kidbeck
Strands Inn
Galesyke
Burnmoor Lodge
Tongue Moor
Eskdale Moor
Eskdale
Sowermyrr
Gaterigghow
Stangends
Easthwaite
▲1755
Whin Rig
▲ 1103
Boat How
Whillan Beck
Park Nook
Hall Bolton
Hollins
Flass
▲ 655
Mecklin Beck
1286 ▲
Miterdale Head
Low Longrigg
Meolbank
Laconby
Burnt House
Crag House
Meckslin Park
Irton Fell
Caddy Well
Great Bank
▲1079
Miterdale Head
Low Place
Stone Circles
Gill Bank
Eel
Santon
Seedhill
Gill House
Ain House
Santon Bridge
Eskdale Corn Mill
820 ▲
Great Barrow
Wardwarrow
Bridge Inn
Cubben
Miterdale
River Mite
Blea Tarn
Siney Tarn
ST CATHERINE
Boot
Scenic Hamlet
Hollins
Snowder
Greenlands
Parkgate Tarn
Plumgarth
Keyhow
Outward Bound School
DALEGARTH
BECKFOOT
Eskdale
Penny
Bir
Holmrook
Greengarth Hall
Aikbank
Irton Cross
Mainsgate
Irton Park
River Mite
Eskdale Green
IRETON ROAD
ST PAUL
Ireton
Mountain Rescue Post
Stanley Force
Gate Crag
Gubbergill
Murthwaite
RAVENGLASS & ESKDALE RAILWAY
Muncaster Head
Forge House
Green How
Low Bir
Whincop
Green How
Moorgate
Muncaster Fell
570
Ross's Camp
Field Head
Garner Bank
Low Grounds
Miteside
Hooker Crag
731
Brant Rake
Rough Crag
High Ground
Smallstone
Cumblands
High Eskholme
Cropple How
Linbeck
Birkerthwaite
Birker

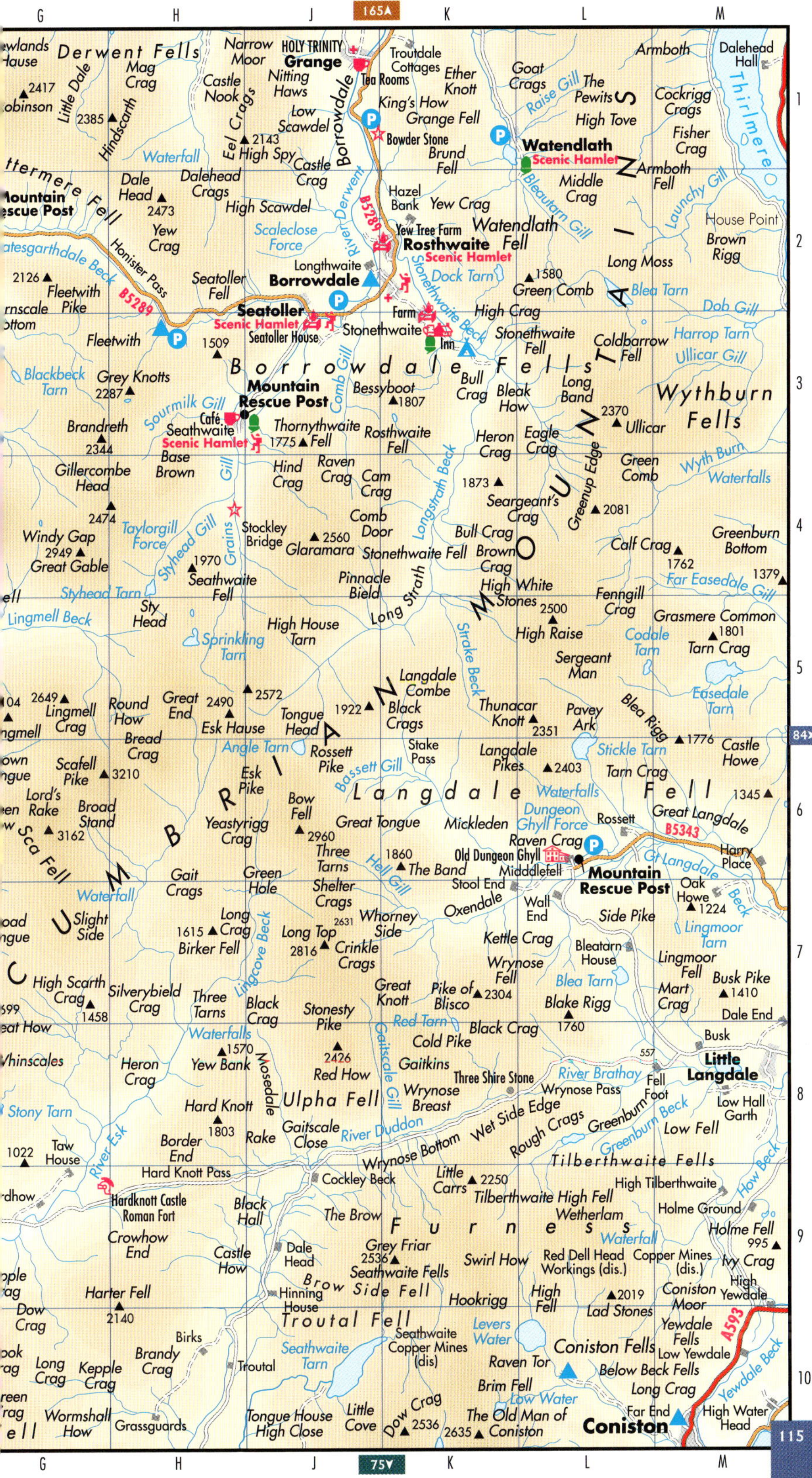

165A
G H J K L M
Derwent Fells
Narrow Moor
HOLY TRINITY
Grange
Tea Rooms
Troutdale Cottages
Ether Knott
Goat Crags
Armboth
Dalehead Hall
Thirlmere
Little Dale
2417
Robinson
Mag Crag
Nitting Haws
Castle Nook
King's How
Grange Fell
The Pewits
Cockrigg Crags
2385
Hindscarth
Low Scawdel
Raise Gill
High Tove
1
Eel Crags
High Spy
2143
Bowder Stone
Brund Fell
Watendlath
Scenic Hamlet
Armboth Fell
Fisher Crag
Waterfall
Castle Crag
Dale Head
Dalehead Crags
2473
High Scawdel
Hazel Bank
Yew Crag
Watendlath Fell
Middle Crag
House Point
Brown Rigg
Scaleclose Force
Yew Tree Farm
Rosthwaite
Scenic Hamlet
Long Moss
Blea Tarn
2
Yew Crag
Honister Pass
B5289
Seatoller Fell
Borrowdale
Longthwaite
Dock Tarn
Green Comb
1580
High Crag
Dob Gill
2126
Fleetwith Pike
Seatoller
Scenic Hamlet
Seatoller House
Farm
Stonethwaite
Stonethwaite Fell
Coldbarrow Fell
Harrop Tarn
Fleetwith
1509
Inn
Ullicar Gill
Blackbeck Tarn
Grey Knotts
2287
Mountain Rescue Post
Café
Seathwaite
Scenic Hamlet
Bessyboot
1807
Bull Crag
Bleak How
Long Band
2370
Ullicar
Wythburn Fells
Brandreth
2344
Base Brown
Thornythwaite
1775 Fell
Rosthwaite Fell
Heron Crag
Eagle Crag
Greenup Edge
Green Comb
3
Gillercombe Head
Hind Crag
Raven Crag
Cam Crag
1873
Seargeant's Crag
2081
Wyth Burn
Waterfalls
2474
Taylorgill Force
Styhead Gill
Stockley Bridge
2560
Comb Door
Bull Crag
Brown Crag
Calf Crag
Greenburn Bottom
Windy Gap
2949
Great Gable
1970
Glaramara
Stonethwaite Fell
High White Stones
1762
Far Easedale Gill
1379
4
Styhead Tarn
Seathwaite Fell
Pinnacle Bield
2500
Fenngill Crag
Grasmere Common
Lingmell Beck
Sty Head
High House Tarn
Long Strath
High Raise
Codale Tarn
1801
Tarn Crag
Sprinkling Tarn
Strake Beck
Sergeant Man
Easedale Tarn
2649
Lingmell Crag
Round How
Great End
2490
2572
Tongue Head
1922
Langdale Combe
Black Crags
Thunacar Knott
Pavey Ark
Blea Rigg
1776
Castle Howe
5
Lingmell
Bread Crag
Esk Hause
2351
Stickle Tarn
Scafell Pike
3210
Esk Pike
Rossett Pike
Bassett Gill
Stake Pass
Langdale Pikes
2403
Tarn Crag
1345
Great Langdale
6
Lord's Rake
Broad Stand
Yeastyrigg Crag
Bow Fell
Great Tongue
Mickleden
Dungeon Ghyll Force
Rossett
B5343
Sca Fell
3162
2960
Three Tarns
Hell Gill
The Band
Raven Crag
Old Dungeon Ghyll
Midddlefell
Mountain Rescue Post
Gt Langdale
Harry Place
Oak Howe
1224
Gait Crags
Green Hole
Shelter Crags
1860
Stool End
Oxendale
Wall End
Side Pike
Lingmoor Tarn
Slight Side
Long Crag
1615
Long Top
2631
Whorney Side
Kettle Crag
Bleatarn House
Lingmoor Fell
Busk Pike
1410
7
Birker Fell
2816
Crinkle Crags
Wrynose Fell
Blea Tarn
Mart Crag
Dale End
High Scarth Crag
1458
Silverybield Crag
Three Tarns
Black Crag
Stonesty Pike
Great Knott
Pike of Blisco
2304
Blake Rigg
1760
Busk
Busk
Little Langdale
8
Great How
Whinscales
Heron Crag
1570
Yew Bank
Moasedale
2426
Red How
Gaitkins
Red Tarn
Three Shire Stone
Black Crag
River Brathay
557
Fell Foot
Low Hall Garth
Low Fell
Stony Tarn
Hard Knott
1803
Gaitscale Close
River Duddon
Wrynose Breast
Wrynose Pass
Greenburn Beck
Low Fell
1022
Taw House
Border End
Rake
Wet Side Edge
Rough Crags
Tilberthwaite Fells
Hard Knott Pass
Cockley Beck
Little Carrs
2250
Tilberthwaite High Fell
High Tilberthwaite
Holme Ground
Holme Fell
995
9
Hardknott Castle Roman Fort
Black Hall
The Brow
Wetherlam
Waterfall
Ivy Crag
Crowhow End
Castle How
Dale Head
Grey Friar
2536
Swirl How
Red Dell Head Workings (dis.)
Copper Mines (dis.)
High Yewdale
Harter Fell
2140
Hinning House
Brow Side Fell
Seathwaite Fells
Hookrigg
High Fell
2019
Lad Stones
Coniston Moor
Yewdale
A593
Dow Crag
Birks
Brandy Crag
Troutal
Troutal Fell
Seathwaite Copper Mines (dis)
Levers Water
Raven Tor
Coniston Fells
Low Yewdale
Below Beck Fells
Yewdale Beck
10
Long Crag
Kepple Crag
Seathwaite Tarn
Little Cove
Dow Crag
2536
Brim Fell
Low Water
Long Crag
Far End
High Water Head
Wormshall How
Grassguards
Tongue House High Close
The Old Man of Coniston
2635
Coniston
G H J K L M
75
115

Eskdale

Villages of Interest...

Boot. A small cluster of cottages has settled beside a stream at the head of the railway. A popular spot for walkers and campers (Hollins Farm) in the shadow of the Scafells and the Gable mountain ranges. Woolpack Inn & (their micro) Harknott Brewery www.woolpack.co.uk hold regular folk singing events. (E9)

Buttermere. A busy start for many walks. Often festooned with cars and hill walkers. Ice cream shop. Hotel and former home of the Maid of Buttermere - see Celebrities. (F1)

Eskdale Green. A pretty village on a bend in the road with post office and Outward Bound Centre. (C9)

Irton Cross. Rare example of a C9 sandstone cross. Rarely marked on maps. (A9)

Santon Bridge. It was at the Bridge Inn that the competition for "The World's Biggest Liar" took place. In the C19, Will Ritson (1808-1890), a publican who lived at the head of the Wasdale Valley would entertain folk with his tall stories. He had great powers of perception and would bewilder his audience into believing that the Lakes were formed by moles and eels! Each year a competition is held here in November. 019467 26221 (B9) www.santonbridgeinn.com

Seathwaite. A tiny group of cottages and farm buildings, and recorded to be the wettest place in England. Venture forth from here to the Gables and Scafell range. Basic tearoom. Remains of old plumbago mines, producers of black lead. (H3)

Seatoller. National Trust car park and a row of cottages amidst an enchanting landscape of dry stone walls and farm buildings. Guesthouse. Inn and tearoom. (J3)

Watendlath. Isolated moorland hamlet with houses built and roofed with stone. The setting for Hugh Walpole's novel Judith Paris. The winding, tortuous road up to the village is bedlam in summer.

It's advisable to walk up from Rosthwaite, or Lodore Falls. Tearooms. (L1)

Wasdale Head. The cradle of British rock climbing and centre for the earliest climbers who were Victorian and Edwardian gentlemen kitted out in tweeds, hobnailed boots and a length of hemp or silk rope. They came, stayed at the hotel, climbed and returned exhausted to the hotel where they flung their gear onto the floor of the hallway. After dinner they were entertained with tall-stories by the hotel-keeper, known as the greatest liar in the world. Drystone walls cover the valley floor in beautifully shaped patterns, best viewed from the path below Wasdale Fell. Climbing shop and climbers' bar. Campsite. The Shepherds' Meet is held every October - a tradition when the farmers would walk down off the fells to exchange stray animals that had gathered in the wrong valley. Much ale and banter was had by all. Today, the Wasdale Show puts on wrestling, dog races and sheep shows. (F5)

A moody Wasdale

1842   Tennyson writes much of Morte d'Arthur at Mirehouse
1845   William Wordsworth is presented to Queen Victoria at the Queen's Fancy Ball
1845   First public steamer launched on Windermere, Lady of the Lake

Dawn, Seathwaite

Wastwater

'The Valley with the Lake' is the deepest, most dramatic and haunting of all the lakes. It draws me to visit it time and time again. No matter what the weather, it is always a thrill to drive up the road towards Wasdale Head. The scenery is rugged, indeed awe-inspiring, especially the Screes overlooking the south-east corner - a mass of rubble rising to nearly 2,000 feet. A quite unforgettable site, for it

appears to drop straight into the lake down a further 600 feet. There is a rugged footpath, tough going in places, which passes beneath the

Screes beside the lake. The view up the valley towards Yewbarrow, Great Gable and Scafell is memorable. No boating allowed. (D6)

Stair
Stonycroft
Skelgill
Hawse End
Keswick
Wallow Crag
▲ 1234
Rowling End
Emerald Bank
y Pike
Old Brandelhow
Victoria Bay
St. Herbert's Island
Lady's Rake
B5289
Barrow Bay
Falcon Crag
Ca
Birkrigg
East Ho
Brandelhow Park
Derwent Water
Youth Hostel
Barrow Ho
Brown Knotts
Bawd Hall
Gillbrow
Keskdale Beck
n tt
Barrow Bay
Waterfalls
Ashness
0
P
▲ 1481
Cat Bells
Black Crag
Little Town
High Crag
Hotel
Lodore Cascade
Gowder Crag
1
Dodd
High Snab
Low Ho
Great Bay
Shepherd Crag
High Lodore
Ashness Fell
Thwaite Ho.
bank
Low Snab
Scope End
Goldscope Lead Mines (disused)
Maiden Moor
1887
Manesty
Borrowdale Gates
B5289
BORROWDALE
Troutdale Cotts
1204 ▲ Brown Dodd
Caffell Sides
Goat Crags
RWENT FELLS
High Crags
Narrow Moor
Tea Shops
Grange
Hollows
River Derwent
Greatend Crag
Ether Knott
Raise Gill
g
Castle Nook
Nitting Haws
King's How
Grange Fell
Watendl
High Spy
▲ 2143
Eel Crags
Low Scawdel
8
Bowder Stone
Brund Fell
▲ 1363
2
Watendlath Tarn
Cafe
P
Waterfall
Lobstone Band
BORROWDALE
Castle Crag
S
Bleatarn Gill
Great Gable
Dale Head ▲ 2473
Dalehead Crags
Rigghead Quarries (disused)
7
Yew Crag
3
Hazel Bank
B5289
Great Crag
arth
High Scawdel
Watendla
nere
Yew Crag
Scaleclose Force
River Derwent
Rosthwaite
Honister Pass
Quarries (disused)
B5289
6
Seatoller Fell
Hause Gill
927 ▲
Longthwaite
Borrowdale
Knotts
Tarn
1580 ▲
Green Comb
Seatoller
B5289
4
Stonethwaite
Stonethwaite Beck
Stonethwaite Fell
High Crag
etwith
5
Youth Hostel
Honister Hause
1509 ▲
Thornythwaite
BORROWDALE FELL
2287
Plumbago Mines (disused)
Borrowdale
High Knott
Bull Crag
Lon Ban
s
Sourmilk Gill
River Derwent
Thornythwaite Fell
Comb Gill
Bessyboot
1807 ▲
Johnny's Ho.
White Crag
Bleak How
Seathwaite
1775 ▲ Capell Crag
Tarn at Leaves
Rosthwaite Fell
Heron Crag
Eagle Crag
Scale
0   500   1000 metres
0   500   1000 yards
oldeneye
Hind Crag
Raven Crag
Cam Crag
Longstrath Beck
Seargeant's Crag
1873 ▲

Watendlath to Honister

12.5 miles (20km);
5 off-road, 7.5 road.
Grade 2.
Riding Time 3-4 hours.

A steep tarmac climb leads past two justly famous views over Derwent Water for a varied tour of Borrowdale, one of Lakeland's most beautifully wooded valleys. The steep climb up to Honister Hause is optional, but opens more dramatic views.

0 Unless you are riding from Keswick, (busy road in summer) park after the Derwent Water Youth Hostel at Kettlewell lakeside car park. **Do not** take your car up to Watendlath.

1 Steeply up to the famous Ashness Bridge which provides a view over Derwent Water to Skiddaw (with clifftop "Surprise View" soon after). Continue straight on to Watendlath (tea-shop).

2 Take right path over the humpy footbridge beside edge of the tarn, forking right up obvious, steep stony track, signposted Bridleway/Rosthwaite. Track flattens out before steep descent, which may be better walked.

3 Below the steep descent ignore the first gate in wall on your right, signposted Keswick / Bowderstone and continue 200m to pass through second gate on right (footpath straight on signposted Stonethwaite.) Easily down to road at Rosthwaite and turn left to Seatoller.

4 Fork right, signposted Honister Pass through Seatoller. Either take bridleway on right in 500m or straight on for steep 1-in-4 to Honister House. A short climb up the obvious quarry track, forking righ after 100m, leads to the old gated quarry tunnel offering superb views down other side of the pass.

5 Descend back into Borrowdale, first by track on right behind hostel, soon crossing to other side of road. Below where it rejoins the road for second time, take obvious track on left, signposted bridleway to descend to gate.

6 After gate, bridleway flattens out as Seatoller comes into view. Just before obvious clump of larch trees (and another gate) take single track forking left above the track, signposted B/way. Make a short climb to gate in wall, then follow wall on R to footbridge.

7 Cross stream and continue straight ahead until a very rough stone-paved track descends behind Castle Crag and through a gate.

8 Cross two successive fords (footbridge at second) to join walled track near campsite. Straight on to Grange (tea-shops). Turn right to cross bridge, then left on valley road back to start.

S *Shortened Route. 6 km (1 off-road.) Turn right at road and follow this for 1 km. Through gate on right, signed bridleway, follow track parallel with road to visit the Bowderstone. Straight on to rejoin road back to start.*

Hardknott Roman Fort

Special Places to Visit...

Eskdale Corn Mill.

An historic water-powered corn mill dating back to 1578 located in breathtaking scenery. Picnic area. Open Mar-Sept Tu-Su & BHs 11-5. (F9) 019467 23335

Hardknott Roman Fort.

Spectacular site, also known as Mediobogdum. Overlooks the Esk Valley, and well placed to defend the route between Ambleside and Ravenglass. Built in Hadrian's time, about AD 120-138. There's visible evidence of the granaries, HQ, parade ground and bathhouse. (H9)

Honister Slate Mine.

Guided tours (10.30, 12.30 & 3.30) explain the history and features of this spectacular mine which has for centuries produced beautiful green roofing slates. Visitor Centre. Coffee shop. Open daily 9-5. (H3) 017687 77230 www.honister-slate-mine.co.uk

Where to Eat, Drink & Be Merry (after a hard day on the fells)...

Wasdale Head Inn. A hostelry known and loved by generations of rock climbers, mountaineers and hill walkers. It is a place of history and refuge after a day on the rock face or the surrounding fells. Old photographs by the legendary Abraham brothers line the walls. The hotel provides bedrooms with bath or showers, and a full English breakfast. You can eat in the Dining Room or in the adjoining Climbers' Bar. Drying room. Self-catering apartments. (F5) 019467 26229 www.wasdale.com

Where to Eat, Drink & Be Merry in Borrowdale...

Grange Tea Rooms. Perfect spot for a light lunch or afternoon tea. The soup and sandwiches were a life-saver. Open daily. (J1)

Seathwaite Café. The last pit stop before you tackle Scafell or the Gables. (H3)

The Flock In, Rosthwaite.

Tearoom adjoining Yew Tree Farm and home to thousands of Herdwick sheep. Serves lunches and afternoon teas. Garden café. Gifts. Open Feb-Nov Th-Tu, Nov F-Tu, 10-5. (K2) 01768 777675 www.borrowdaleherdwick.co.uk

Where to Stay...

Old Dungeon Ghyll, Great Langdale.

An old favourite of the mountaineer and hill walker, and for well over 300 years an inn of great hospitality and sustenance. Today the hotel has 13 bedrooms and a comfortable residents' lounge. Hikers' bar, next door. (L6) 01539 437272 www.odg.co.uk

Seatoller House, Borrowdale.

A guest house for more than 100 years patronised by the same groups of families for more than 70 years. Home to the twice-yearly Man Hunts, an event which was started by three Cambridge undergraduates in the late C19 and was based on the manhunt in RL Stevenson's Kidnapped. The bedrooms are comfortable, the dining is communal around two large oak tables, and the library is impressive. TVs and radios are banned. Families and dogs are welcome but there is an age limit. The cuisine is home cooked and wholesome. (J3) 017687 77218 www.seatollerhouse.co.uk

Stonethwaite Farm, Borrowdale.

The quintessential cottage garden draws you down the path into this farmhouse B&B. Set within arguably the most beautiful (and wettest) corner in England, and a walker's paradise. The rooms are simply and practically furnished. Next door, the local inn serves home-made fare and local brews. It all makes for a winning combination. (K3) 017687 77234

The Strands Inn & Brewery, Nether Wasdale.

Cosy bar, comfy bedrooms and real ale brewed on the premises -just what Matron ordered after a full day in Lakeland. (C7) 019467 26237 www.strandshotel.co.uk

Yew Tree Farm, Rosthwaite.

Traditional Borrowdale farm (with over 2,000 Herdwick sheep) provides comfortable B & B. Joe and Hazel hit the headlines when Prince Charles came to stay here. (J2) 017687 77675 www.borrowdaleherdwick.co.uk

Honister Slate Mine ss

Stonethwaite Fell

An enchanting and picturesque landscape, and perhaps the most visited and photographed area of Lakeland. A place of steep wooded banks, and in the Autumn a kaleidoscopic range of colour. This is splendid and easy walking country. Wander up the Langstrath Valley, or to Greenup Ghyll, all accessible valleys. A more arduous path leads to Styhead Pass and on to the Scafells and Gables. The weather is forever changing. Storm clouds billow up around the mountain tops and the sudden shafts of light are a photographer's dream. The Bowder Stone is a much-visited attraction: a gigantic stone, finely balanced and weighing about 2,000 tons, lies in a pretty woodland setting, most probably left by retreating glaciers in the Ice Age. (J1)

Bowder Stone, Borrowdale

Single Tree, Stonethwaite

Honister Pass

Ennerdale.
Remote, wild, isolated and not too accessible. Plenty of forest trails waymarked by the Forestry Commission. Many conifers. A good base for climbing Pillar and Steeple. (B2)

Eskdale.
Green pastures and gentle slopes of ethereal beauty provide a marked contrast to the rugged high slopes of Hardknott Pass. Look out for evidence of the pink granite unique to this valley. Its industrial past is hidden by the picturesque landscape for today it is a refuge of small hamlets, farms and quiet hotels. (E9)

Langdale.
Dramatic scenery and easy access from Ambleside and Windermere. No wonder it's such a popular valley. The Langdale Pikes rise sheer from the valley floor of Great Langdale. The Old Dungeon Ghyll Hotel is a welcome refuge after a day on the fells. Nearby, Stickle Barn, a cafe and bar. Little Langdale is not so spectacular but offers less strenuous walks. (M6)

Hardknott Pass (394m/1291ft).
The most notorious and exciting motoring challenge in the Lakes. Sharp bends, spectacular drops and a 1 in 3 gradient might make you think twice before you venture here especially when the roads are wet. Not for the faint hearted. It's congested in summer, with passing places, not parking spaces. Caravans are banned. Winter travel is not advised. Check your brakes, and pulse! (H9)

Honister Pass (359m/1176ft).
Fairly easy to navigate. At times a 1 in 4 gradient provides added interest and concentration. The most direct of all routes to Buttermere from Borrowdale. Working slate quarry at the head of Pass with shop/cafe and guided tours. (H2)

Wrynose Pass (391m/1281ft).
Notoriously steep and narrow. At times only space for single cars. There are passing places not parking places. Caravans are banned. Winter travel can be treacherous, and is not advised. The Three Shires Stones rest on the summit. (L8)

1850	William Wordsworth dies at Rydal Mount	1852 First recorded Grasmere Sports meeting
1850	Hoad Monument built overlooking Ulverston to honour Sir John Barrow	1855 Publication of Harriet Martineau's Complete Guide to the English Lakes

Entering Eskdale

Buttermere, 'The Lake of the Dairy Pastures'. There are few places so beautiful in this world as Buttermere and no surprise that it is considered by many to be the most picturesque of the 16 main bodies of water. Listen for the sound of running water, its soothing sound will haunt you for hours. The becks rush down the hillside and Sour Milk Ghyll thunders down from Bleaberry Tarn. Try the easy 6 mile / 8km circular walk from Buttermere village. (F1)

Summit of Great Gable

Ennerdale Water. The westerly location and inaccessibility provide peace and solitude for the serious walker. This wild and remote area is popular with mountaineers intent on scaling Pillar, Great Gable and the High Stile range. A circular walk of the lake takes about four hours. The best viewpoint is near the car park at Bowness Point. No amenities. (B2)

Waterfalls...

Dungeon Ghyll. Accessible walk up from car park, to this 52 feet fall, hidden under a rock bridge beneath a dark chasm. (L6)

Galleny Force. A short walk up river from Stonethwaite. The fall enters a clear pool surrounded by trees and tall rocks. (J3)

The Mountains...

Bow Fell, 2960ft/902m. (J6)
A pyramid shaped mountain at the head of the Great Langdale, Eskdale and Langstrath valleys. Not an easy ascent compared to the many, smaller fells yet a popular and easier introduction to walking the higher fells.

Route 1. Park in Langdale. Walk up Mickleden until you reach the Guide Stone. Up to Rossett Gill to Angle Tarn. Then left up to Ore Gap and on to Bow Fell. Return via the Three Tarns, and down beside Buscoe Silk and Oxendale Beck to Langdale. (L6)

Crinkle Craggs, 2816ft/858m. (J7)
Route 1. Simple and direct route starts from the Three Shire Stone on Wrynose Pass. Up to Cold Pike, and across fell to summit. (K8)
Route 2. Set out from Langdale car park. Follow track to Stool End Farm, bear left up Oxendale, over Brown Hose, scrambling up Browney Gill, and up to Great Knott. Return via the Three Tarns, descending beside Buscoe Silk, and Hell Gill to Oxendale. Superb views. (L6)

Great Gable, 2949ft/899m.
A most impressive looking mountain. Pyramid shaped, in imperious symmetry. Fine, panoramic views from the summit. A memorial service is held by Lakeland's Fell & Rock Climbing Club on the summit every Remembrance Sunday to commemorate the mountaineers who died in World War I. The

mountain provided the venue for some of the earliest rock climbs: Nape's Needle, Eagle's Nest Ridge and White Napes. (G4)

Route 1. From Seathwaite, follow the path beside Sour Milk Ghyll, and up to Green Gable. Cross Windy Gap to summit. (H3)

Route 2. Easiest route is from Honister Pass, over Grey Knotts, Brandreth and Green Gable. (H3)

Route 3. Direct route from Wasdale Head. (F5)

Langdale Pikes, 2403ft/736m. An impressive range of crags made up of Pike of Stickle, Harrison Stickle, Loft Crag, Gimmer Crag and Thorn Crag. Popular climbing and walking area. The neolithic axe factory was sited on Pike of Stickle. (L6)

Route 1. Start from the National Trust car park. Follow path up beside Stickle Ghyll to Stickle Tarn. The path leads around to the summit. Wonderful views. (L6)

Pillar, 2927ft/892m. A climbing area that in recent years has lost its popularity despite the early fame for the rock climb of Pillar Rock's spire. (E3)

Route 1. From Wasdale follow the right side of Mosedale up to Gatherstone Head to Black Sail Pass. From here an easy trek to summit. Return via the same route. Other routes are difficult and steep. (F5)

Route 2. Several paths lead towards the summit from Ennerdale Forest. (C2)

Scafell, 3162ft/964m & Scafell Pike, 3210ft/978m. England's highest mountain holds a popular fascination with walkers. These two must be treated with respect and caution; beware sudden changes in the weather. The summit is strewn with untidy boulders. Allow 6-8 hours for the whole journey. (G6)

Route 1. The shortest, and quickest ascent starts from Wasdale. Follow path up Lingmell Gill to the summit. (F5)

Route 2. From Seatoller, or Seathwaite, follow the routes to Styhead Pass. Cross the open space towards the western flank of Scafell Pike, which leads to the route known as the Corridor, or Guides Walk. This route leads up rocky ground to the summit. (H3)

Taylorgill Force

Short, Easy Walks...

Buttermere Circuit from Buttermere Village. (F2) An easy 4.5 miles/7.3 km along a flat, lakeside path with a short section of tarmac, but first start from the car park alongside the Fish Hotel. Then set out along the south-west shore of Buttermere. An ideal circuit for those wishing to be surrounded by the mountains without exerting too much energy.

Wasdale Valley from Wasdale Head. (F5) An easy-medium grade walk of 2-2.5 miles/ 4 km that takes in some uphill sections. From the car park strike out toward Wast Water. Just after old school building on left, take stile on left and cross field to footbridge over beck. Head diagonally up flanks of Lingmell Fell until at Brown Tongue you meet path to National Trust campsite in valley from whence you return to Wasdale Head alongside the stream.

Hardknott Pass Roman Fort. (G9) Hardknott Roman Fort is situated on the western side of Hardknott Pass with commanding views down the Eskdale valley. Having spent time in the car negotiating the steep, winding, narrow road through Hardknott and Wynose passes, it is worth getting out and walking round

this ancient site, as the setting of the fort is spectacular and the scenery incredible. The terrain is grassy and can be slippery.

Seathwaite to Stockley Bridge. (H3) A short 2 mile/3 km linear route that starts from the car park at Seathwaite. Take the footpath through farm buildings to wooden footbridge. Continue on farm road to Stockley Bridge. Taylorgill Force is an impressive sight on the right. Retrace your steps to return to Seathwaite.

Stonethwaite Valley (Cumbria Way). (K3) Find a place to park in Stonethewaite village. Cross the bridge and turn right. Follow this path as far as you will. There can be few more beautiful valleys than this, anywhere and retrace your steps. It is a valley to wander in, slowly and to be happy that you are alive to witness it.

Ennerdale Forest Trails. (B2) There is a 7-mile circular walk described as easy along forest paths, plus a full range of walking and cycling opportunities in 20 miles of forest roads, tracks and trails. Maps are available from the service boxes in the car park. Roe deer and red squirrel inhabit the forest. Park at Bowness Knot car park.

1869   Kendal Mintcake first produced (by accident)
1871   John Ruskin buys Brantwood for £1,500

1875   Whitehaven Iron Mines Ltd Company build a gauge railway to link Ravenglass with their Nab Gill Mines at Boot
1876   The Ravenglass & Eskdale Railway opens for public use

Buttermere

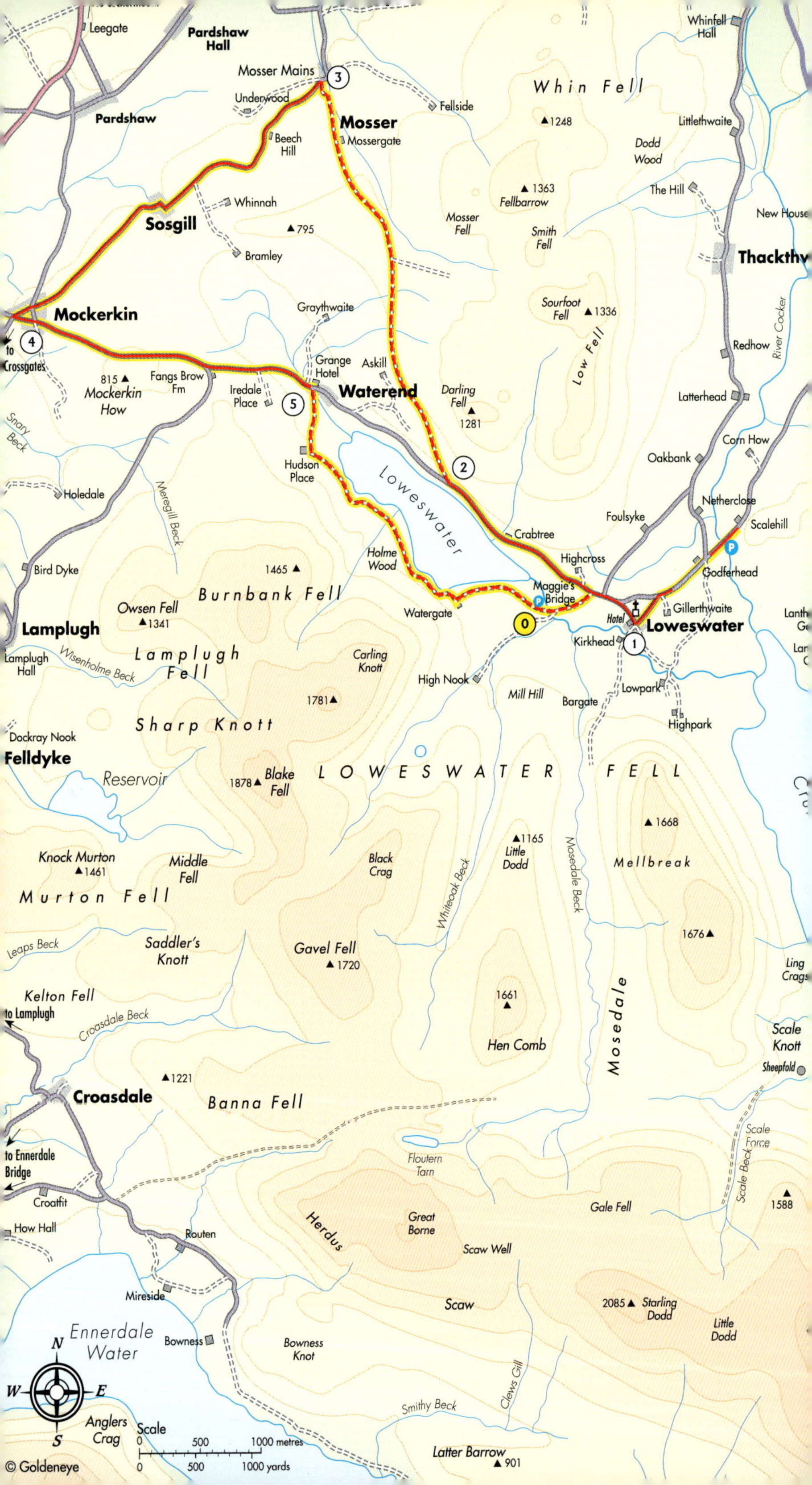

Leegate
Pardshaw Hall
Pardshaw
Whinfell Hall
Mosser Mains
Underwood
Mosser
Whin Fell
1248
Fellside
Littlethwaite
Beech Hill
Mossergate
Dodd Wood
The Hill
New House
Whinnah
795
Sosgill
Mosser Fell
1363
Fellbarrow
Smith Fell
Thackthv
Bramley
Graythwaite
Sourfoot Fell
1336
Low Fell
Redhow
River Cocker
Mockerkin
to Crossgates
4
Grange Hotel
Askill
Waterend
Darling Fell
1281
Latterhead
Corn How
Oakbank
815
Fangs Brow Fm
Mockerkin How
Iredale Place
5
Loweswater
2
Netherclose
Scalehill
Holedale
Hudson Place
Foulsyke
Godferhead
Snary Beck
Meregill Beck
Bird Dyke
Holme Wood
Crabtree
Highcross
Maggie's Bridge
P
Gillerthwaite
Lamplugh
Owsen Fell
1341
1465
Burnbank Fell
Watergate
0
Hotel
Kirkhead
Loweswater
1
Lanth
Lamplugh Hall
Wisenholme Beck
Lamplugh Fell
Carling Knott
High Nook
Mill Hill
Bargate
Lowpark
Highpark
Dockray Nook
Sharp Knott
1781
Felldyke
Reservoir
1878
Blake Fell
L O W E S W A T E R   F E L L
1668
Knock Murton
1461
Middle Fell
Black Crag
Little Dodd
1165
Mellbreak
Murton Fell
Whiteoak Beck
Mosedale Beck
1676
Leaps Beck
Saddler's Knott
Gavel Fell
1720
1661
Ling Crags
Kelton Fell
to Lamplugh
Croasdale Beck
Hen Comb
Mosedale
Scale Knott
Sheepfold
1221
Croasdale
Banna Fell
to Ennerdale Bridge
Floutern Tarn
Scale Force
Scale Beck
Croatfit
How Hall
Routen
Herdus
Great Borne
Scaw Well
Gale Fell
1588
Mireside
Scaw
2085
Starling Dodd
Little Dodd
Ennerdale Water
Bowness
Bowness Knot
Clews Gill
Smithy Beck
N
W   E
S
Anglers Crag
Scale
0   500   1000 metres
0   500   1000 yards
Latter Barrow
901
© Goldeneye

Loweswater to Mosser

9 miles (14km)
1.5 off-road, 7.5 road.
Grade 1.
Riding Time 1.5 hours.

An easy, scenic country ride through quiet lanes and woodland on the fringe of the National Park. With the only real off-road section almost flat, its an excellent route for beginners. A simple circuit of the lake is just over 3km.

0 Park at Maggie's Bridge National Trust car Park where the Bridleway begins. Ride back to lake road and turn left.

1 Take the Lakeside road for Ullock from Loweswater village, turning left after 130m, fingerpost indicates bridleway. Park at the Maggie's Bridge National Trust car park where the bridleway begins. Ride back to lake road and turn left.

2 Halfway along the lake (after approximately 1km) turn right up lane, (signposted Mosser Unfit for Cars) and follow the single track tarmac with grass up the centre. Climb steadily for 1km, then another level km to descend to the hamlet of Mosser Mains.

3 Turn sharp left signposted Sosgill/Mockerkin to follow narrow country lane through hamlet of Sosgill (don't blink) to Mockerkin.

4 Turn left and follow the road, signposted Loweswater bearing left after 500m at Fangs Brow Farm. Continue for another 500m to the Grange Hotel (coffee/bar-snacks etc).

5 Take farm track opposite hotel, signposted The Place, B/way Holme Wood, etc. climbing to Hudson Place. Bear left through gate to narrow walled descent **(control speed, walkers likely)** down to good flat track through beautiful beeches around Loweswater back to start.

Styhead Gill, Alison Critchlow, Blencathra Arts

George Fishers, Keswick

Despite their very modest height, the mountains of the Lake District had a profound influence on the development of mountaineering as a sport. Until the first ascent of Napes Needle in1886, the English pioneers who first established mountaineering as a sport focussed entirely on the European Alps. As alpinists they saw the Lakeland crags as nothing, but a training ground for their alpine expeditions. It was in 1884 and in this alpine context, that Walter Parry Haskett Smith made the first exploration of Great Gable's Needle Ridge. As a climb it is largely alpine in character, an obvious line to a summit - ideal training for the type of route then undertaken in the Alps. During his climbs (both in ascent and descent) on the ridge he noticed the spectacular, free-standing obelisk after which it was named - Napes Needle. Two years later Haskett-Smith would return, to make the first ascent of "The Needle". Even today it remains a challenging and intimidating route, Haskett Smith's first ascent was even more remarkable for having been a solo climb. This event caused a seismic shift in mountaineering attitudes. Henceforth it became acceptable to climb a section of rock for its own sake, the pre-requisite of reaching a summit was no longer required and British crags were viewed a worthy challenge in their own right. No longer were our mountains seen as just an alpine training ground - the sport of rock climbing was born. A private income and the extended

Napes Needle, Abraham Brothers

leisure time a trip to the Alps demanded was no longer a pre-requisite to becoming a mountaineer. The cliffs of the Lake District - and shortly after those in Snowdonia and the Highlands - would open up mountaineering to a much wider spectrum of society. Throughout the late Victorian and the Edwardian eras, the upper middle-class gentlemen of The Alpine Club gradually lost their dominance of mountaineering, giving way to sportsmen from the lower middle-classes. In the decades before the First World War, rock climbs on the Lake District crags were amongst the most technically demanding and difficult of those found anywhere in mountaineering. Wasdale Head, complete with its famous hotel, became the base from which the finest climbers of a generation sallied forth to find real, cutting-edge adventure on the cliffs of Scafell, Great Gable and Pillar. They made this amphitheatre of Lakeland rock their arena, their efforts were Olympian. Names such as O.G. Jones, Frederick Botterill and Siegfried Herford deserve to be ranked alongside Hillary, Messner and Bonington. Their climbs, routes like Kern Notts Crack, Botterill's Slab and Central Buttress were at the absolute forefront of what was deemed possible. Even today, they still generate great respect amongst modern climbers.

Robin Ashworth

George Fishers, Keswick

For solitude, mountains, walks, valleys.

It is to the Northern Fells and lakes that the regular Lakeland visitor is often drawn. The streets of Keswick can be a colourful scene when the pavements are festooned with walkers and climbers dressed in all manner of mountain equipment. Visitors also flock to Keswick for its annual jazz and film festivals and the more permanent artistic presence of the beautiful Theatre by the Lake. Keswick also lays claim to being the birthplace of the pencil industry due to the deposits of and extremely pure and solid form of graphite found in nearby Borrowdale.

Surrounded by fells on all sides, and to the south, the ethereal beauty of Borrowdale, lie the magical waters of Derwent Water which has seven lakeside marinas and dozens of small islands. The natural beauty of the region can as easily be viewed from aboard a sea craft as from on high after the rewarding climb up to Sty Head or one of the other fells.

Derwent Water itself is home to Britain's rarest fish, the Vendace Coregonus Vandesius. The freshwater fish inhabits deep and cold lakes and has died out from all its other known habitats in England.

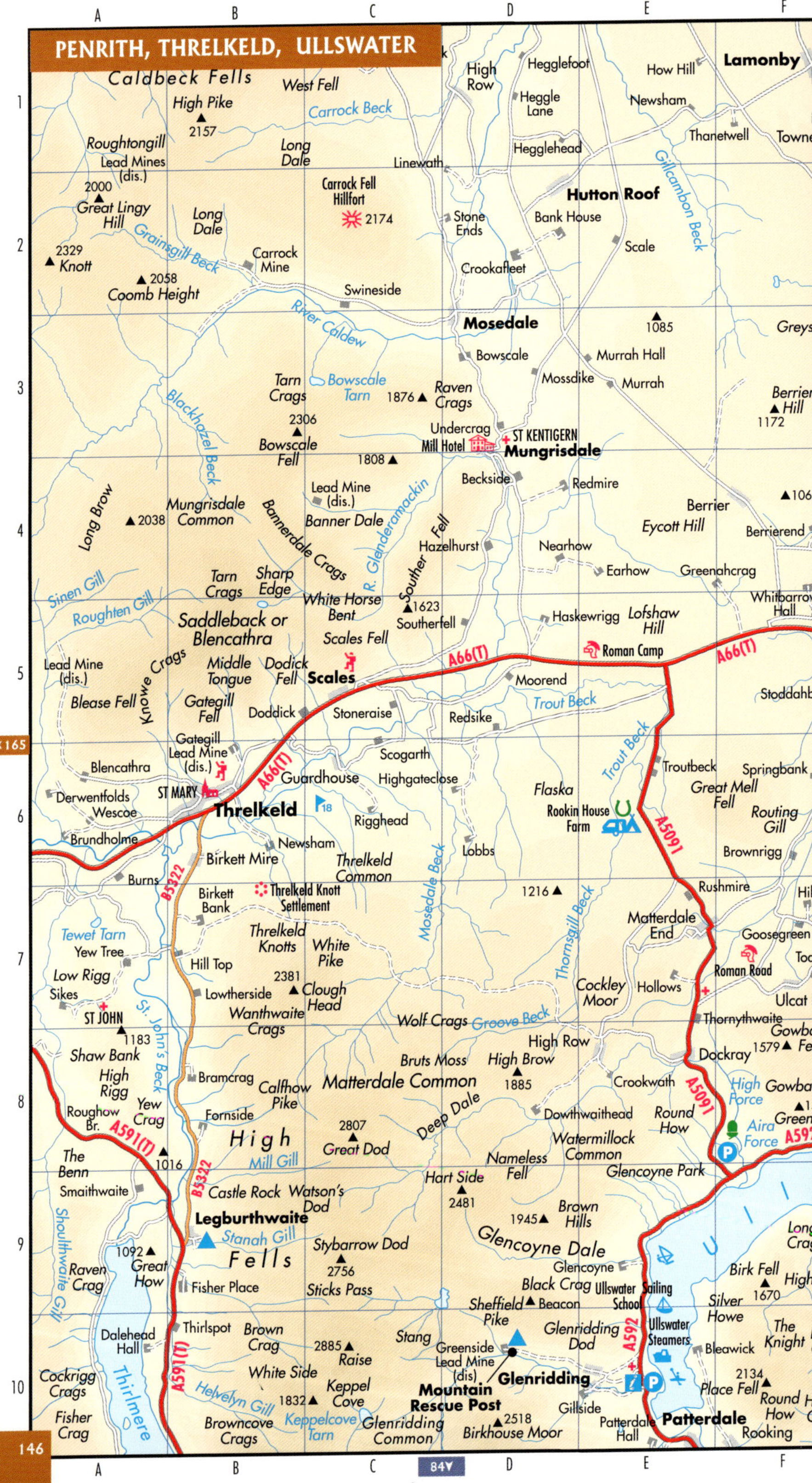
PENRITH, THRELKELD, ULLSWATER
Caldbeck Fells
West Fell
High Pike
2157
Roughtongill
Lead Mines (dis.)
2000
Great Lingy Hill
Long Dale
Long Dale
Carrock Beck
Carrock Fell Hillfort
2174
Linewath
High Row
Hegglefoot
Heggle Lane
Hegglehead
How Hill
Newsham
Thanetwell
Lamonby
Towne
Hutton Roof
Stone Ends
Bank House
Scale
2329
Knott
Grainsgill Beck
Carrock Mine
Swineside
Crookafleet
Mosedale
1085
Murrah Hall
Murrah
Greyst
2058
Coomb Height
River Caldew
Bowscale
Mossdike
Blackhazel Beck
Tarn Crags
Bowscale Tarn
1876
Raven Crags
Berrier Hill
1172
2306
Bowscale Fell
1808
Undercrag
Mill Hotel
ST KENTIGERN
Mungrisdale
Beckside
Redmire
Berrier
1063
Long Brow
2038
Mungrisdale Common
Bannerdale Crags
Banner Dale
R. Glenderamackin
Lead Mine (dis.)
Souther Fell
Hazelhurst
Nearhow
Earhow
Eycott Hill
Greenahcrag
Berrierend
Sinen Gill
Roughten Gill
Tarn Crags
Sharp Edge
White Horse Bent
1623
Southerfell
Haskewrigg
Lofshaw Hill
Whitbarrow Hall
Saddleback or Blencathra
Scales Fell
Knowe Crags
Middle Tongue
Dodick Fell
Scales
A66(T)
Roman Camp
A66(T)
Lead Mine (dis.)
Blease Fell
Gategill Fell
Doddick
Stoneraise
Moorend
Redsike
Trout Beck
Stoddahb
Gategill Lead Mine (dis.)
Blencathra
Derwentfolds
Wescoe
ST MARY
Threlkeld
A66(T)
Guardhouse
Highgateclose
Scogarth
Flaska
Trout Beck
Troutbeck
Great Mell Fell
Springbank
Routing Gill
18
Rigghead
Lobbs
Rookin House Farm
A5091
Brownrigg
Brundholme
Burns
B5322
Birkett Mire
Newsham
Threlkeld Common
Mosedale Beck
1216
Rushmire
Hill
Birkett Bank
Threlkeld Knott Settlement
Matterdale End
Goosegreen
Tod
Tewet Tarn
Yew Tree
Low Rigg
Sikes
Hill Top
Threlkeld Knotts
White Pike
2381
Clough Head
Thornsgill Beck
Roman Road
Ulcat R
ST JOHN
1183
Shaw Bank
High Rigg
Lowtherside
Wanthwaite Crags
Wolf Crags
Groove Beck
Cockley Moor
Hollows
Thornythwaite
Gowba
St. John's Beck
Bramcrag
Calfhow Pike
Fornside
Matterdale Common
Bruts Moss
Deep Dale
High Row
High Brow
1885
Crookwath
High Row
Dockray
1579
Fel
A591(T)
Roughow Br.
Yew Crag
1016
B5322
High
Mill Gill
2807
Great Dod
Dowthwaitehead
Watermillock Common
Round How
A5091
High Force
Aira Force
Gowbar
Green
14
A592
The Benn
Smaithwaite
Castle Rock
Watson's Dod
Hart Side
2481
Nameless Fell
Glencoyne Park
Legburthwaite
Stanah Gill
Fells
Stybarrow Dod
2756
Brown Hills
1945
Glencoyne Dale
Glencoyne
Long Crag
Birk Fell
1670
High
Shoulthwaite Gill
1092
Great How
Raven Crag
Fisher Place
Sticks Pass
Black Crag
Sheffield Pike
Beacon
Ullswater Sailing School
Silver Howe
The Knight
B
C
Dalehead Hall
Thirlspot
Brown Crag
2885
Raise
White Side
Stang
Greenside Lead Mine (dis.)
Glenridding Dod
Glenridding
A592
Ullswater Steamers
Bleawick
2134
Place Fell
Round Ho
How C
Cockrigg Crags
Fisher Crag
Thirlmere
A591(T)
Helvelyn Gill
1832
Browncove Crags
Keppel Cove
Keppelcove Tarn
Glenridding Common
Mountain Rescue Post
2518
Birkhouse Moor
Gillside
Patterdale Hall
Patterdale
Rooking

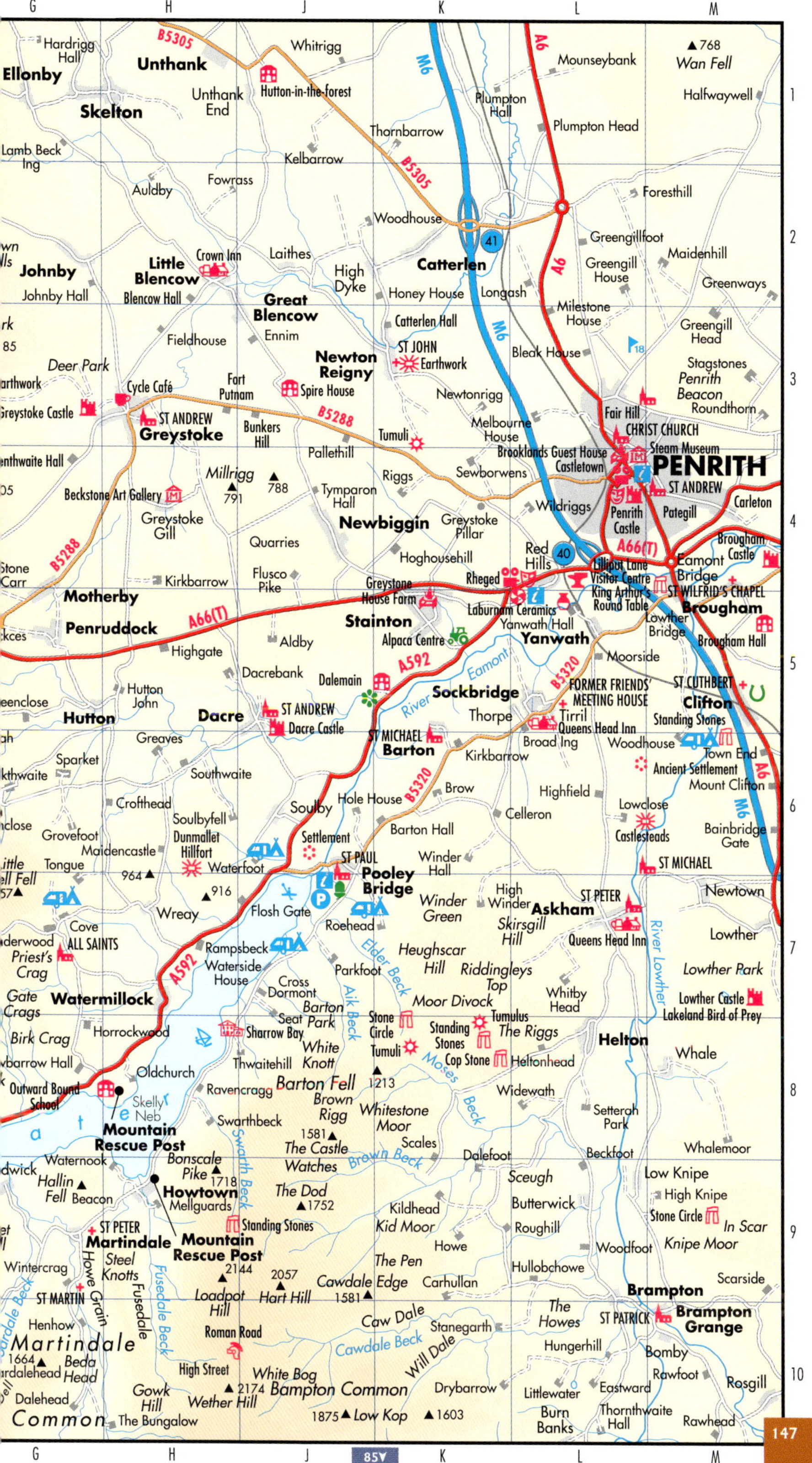

G   H   J   K   L   M

B5305
Hardrigg Hall
Ellonby
Unthank
Whitrigg
Hutton-in-the-forest
Mounseybank
768
Wan Fell
Skelton
Unthank End
Halfwaywell
Lamb Beck Ing
Kelbarrow
Plumpton Hall
Thornbarrow
Plumpton Head
B5305
Auldby
Fowrass
Woodhouse
41
Foresthill
Johnby
Little Blencow
Crown Inn
Laithes
High Dyke
Catterlen
Greengillfoot
Maidenhill
Johnby Hall
Blencow Hall
Honey House
Longash
Greengill House
Greenways
Great Blencow
Ennim
Catterlen Hall
Milestone House
Greengill Head
Fieldhouse
Newton Reigny
ST JOHN
Earthwork
Bleak House
18
Stagstones
Deer Park
Cycle Café
Fort Putnam
Spire House
Newtonrigg
Penrith Beacon
Greystoke Castle
ST ANDREW
Melbourne House
Fair Hill
CHRIST CHURCH
Roundthorn
Greystoke
Bunkers Hill
B5288
Tumuli
Sewborwens
Brooklands Guest House
Castletown
Steam Museum
PENRITH
ST ANDREW
Beckstone Art Gallery
Millrigg
791
788
Tymparon Hall
Riggs
Wildriggs
Penrith Castle
Pategill
Carleton
Pallethill
Brougham Castle
Greystoke Gill
Newbiggin
Greystoke Pillar
40
A66(T)
Eamont Bridge
ST WILFRID'S CHAPEL
B5288
Quarries
Hoghousehill
Red Hills
Rheged
Lilliput Lane Visitor Centre
King Arthur's Round Table
Brougham
Stone Carr
Kirkbarrow
Flusco Pike
Greystone House Farm
Laburnam Ceramics
Yanwath Hall
Lowther Bridge
Brougham Hall
Motherby
Stainton
Alpaca Centre
Yanwath
Moorside
ST CUTHBERT
Penruddock
Highgate
Aldby
A592
Dacrebank
Dalemain
Sockbridge
Thorpe
FORMER FRIENDS' MEETING HOUSE
Tirril
Clifton
Hutton
Hutton John
ST ANDREW
Dacre Castle
ST MICHAEL
Queens Head Inn
Standing Stones
Dacre
Barton
Kirkbarrow
Broad Ing
Woodhouse
Town End
Greaves
Sparket
Southwaite
Hole House
B5320
Brow
Highfield
Lowclose
Ancient Settlement
Mount Clifton
Crofthead
Soulby
Barton Hall
Celleron
Castlesteads
M6
Grovefoot
Maidencastle
Soulbyfell
Dunmallet Hillfort
Settlement
ST PAUL
Winder Hall
Bainbridge Gate
Tongue
964
916
Waterfoot
Pooley Bridge
High Winder
Askham
ST PETER
ST MICHAEL
Newtown
Wreay
Flosh Gate
Winder Green
Queens Head Inn
Lowther
Cove
ALL SAINTS
Rampsbeck
Roehead
Heughscar Hill
Riddingleys Top
Whitby Head
Lowther Park
Priest's Crag
Waterside House
Parkfoot
Moor Divock
Lowther Castle
Lakeland Bird of Prey
Gate Crags
Watermillock
Cross Dormont
Barton Park
Stone Circle
Standing Stones
The Riggs
Helton
Whale
Birk Crag
Horrockwood
Sharrow Bay
Seat Bay
White Knott
Tumuli
Cop Stone
Heltonhead
Oldchurch
Thwaitehill
Barton Fell
1213
Widewath
Outward Bound School
Skelly Neb
Ravencragg
Brown Rigg
Whitestone Moor
Setterah Park
Waternook
Swarthbeck
1581
Scales
Dalefoot
Beckfoot
Whalemoor
Hallin Fell
Beacon
Bonscale Pike
1718
The Castle
Watches
Brown Beck
Sceugh
Low Knipe
Howtown
Mellguards
The Dod
1752
Kildhead
Butterwick
High Knipe
Stone Circle
In Scar
ST PETER
Martindale
Standing Stones
Kid Moor
Howe
Roughill
Woodfoot
Knipe Moor
Steel Knotts
Mountain Rescue Post
The Pen
Hullobchowe
Scarside
Wintercrag
2144
2057
Cawdale Edge
Carhullan
The Howes
Brampton
ST MARTIN
Loadpot Hill
Hart Hill
1581
ST PATRICK
Brampton Grange
Henhow
Roman Road
Caw Dale
Stanegarth
Hungerhill
Bomby
Martindale
High Street
Will Dale
Littlewater
Eastward
Rawfoot
Rosgill
1664
Beda Head
Gowk Hill
White Bog
Bampton Common
Drybarrow
Burn Banks
Thornthwaite Hall
Rawhead
Dalehead
Common
The Bungalow
Wether Hill
1875
Low Kop
1603
85
147

Penrith

PENRITH

Penrith was the ancient capital of Cumbria in the C9 and C10s and unfortunately for the inhabitants a favourite of the marauding Scots. Legend has it that the C10 King of Cumbria, Owen Caesario, lies buried in a grave on the north side of St Andrews Church. It is a town with many attractions, not least its old inns, alleyways and modern amenities where it's possible to idle away the hours if the weather is not suitable for exploring the nearby lakes and mountains. The buildings are impressive and look as if they were meant to stay (perhaps to deter the Scots). It has become a prosperous market town in the Eden Valley and is just a stone's throw from the borders of the National Park. If you are feeling energetic there are superb views to be gained from Penrith Beacon. (M4)

Special Places to Visit in Penrith...

Lilliput Lane Visitor Centre. World-famous Lilliput Lane miniature cottage sculptures. See production, guided tour, shop and tearoom. Open M-F 9-4.30. (M4) 01768 212692. www.lilliputlane.co.uk

Penrith Castle. Built by William Strickland, later the Bishop of Carlisle, to repel Scottish raiders. Later the home of Warwick the Kingmaker, and the Duke of Gloucester, (Richard 111). Partly demolished in 1648. (L4)

Penrith Museum, Middlegate.

Housed in building established for the education of poor girls in 1670, the museum describes the history, geology and archaeology of the district. TIC. Open all year M-Sa 10-5 (Su in Apr-Oct 1-4.45). (L4) 01768 212228 www.eden.gov.uk

Sharrow Bay ss

1877	Launching of steamer Lady of the Lake on Ullswater	1884
1879	Manchester Corporation granted powers to create Thirlmere	
		1885

1884 The trade of flax hand-spinning is revived in Elterwater by Marion Twelves, a disciple of Ruskin

1885 Beatrix Potter first travels to Near Sawrey

Rheged - The Village In The Hill, Redhills. Spectacular attraction featuring 1,500 years of Cumbria's magical heritage in the Discovering Cumbria Exhibition plus the National Mountaineering Exhibition, 180 degree Cinerama Theatre. Restaurants. Café. Shops. Open daily all year. (L4) 01768 868000 www.rheged.com

Where to Stay Just Outside Penrith...

Sharrow Bay. Without doubt one of England's great hotels, and perhaps the first to define and set the style of the English country house hotel. It is a place of legend and the story behind its success matches its brilliance. The views from the Drawing Room, gardens and Bank House are magical. The place embraces enthusiasm and adjectives. The décor may be a little over the top for some of us. Its exuberance and colour only matched by the two late gentlemen, Francis Coulson and Brian Sack, who started this business after World War II. This hotel invites loyalty and a passion for service. The staff have worked here for years and will treat you like royalty. If you can't afford to stay the night then drop in for afternoon tea and share the experience. See Celebrities for biographical notes. (H8) 01768 486301 www.sharrowbay.co.uk

Large Lounge, Sharrow Bay ss

Large Bedroom, Sharrow Bay ss

1886   Napes Needle's first ascent by Haskett Smith – the birth of rock climbing

1889   Launching of steamer Raven on Ullswater
1890   Birth of Stan Laurel
1892   First ascent of Eagle's Nest by Godfrey Allan Solly

Where to Eat, Drink & Be Merry Outside Penrith...

Carleton Farm Shop, Carleton.
Carleton Farm Shop. You can purchase vegetables from their working farm and a variety of locally produced meats, james etc (gluten free). (M4) 01768 210027 www.carletonfarmshop.co.uk

Fusion Café, Brougham Hall.
A welcome watering-hole on one's travels around the Penrith area. Just the place for a snack or lunch; baguettes, paninis, coffees, all surrounded by arts and crafts. Special Music and Food Evenings. (M5) 07933 177234 www.allfusedglass.co.uk

Gate Inn, Yanwath. This is a popular foodie pub serving lunch and dinner. Be prepared for their Ribeye Steaks, Sea Bass or Braced Lamb Shank. The inn dates from 1683 and was formerly known as the "Yanwath Yat" (toll gate). (L5) 01768 862386 www.yanwathgate.com

Granny Dowbekin's. Established in 1687 would you believe. Set in a pretty spot overlooking the river serves all-day breakfasts, lunches and cream teas. (J6) 01768 486453

Greystoke Cycle Café Tea Garden. This is much more than your usual café. It has the lovely Annie, it's quirky and you can enrol in day courses of painting, cookery and willow weaving. Leave your bike here, camp, borrow an inner tube. And it's open to all especially the garden given to fine views of the Castle. Open Apr-Sept F 12-6, Sa 10-6 and 2nd Su of month. (H3) 01768 483984 www.greystokecyclecafe.co.uk

Greystone House Farm Shop & Tea Room Stainton. The Dawsons have farmed here since 1752 and in 2003 the farm was converted into an organic system. It is a traditional tearoom and butcher's shop where you can buy home-reared beef and lamb. Open daily 10-5.30. (K5) 01768 866952 www.greystonehousefarm.co.uk

Queens Head Inn, Tirril. Home of the Tirril Brewery and traditional tavern dating from 1719. A popular dining pub offering home cooked food and real ales. Blessed with log fires, flagstone floors and comfy rooms. No wonder it is always full to the rafters. (L5) 01768 863219 www.queensheadinn.co.uk

Queens Head Inn, Askham.
This is a charming old inn in an exceptionally pretty village. There are 4-poster beds and a family room, and pets are welcome, too. (L7) 01931 712225 www.queensheadaskham.com

Villages of Interest...

Askham. The ancient home of the Earls of Lonsdale and on the east side of the village the sad site of the Gothic ruin, Lowther Castle. Only the church remains from the original Lowther Old Village. The village spoilt the Earl of Lonsdale's view from Lowther Castle so he had the cottages torn down and the villagers re-housed in Newtown, a "model village" based on a real village designed by Robert Adam. The wide village green is lined with attractive C17 houses. Often referred to in mythology as "the place of the ash trees" for the area abounds in ancient monuments, earthworks and stone circles. (L7)

Brougham. The Roman fort Brocavum was built here to protect the north-south and east-west routes. Its remains were used in the building of Brougham Castle which was restored by Lady Anne Clifford. This village and its neighbour, Clifton, is often overlooked by Cumbrian visitors because of their urgent need to get to the Lakes, and because they rush by on the busy A6 and M6 ignorant of what has happened on the nearby fields. (M5)

Askham

Brougham Hall

Clifton. The last battle on English soil was fought here between the retreating Scottish Jacobites of Bonnie Prince Charlie and the notorious Duke of Cumberland on the night of 18 December, 1745. There are various plaques and memorials around the village, and in the churchyard. The Prince's dream was later destroyed on the fields of Culloden soon after, considered the bloodiest of all battles on Scottish soil. (M5)

Dacre. A lovely village dominated by Dacre Castle, a former C14 Pele Tower of immense proportions for the walls reach out to a girth of eight feet. With its turret and battlements it became a refuge from invading Scots during the Middle Ages. Leonard Dacre led an unsuccessful rebellion in 1570 on behalf of Mary Queen of Scots against her cousin Elizabeth I. Next door, one of the finest churches in Cumbria, famous for the stone bears. (J5)

Greystoke. A beautiful estate village of solid, stone built C19 houses. It has much going for it. A fine C16 inn, cycle café, village shop and a major collegiate church (see Churches). It's a fine place to live in and the village has a buzz with its many young families. There is a plague stone on the old Roman road from Voreda (Penrith) to Keswick. All comic and film buffs will know that Tarzan was descended from a long line of Lord Greystokes. The park is now the venue for a host of outdoor activities. (H3)

Pooley Bridge.
Set at the north-east corner of Ullswater - the moody (or magical) lake. A centre with village store, gift shops and a couple of pubs. It has one of Lakeland's traditional tearooms in Granny Dowbekin. You can rent boats, but if you wish to explore the country to the south of Ullswater, best to stock up on provisions from the village store. (J6)

St Johns in the Vale.
A farming community of scattered hamlets and farms set between the reservoirs, Thirlmere and Threlkeld., The origins of this vale are believed to come from the Knight Hospitallers, of the Order of St John. The church has C13 origins and some of the headstones are enchanting. (A8)

Threlkeld.
A former lead mining centre but now by-passed by the busy A66. The village has two inns, but it is the Horse & Farrier which provides comfortable accommodation and better than average pub grub. There are a number of paths leading out towards the towering Blencathra. It is also the home of the Blencathra Foxhounds (John Peel Hunt) whose activities under the current law allow them to "Exercise and Drag". To follow you need to be super fit, for you follow on foot. See the local inns for details. (B6)

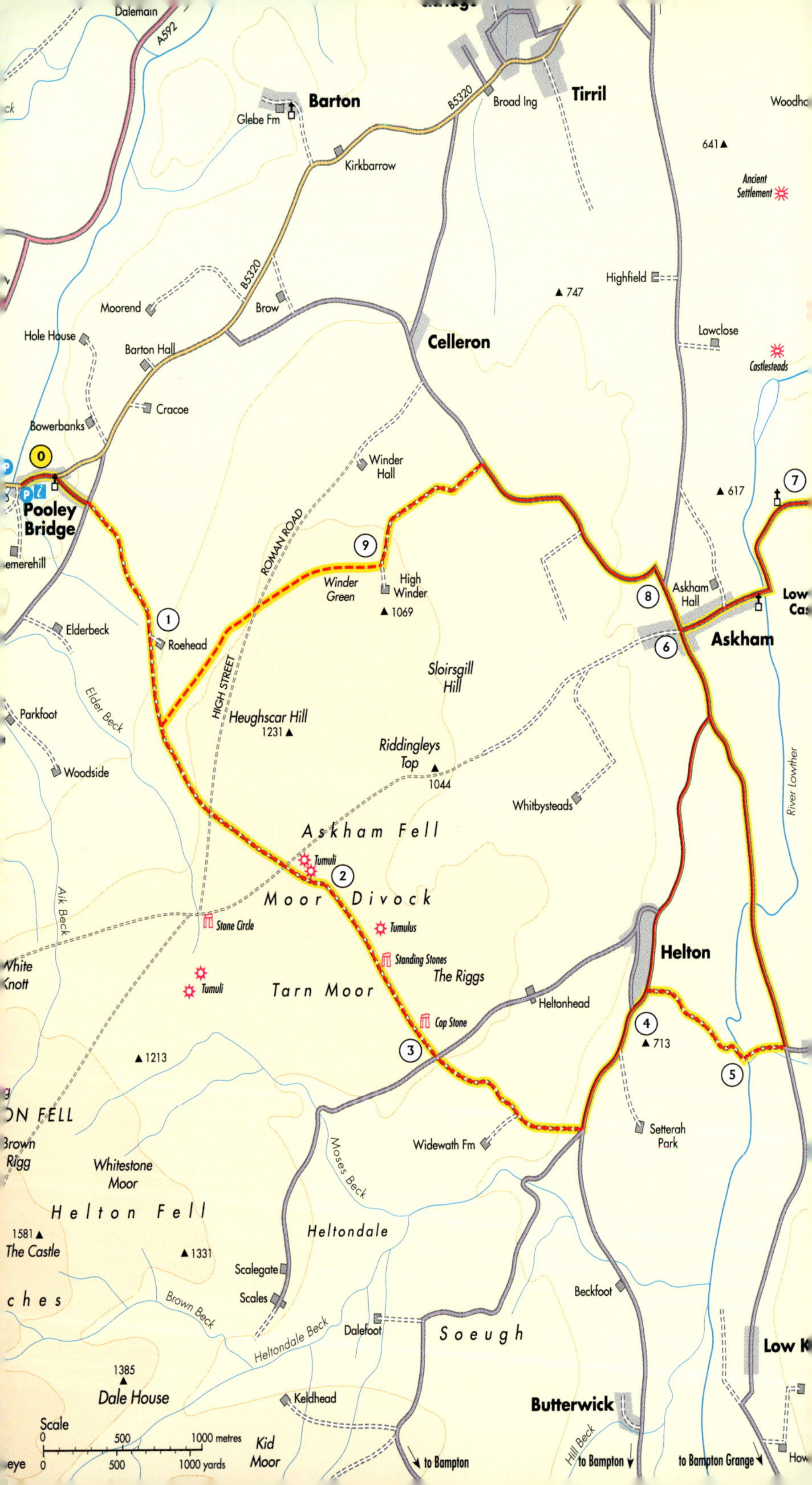

Dalemain
A592
Barton
Glebe Fm
Kirkbarrow
B5320
Broad Ing
Tirril
Woodho
641
Ancient Settlement
747
Highfield
Moorend
Brow
B5320
Celleron
Lowclose
Hole House
Barton Hall
Castlesteads
Cracoe
Bowerbanks
0
Winder Hall
P
Pooley Bridge
emerehill
ROMAN ROAD
9
617
7
Winder Green
High Winder
8
Askham Hall
Low Ca
1
Roehead
1069
6
Low Cas
Elderbeck
HIGH STREET
Askham
Sloirsgill Hill
Parkfoot
Heughscar Hill
1231
Riddingleys Top
Woodside
1044
River Lowther
Whitbysteads
Askham Fell
Aik Beck
Tumuli
2
White Knott
Moor Divock
Helton
Stone Circle
Tumulus
Tarn Moor
Standing Stones
The Riggs
Tumuli
Heltonhead
1213
Cop Stone
4
713
3
5
ON FELL
Moses Beck
Widewath Fm
Setterah Park
Brown Rigg
Whitestone Moor
Helton Fell
Heltondale
1581
The Castle
ches
1331
Beckfoot
Scalegate
Scales
Low K
Brown Beck
Dalefoot
Soeugh
Heltondale Beck
1385
Keldhead
Butterwick
Dale House
eye
Kid Moor
Scale
500
1000 metres
500
1000 yards
to Bampton
to Bampton
to Bampton Grange

Pooley Bridge to Askham Fell

13 miles (20.8km)
6 off-road, 7 road.

Grade 1.

Riding Time 2 hours.

An easy, yet hugely enjoyable route over grassy moorland above Ullswater, which thanks to the rain-shadow of the high fells to the west, is often drier and sunnier. Good, rideable surfaces and moderate gradients make this an excellent route for beginners, or a relaxing cruise.

0 From the National Trust car park in Pooley Bridge, ride through the village for 100m, then turn right, signposted Howton, Martindale. Straight over at X-roads climbing steadily to gate at end of tarmac.

1 Through the gate, signposted Barton Fell Common, Public Bridleway Helton up stony track. becoming grassy. Straight ahead towards Helton at signpost Bridleway continuing over two X-roads. Track levels out at first of these.

2 Moor Divock 1,066ft is highest point of route, now descends to junction with road.

3 Straight ahead to follow less distinct grassy bridleway, signposted Public Bridleway Bampton down to gate and walled track, joining tarmac lane from farm on right. Straight on past stone barn on left to road. Turn left for Helton, passing turning on right, signposted Setterah Park.

4 Fork right just before village, then narrow, fenced bridleway leading downhill on right to gate. **Slow, be prepared for walkers**. (If too muddy, continue by road to Askham.) Through gate by stream onto indistinct bridleway through meadow to gated bridge over wide river.

5 Across bridge and walk immediately right through another gate to bear left (still indistinct) to more obvious track ahead. Follow track to road and turn left on to pleasant lane to pretty village of Askham.

6 Askham. Route goes straight on to junction in 300m. First, turn right down village street between greens & C17 cottages, past Askham Hall to church and stone bridge. Turn left by river along rocky gorge to climb up into "Capability Brown" Lowther Deer Park with tiny church.

7 Go past church for view to right side of magnificent folly, Lowther Castle. Return to Askham & turn right. (Diversion 1km).

8 Turn left signposted Celleron. Ignore the first bridleway on left and take second at metal 5-bar gate and cattle grid in 500m signposted Public B/way, begins as tarmac farm-lane, becoming gravel through gate just before stone barn on left. Through second gate just before trees to turn immediately right up grassy bridleway weaving up hillside towards trees and gate.

9 Through gate onto more obvious track through middle of bracken and below small crag on left. Fork right after crag turning diagonally down hillside towards the lake. Bear left (easier) or right (steeper and rougher) at next junction to original bridleway just above Roehead.

Home of Lord Inglewood's family since 1605. The mansion was originally based on a medieval Pele Tower but, with substantial additions in the C17, C18 and C19, it has become the splendid building of today. A major attraction is the beautiful walled garden with topiary. Woodland walk. House open 2 May-30 Sept W, Th, Su & BH Ms, 12.30-4. Garden open daily except Sa Apr-Oct 11-5. (J1) 017684 84449. www.hutton-in-the-forest.co.uk

Dalemain

Brougham Hall

Brougham Castle

Special Historic Buildings to Visit...

Brougham Castle (EH). The impressive remains, easy to view, stand beside the River Eamont. What is left is the C13 Keep and the paved courtyard. The castle was restored to its former glory in the C17 by Lady Anne Clifford. Open daily, 10-5. (M4)

Brougham Hall. Now undergoing one of the largest country house restorations in Britain, all achieved by private fundraising and donation.

A fortified home since 1307 and with a chequered history to confuse the most able of historians, the house came into its own during the Victorian era when it became known as the Windsor of the North. As half-way house between Windsor and Balmoral, the King took overnight stops here and it was the home of the Lord Chancellor. It fell into disrepair in 1934 to be rescued from dereliction in 1985. Craft Centre. Open daily. 9-dusk. (M5) 01768 868184 www.broughamhall.co.uk

Dalemain. Historic house and gardens owned by the Hasell family since 1679. The house's history stretches from Saxon times to early Georgian. It has amassed a fine collection of furniture, portraits, ceramics and in the Chinese Room displays of original hand-painted Chinese wallpaper. The garden is a plantsman's delight with its richly planted herbaceous borders and very much the pride and joy of the Hasell-McCosh women. Open Apr-Oct Su-Th 10.30-5 (House 11-4). Restaurant. (J5) 017684 86450 www.dalemain.com

1898   Abraham Brothers of Keswick publish a series of Lakeland postcards

1899   Owen Glynn Jones (Genuine Jones) falls and dies during an Alpine climb of the Dente Blanche
1899   Building of Brockhole by Manchester businessman

Greystoke Castle Estate.
The former home of Lord Greystoke covers three thousand acres of rugged upland terrain and is the centre for "Adventure Activities". Specific tasks are designed for enhancing team building skills and you can tackle off-road driving, quad treks, rifle shooting and abseiling, to name a few. As a matter of interest, the Castle was not used as Tarzan's home in the film Greystoke. (It was in fact Floors Castle in the Scottish Borders, the home of the Duke of Roxburghe). (G3) 01768 483722
www.greystoke.com

Lowther Castle. A spectacular C19 ruin now sadly a shadow of its former glory with turrets and battlements. Once the dream of Sir Robert Smirke, architect of the British Museum. Closed to public viewing. However, a road passes through the estate, and there are plans afoot to develop the site into the "Tate of the North" with exhibitions from the Tate Gallery and the V&A museum. We await developments with interest. (M7) 01931 712577 www.lowther.co.uk

Churches of Interest...

Brougham, St Ninian. Known as 'Nine-Kirks'. Stands isolated in field. Saxon, later rebuilt by Lady Anne Clifford in 1660. (M4)

1900   Blackwell, the Arts & Crafts Movement house, is built by Mackay Hugh Baillie Scott

1901   Beatrix Potter publishes at her own expense The Tale of Peter Rabbit

1900   John Ruskin dies aged 80

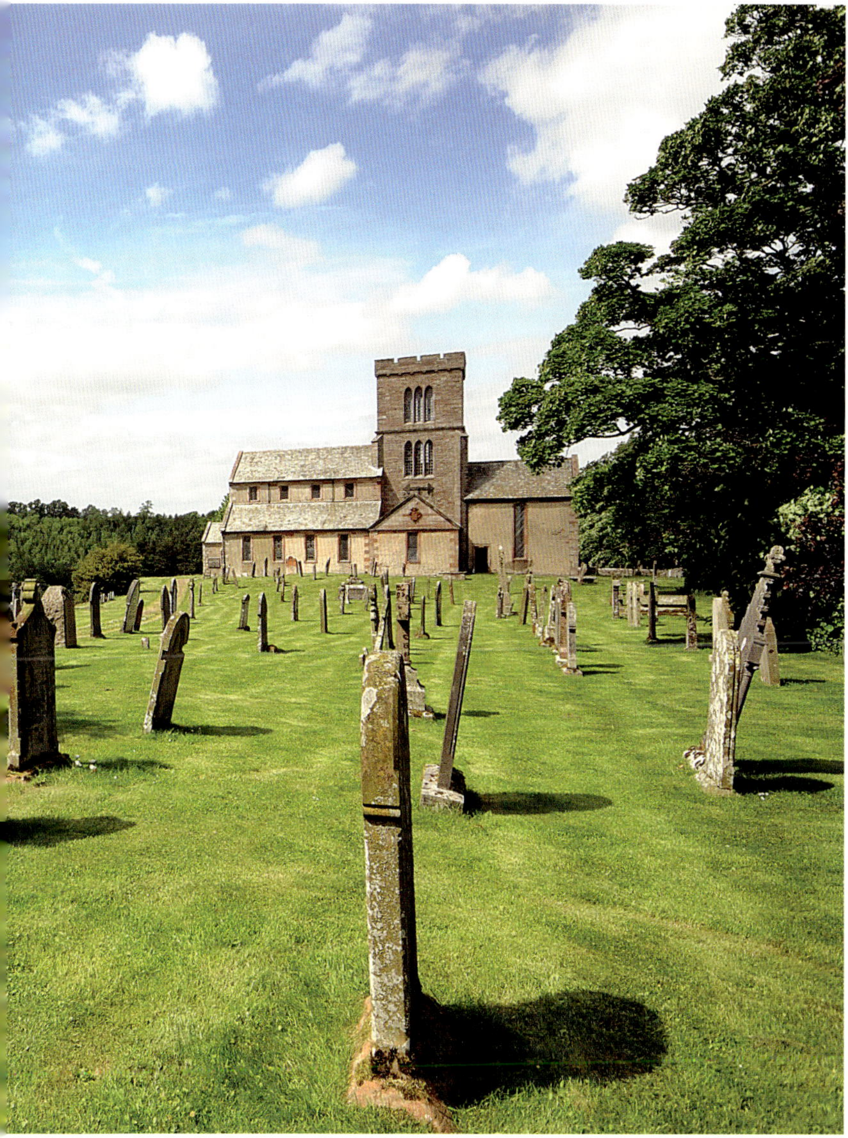

Lowther Church & Mausoleum

Brougham, St Wilfrid. Wonderful contrast between the simple exterior and the rich carvings within. (M4)

Dacre, St Andrew. One of the great churches of Cumbria emboldened with a long and varied history. C10 Viking Cross Shafts. C13 effigy. Chancel window by Lawrence Whistler. Stone bears on each side of the churchyard, all within an attractive village. (J5)

Lowther Castle

Martindale in Spring

1901 Beatrix Potter publishes (again) at her own expense The Tailor of Gloucester

1902 The National Trust acquires much of Derwent Water and Borrowdale

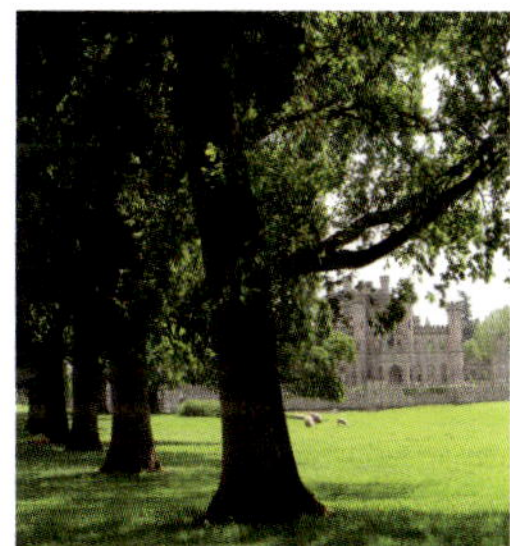

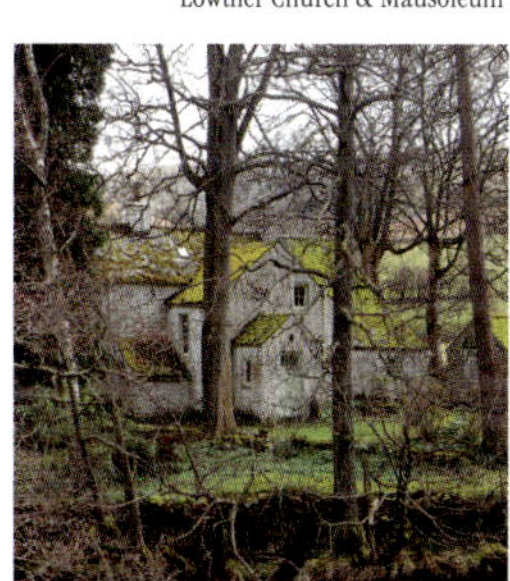

Greystoke, St Andrews

St Martin's Yew Tree, Martindale

Greystoke, St Andrews. Former Collegiate church enjoys a large and gracious interior. Much is C15, notably the fine stained glass and misericords. Effigy of Baron William Dacre. It is large because in the C13 it was second in importance to Carlisle Cathedral and because the 14th Baron Greystoke added chantries where Masses for the dead would frequently be said. He was thinking about his own immortal soul. (J5)

Lowther. Mix of C12, C13 and C17s. Strange mausoleum outside. (L6)

Martindale, St Martin (The old church). Isolated thus rarely used but for the occasional wedding. The yew tree is an extraordinary shape and a delight. It hangs over a former vicar's tomb. (G9)

Matterdale. In picturesque spot. Quaint tower. Panelled woodwork. (E7)

Mungrisdale. Tiny with pannelled double-decker pulpit. (D3)

Arts & Crafts...

Beckstones Art Gallery. Traditional work by 40 artists and over 300 original paintings. Subjects range from Still Life to Wild Life, Landscapes to Figurative, in a variety of media. Open daily Mar-Nov 10-5, Dec-Feb, F & W/Es 10.30-4.30. (H4) 01768 483601 www.beckstonesartgallery.co.uk

Brougham Hall Craft Centre. Thriving craft centre, art gallery, teashop and bicycle rental centre, smokehouse, furniture restoration, stonemasonry, art metalwork, nail and beauty therapy. Cromwellian Chapel. Cafe. Open daily. (M5) 01768 868184. www.broughamhall.co.uk

The Old Smokehouse, Brougham Hall. Highest quality smoked local food. Handmade chocolates from local cream, real fruit and alcohol. Open Oct-Mar M-F 10-4, Mar-Sept daily, 10-5. (M5) 01768 890270 www.the-old-smokehouse.co.uk

Laburnum Ceramics, Yanwath. Gallery devoted to quality work, from established artists to graduates 'bursting with talent'. Open W-Su 10-4.30. (L5) 01768 864842

Animals...

Alpaca Centre, Stainton. South American Alpacas in paddocks, products of the ancient Andean civilisation. Unique centre with shop and cafe. Home-made cakes. Open daily 10-5. (K5) 01768 891440 www.thealpacacentre.co.uk

Lakeland Bird Of Prey Centre. Set in the former walled garden of Lowther Castle. Aviary walk. Flying displays at 11.30, 2 & 4 pm. Tearoom. Open daily Apr-Oct 11-5. (M7) 01931 712746

Rookin House Farm Equestrian & Activity Centre, Nr Ullswater. Quad bike treks, go-karts, archery, horse riding (trekking & lessons), Clay pigeon shooting. Open all year, 9-5.30. (E6) 017684 83561 www.rookinhouse.co.uk

Lake Cruises...

Ullswater Steamers. The four steamers, M Y Raven, M Y Lady of the Lake and M V Lady Dorothy were built over 100 years ago in Glasgow and they, together with the more recently commissioned "Lady Wakefield", run on a scheduled service from Glenridding to Howtown, and Pooley Bridge. Beautiful lakeside walks of 1-10 miles length. Bar. The service runs daily, all year. (E10) 017684 82229 www.ullswater-steamers.co.uk

Dacre Church Bear

Thirlmere

The Thirlmere Reservoir was formerly two lakes, Leatheswater and Brackmere, until their marriage (of convenience) in the 1880s. Its formation was controversial and had many opponents but the Manchester Corporation eventually had their way and the two farming hamlets of Armboth and Wythburn were submerged in 1894. The west side is planted with coniferous woodland and there are forest trails on each side. From Wythburn church on the east bank a steep and direct path leads up to the summit of Helvellyn. Allow three hours for this walk which may reward you, if your luck's in, with fine panoramic views but don't be surprised if the mist comes down. First check the weather forecast. (A1)

Ullswater Steamer from the Sharrow Bay ss

For sheer grandeur, variety, magnificent scenery and ever changing moods, Ullswater is considered to be 'The Lake' of the Lake District. It is best appreciated if approached from Pooley Bridge, for as one journeys towards Glenridding the landscape grows even finer. The walk from Howtown, on the east bank, to Glenridding is full of surprises. But, on the west side in a field close to Aira Beck and Lyulph's Tower, William Wordsworth lay admiring the daffodils and was inspired to write the verse 'I wandered lonely as a cloud..' This serpentine lake offers fine sailing. A sailing school, Outward Bound Centre and the Ullswater Steamers are based at Glenridding. But, if you have the wherewithal, and are in need of a special lunch or cream tea, stop off at the Sharrow Bay hotel on the east side for a memorable and mouth watering experience. If feeling adventurous you may wish to explore the south-east corner by car. If you do, take a picnic and refreshments, for there is nothing but sheep, long vistas of mountains and two quite enchanting valleys (Boardale and Howe Grain), and the isolated villages Howtown and Martindale. The view from Hallin Fell is not so dramatic as from the other side on Gowbarrow Fell. Nevertheless, the walk up Hallin Fell is a relatively easy family walk. (E9)

Aira Force

Blencathra

The Mountains...

Blencathra or Saddleback, 2847ft/868m. A mountain of great individual appearance that has, with time, been moulded into a strange and beautiful shape. The name Saddleback is an obvious one, for depending from where you view it, it takes on the shape of a horse's saddle and it is surely shaped for the gods who live in these mountains. The major challenge is Sharp Edge, a rocky traverse that provides the most exciting ridge walk in the area. Dangerous in the wet and ice, and recommended only for the most experienced of hill walkers and mountaineers. The great Alf Wainwright described five routes. Herewith are two:

Route 1. Easy route starts from Blencathra Centre via Threlkeld. Follow path over Knowe Crags on to the top. Return the same way. (A6)

Route 2. The adventurous route starts behind the Black Horse Inn at Scales. Follow path up the left side of Mousthwaite Combe to Scales Fell, and on to Sharp Edge with Scales Tarn on one's left. It's a steep climb to the top. (C5)

Prehistoric...

High Street. Roman road crosses the fells, giving fine panoramic, Lakeland views. It is also a wonderful traverse by mountain bike. (H2)

King Arthur's Round Table. Late Neolithic circular henge monument dates from 1,000 BC. Charles 11's army camped here. Excavations in the C19 revealed cremated skeletons. (M4)

Mayburgh Henge Monument. A vast, circular embankment (or encampment) of earth that rises to fifteen feet and is considered to be Late Neolithic. Archaeologists have discovered Bronze and Stone Age axes. (M4)

Short Easy Walks...

Aira Force Waterfall. (F8) An easy, short walk of .05 mile/.75 km along a tarmac path suitable for pram and wheelchair access to Aira Beck. Start from the National Trust car park with café & toilets on hand. This was a Victorian beauty spot now owned by the National Trust. The waterfall falls beneath a stone bridge.

Lowther Castle Estate. (M7) Park outside St Peter's Church and wander along the tree-lined avenues and marvel at the ruin, or if feeling adventurous join one of the Guided Wildlife outings where you will encounter all forms of wildlife. For details contact the Estate Office 01931 712577.

Hallin Fell from Martindale Church, Sandwick. (G9) Park opposite the church and follow the natural (steep) pathway that leads straight up the hill onto Hallin Fell. A 4-year old can manage this 2 mile/3.3 km jaunt which delivers great views of almost all of Ullswater. Paths can be slippery.

Great How, Thirlmere. (A9) A short, easy woodland walk of 2 miles/3.2 km that starts from the car park on west side of the dam. On leaving, cross the dam and follow path up steps into the wood. Follow the paths in an anti-clockwise direction around the hill. A waymarked sign indicates the path leading to the summit.

Penrith Beacon. (M3) If you seek fine views over Penrith then try this 1 mile/1.75 km easy hike on the north-east edge of the town. The monument was built in 1719 and beacons have been lit here in times of war and emergency since Henry VIII.

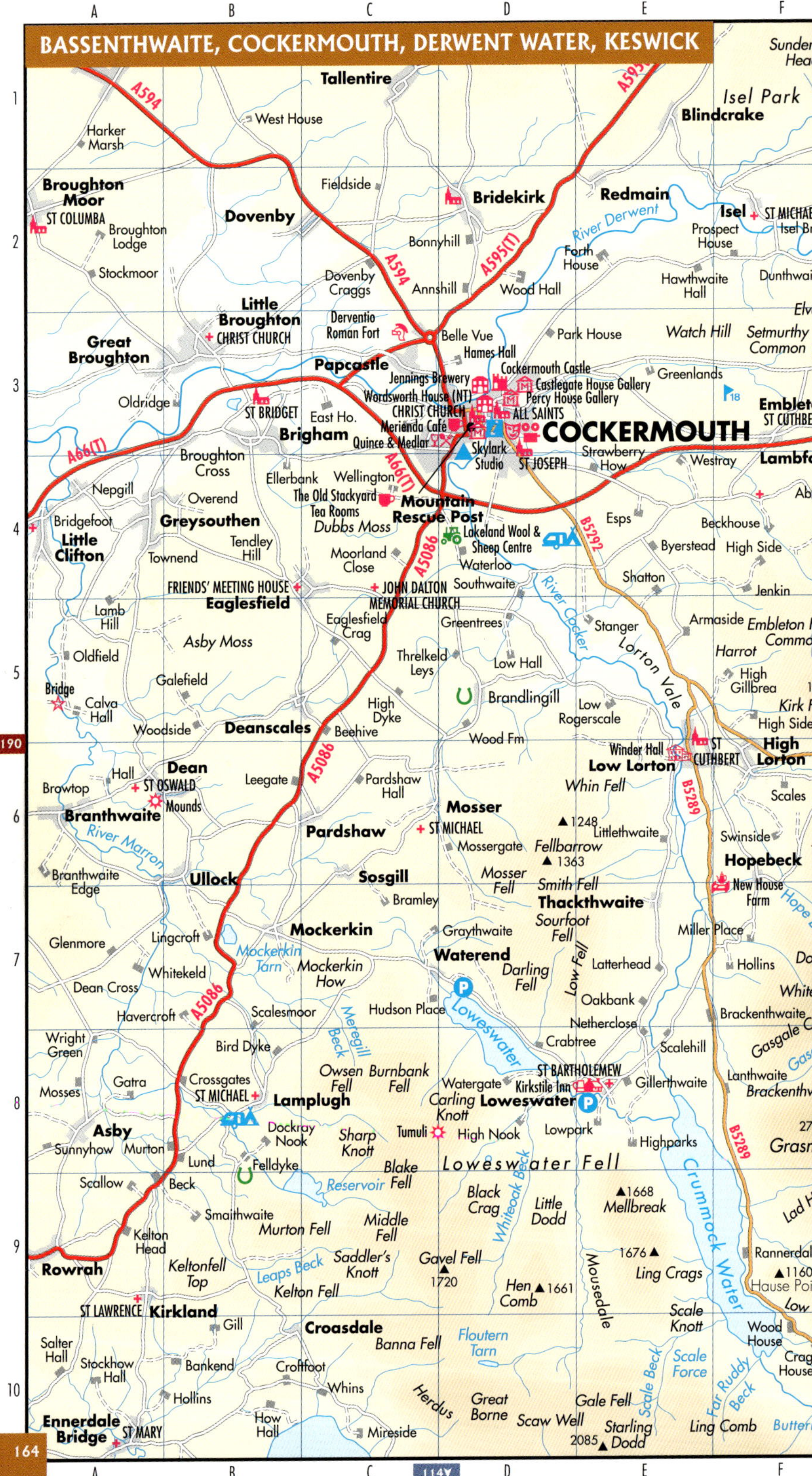

BASSENTHWAITE, COCKERMOUTH, DERWENT WATER, KESWICK
164
190
114
Tallentire
West House
Harker Marsh
Broughton Moor
ST COLUMBA
Broughton Lodge
Stockmoor
Dovenby
Fieldside
Bonnyhill
Bridekirk
Redmain
Blindcrake
Isel Park
Isel
ST MICHAEL
Isel Br
River Derwent
A594
A595(T)
A595(T)
Dovenby Craggs
Annshill
Forth House
Wood Hall
Prospect House
Hawthwaite Hall
Dunthwait
Elva
Little Broughton
CHRIST CHURCH
Derventio Roman Fort
Belle Vue
Hames Hall
Park House
Watch Hill
Setmurthy Common
Great Broughton
Papcastle
Jennings Brewery
Cockermouth Castle
Castlegate House Gallery
Greenlands
18
Embleto
ST CUTHBER
Oldridge
ST BRIDGET
East Ho.
Wordsworth House (NT)
CHRIST CHURCH
Percy House Gallery
ALL SAINTS
COCKERMOUTH
Brigham
Merienda Café
Quince & Medlar
Skylark Studio
ST JOSEPH
Strawberry How
Westray
Lambfo
A66(T)
A66(T)
Broughton Cross
Ellerbank
Wellington
Mountain Rescue Post
The Old Stackyard Tea Rooms
Nepgill
Overend
Esps
Beckhouse
Abb
Bridgefoot
Dubbs Moss
Moorland Close
Lakeland Wool & Sheep Centre
Waterloo
Byerstead
High Side
Little Clifton
Greysouthen
Tendley Hill
A5086
Shatton
Jenkin
Townend
Waterend
Southwaite
B5292
FRIENDS' MEETING HOUSE
Eaglesfield
JOHN DALTON MEMORIAL CHURCH
Greentrees
Stanger
Armaside
Embleton
Common
Lamb Hill
Eaglesfield Crag
Low Hall
Harrot
High Gillbrea
Oldfield
Asby Moss
Threlkeld Leys
River Cocker
Lorton Vale
Kirk F
Bridge
Galefield
High Dyke
Brandlingill
Low Rogerscale
High Side
Calva Hall
Beehive
Wood Fm
Winder Hall
ST CUTHBERT
High Lorton
Woodside
Deanscales
Low Lorton
Whin Fell
Scales
Dean
ST OSWALD
Leegate
Pardshaw Hall
Mosser
ST MICHAEL
1248
Fellbarrow
Littlethwaite
Swinside
Browtop
Hall
Mounds
Mossergate
1363
Hopebeck
Branthwaite
Pardshaw
Smith Fell
New House Farm
River Marron
Sosgill
Mosser Fell
Thackthwaite
Hope be
Branthwaite Edge
Ullock
Bramley
Sourfoot Fell
Miller Place
Lingcroft
Mockerkin
Graythwaite
Low Fell
Hollins
Glenmore
Mockerkin Tarn
Mockerkin How
Waterend
Darling Fell
Latterhead
White
Whitekeld
Oakbank
Brackenthwaite
Dean Cross
A5086
Scalesmoor
Hudson Place
Netherclose
Gasgale
Havercroft
Meregill Beck
Loweswater
Crabtree
Scalehill
Lanthwaite
Brackenthw
Wright Green
Bird Dyke
Owsen Fell
Burnbank Fell
Watergate
ST BARTHOLEMEW
Kirkstile Inn
Gillerthwaite
Mosses
Gatra
Crossgates
ST MICHAEL
Lamplugh
Carling Knott
Loweswater
Lowpark
Grasm
Asby
Dockray Nook
Sharp Knott
Tumuli
High Nook
Lowpark
Highparks
279
Sunnyhow
Murton
Lund
Felldyke
Blake Fell
Loweswater Fell
B5289
Grasm
Scallow
Beck
Reservoir
Black Crag
Little Dodd
Mellbreak
1668
Smaithwaite
Murton Fell
Middle Fell
Crummock Water
Lad H
Kelton Head
Saddler's Knott
Gavel Fell
Ling Crags
1676
Rannerdale
1160
Rowrah
Keltonfell Top
Kelton Fell
1720
Hen Comb
1661
Mousedale
Scale Knott
Hause Poin
Low
ST LAWRENCE
Kirkland
Gill
Croasdale
Banna Fell
Floutern Tarn
Gale Fell
Wood House
Crag House
Salter Hall
Stockhow Hall
Bankend
Croftfoot
Whins
Herdus
Great Borne
Scaw Well
Scale Beck
Scale Force
Far Ruddy Beck
Ling Comb
Butter
Hollins
Ennerdale Bridge
ST MARY
How Hall
Mireside
2085
Starling Dodd

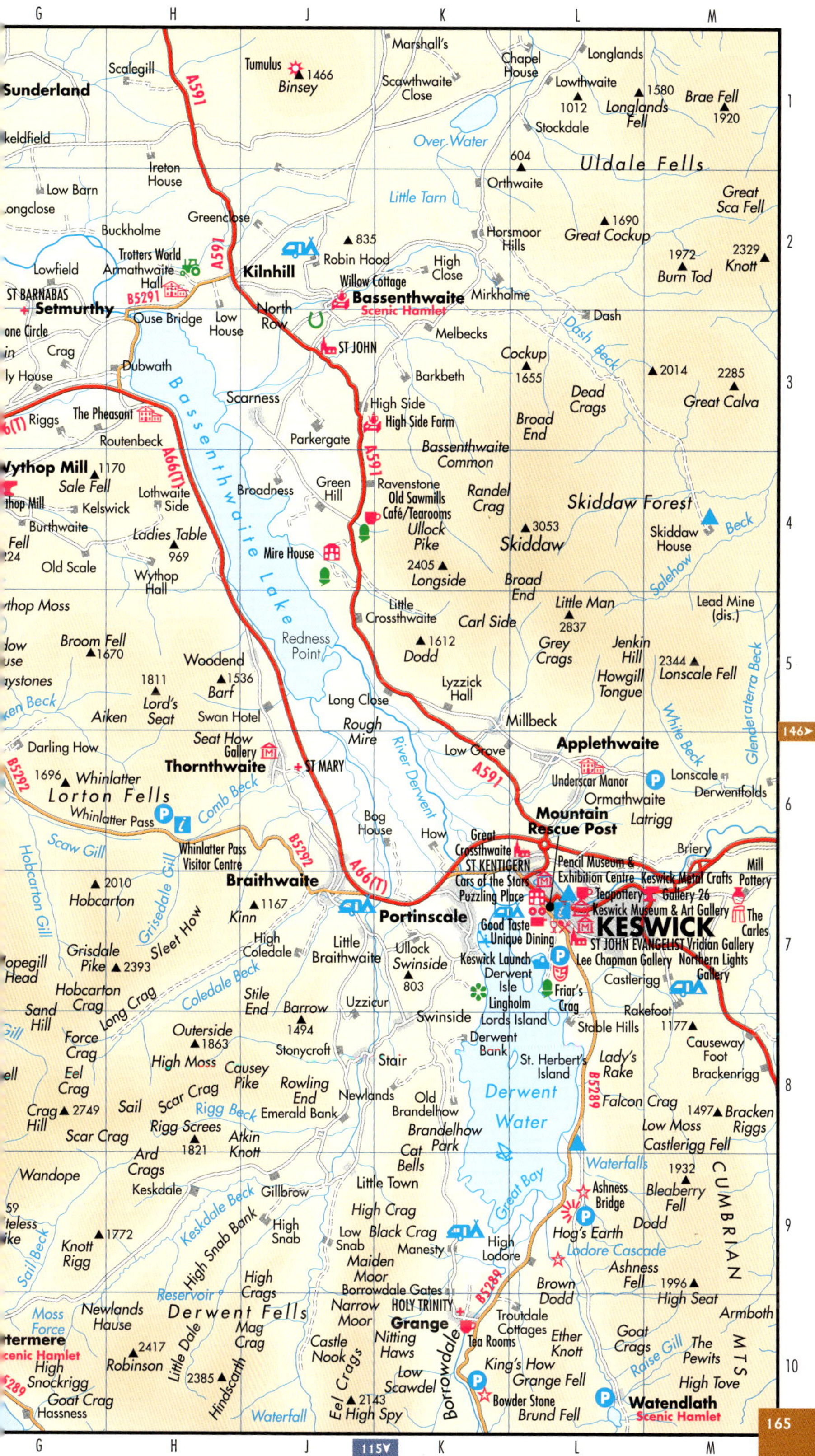

G H J K L M
Sunderland
Scalegill
A591
Tumulus
1466
Binsey
Marshall's
Scawthwaite Close
Chapel House
Longlands
Lowthwaite
1012
Longlands Fell
1580
Brae Fell
1920
1
keldfield
Low Barn
Ireton House
Over Water
604
Stockdale
Orthwaite
Uldale Fells
Great Sca Fell
Longclose
Greenclose
Little Tarn
Buckholme
835
Robin Hood
High Close
Horsmoor Hills
Great Cockup
1690
1972
Burn Tod
2329
Knott
2
Lowfield
Trotters World
Armathwaite Hall
Kilnhill
Willow Cottage
Bassenthwaite
Scenic Hamlet
Mirkholme
Dash
2014
2285
ST BARNABAS
Setmurthy
B5291
Ouse Bridge
Low House
North Row
ST JOHN
Melbecks
Cockup
1655
Dash Beck
Great Calva
3
one Circle
Crag
ly House
Dubwath
Scarness
Barkbeth
High Side
High Side Farm
Dead Crags
Broad End
Riggs
The Pheasant
Routenbeck
A66(T)
Bassenthwaite Lake
Parkergate
Ravenstone
Old Sawmills
Café/Tearooms
Randel Crag
Skiddaw Forest
Beck
4
Wythop Mill
1170
Sale Fell
Lothwaite Side
Broadness
Green Hill
A591
Ullock Pike
3053
Skiddaw
Skiddaw House
hop Mill
Kelswick
Burthwaite
Ladies Table
969
Mire House
2405
Longside
Broad End
Little Man
2837
Lead Mine (dis.)
Fell
224
Old Scale
Wythop Hall
Little Crossthwaite
Carl Side
Grey Crags
Jenkin Hill
2344
Lonscale Fell
Glenderaterra Beck
5
thop Moss
Broom Fell
1670
Woodend
1536
1811
Barf
1612
Dodd
Howgill Tongue
dow use
ystones
Aiken
Lord's Seat
Swan Hotel
Redness Point
Long Close
Lyzzick Hall
Millbeck
146
ken Beck
Darling How
Seat How Gallery
Thornthwaite
ST MARY
Rough Mire
River Derwent
Low Grove
Applethwaite
Underscar Manor
Ormathwaite
Lonscale
Derwentfolds
White Beck
6
B5292
1696
Whinlatter
Lorton Fells
Whinlatter Pass
Scaw Gill
Comb Beck
B5292
A66(T)
Bog House
How
Great Crossthwaite
ST KENTIGERN
Mountain Rescue Post
Latrigg
Briery
Mill Pottery
Hobcarton Gill
2010
Hobcarton
Grisedale Gill
Sleet How
B5292
Whinlatter Pass Visitor Centre
Braithwaite
1167
Kinn
Portinscale
Cars of the Stars
Puzzling Place
Good Taste Unique Dining
Pencil Museum & Exhibition Centre
Teapottery
Keswick Museum & Art Gallery
ST JOHN EVANGELIST
Keswick Metal Crafts
Gallery 26
KESWICK
Vridian Gallery
The Carles
7
Hopegill Head
Grisdale Pike
2393
Long Crag
Coledale Beck
High Coledale
Little Braithwaite
Ullock
Swinside
803
Keswick Launch
Derwent Isle
Lingholm
Lee Chapman Gallery
Friar's Crag
Castlerigg
Northern Lights Gallery
Sand Hill
Hobcarton Crag
Stile End
Barrow
1494
Uzzicur
Swinside
Lords Island
Derwent Bank
St. Herbert's Island
Stable Hills
Rakefoot
1177
Causeway Foot
Brackenrigg
8
Force Crag
Eel Crag
High Moss
Outerside
1863
Stonycroft
Causey Pike
Rowling End
Stair
Newlands
Old Brandelhow
Derwent Water
Lady's Rake
Falcon Crag
1497
Bracken Riggs
Crag Hill
2749
Sail
Scar Crag
Rigg Beck
Emerald Bank
Brandelhow Park
Great Bay
Low Moss
Castlerigg Fell
Eel Crag
Scar Crag
Rigg Screes
Atkin Knott
1821
Cat Bells
Waterfalls
1932
CUMBRIAN
9
Wandope
Ard Crags
Keskdale
Gillbrow
Little Town
High Crag
Low Black Crag Snab
Ashness Bridge
Hog's Earth
Bleaberry Fell
Dodd
59
teless ike
1772
Knott Rigg
Keskdale Beck
High Snab Bank
High Snab
Manesty
High Lodore
Lodore Cascade
Ashness Fell
1996
High Seat
Armboth
Moss Force
Newlands Hause
Derwent Fells
Maiden Moor
Borrowdale Gates
Narrow Moor
HOLY TRINITY
Grange
Brown Dodd
Troutdale Cottages
Ether Knott
Goat Crags
The Pewits
termere
cenic Hamlet
2417
Robinson
Little Dale
2385
Hindscarth
Mag Crag
Castle Nooks
Nitting Haws
Borrowdale
Tea Rooms
King's How
Grange Fell
Raise Gill
High Tove
10
High Snockrigg
Goat Crag
Hassness
Eel Crags
2143
High Spy
Low Scawdel
Bowder Stone
Brund Fell
Watendlath
Scenic Hamlet
MTS
B5289
Waterfall
115
165

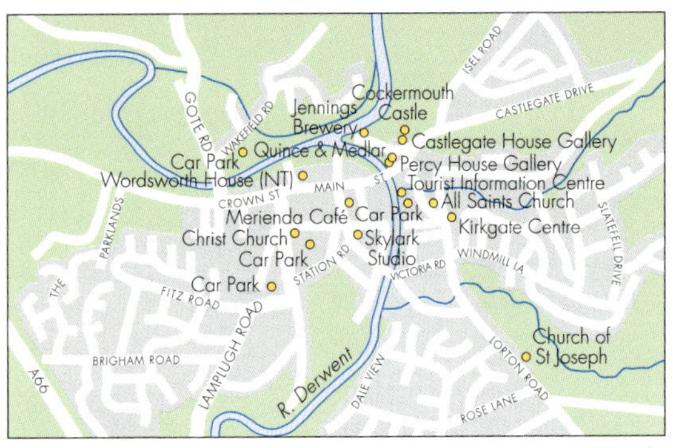

Cockermouth

COCKERMOUTH

A quiet, ancient market town set at the confluence of the rivers Derwent and Cocker. It's a busy place with a host of independent businesses and its attraction is that the main street mirrors Cockermouth's true worth. It is not plagued by the same, standardised modern shop fronts like so much of England, and bravo for that. The tree-lined main street runs parallel with the River Derwent, crosses the Cocker and descends amid some interesting buildings up to the Church of All Saints where an enormous window celebrates the life of William Wordsworth. Cattle auctions are held each Monday and alternate Wednesdays, and there are sheep sales on Fridays in the autumn. For lovers of a bargain, market stalls are placed in the Market Place on Mondays. The town is famous as the birthplace of William Wordsworth and Fletcher Christian (of 'Bounty' fame), and as one would expect the town's burghers plug this for all its worth, and who can blame them? And for those who enjoy a quiet pint of ale your taste buds will surely be tempted to savour a measure of Jennings, the local brew. The town must have one of the highest number of pubs in proportion to population as anywhere in the UK, and bottoms up to that fact! Carnival and Festival of Drama in June, the Music & Arts Festival in August. (D3)

Special Places to Visit...

Castlegate House Gallery.
Contemporary paintings, sculpture and ceramics from English, Scottish and world artists. Open F-M 10.30-5, Su 2.30-4.30. (D3) 01900 822149
www.castlegatehouse.com

Cockermouth Castle.
C12 fortification well protected by the rivers Derwent and Cocker. Built by William de Fortibun in the mid-C13. Little survives. Rarely open to the public. (D3)

Jennings Brewery Tour, Castle Brewery. Brewers since 1828, and the last independent Cumbrian brewery producing Cumberland Ale, Cocker Hoop and Sneck Lifter. Tours Feb-Oct daily 11 & 2, (12.30 mid-July to Aug) and winter tours M-Sa 2pm. (D3) 0845 1297185
www.jenningsbrewery.co.uk

Lakeland Wool & Sheep Centre, Egremont Rd. Live presentation of rare breeds. Shearing demos and sheepdog skills staged. Cumwest Visitors Centre. Open daily, all year 9-5.30. (C4) 01900 822673
www.shepherdshotel.co.uk

Mineral & Fossil Museum.
Shop with original stone gifts, natural stone jewellery, mineral and fossil specimens. Museum of mining, fossil collection. Open 10-5 M-Sa East-Oct. (D3)

Wordsworth House

1913   Castlerigg Stone Circle bought by Canon Rawnsley for the National Trust

1913   Beatrix Potter marries William Heelis, a local solicitor

1913   Closure of Boot's iron ore mines and the Ravenglass Railway

Castlegate House Gallery ss

Lakeland Wool & Sheep Centre ss

Percy House Gallery, 38 Market Place. Work of young Cumbrian artists: sculpture, ceramics, paintings in all styles, in exceptional building dating from 1390. Open M-Sa 10-5. (D3) 01900 82966/
www.percyhouse.com

Skylark Studio. 9 South St. Paintings and etchings by Rolf Parker, and a fine range of quality British crafts and jewellery. Open Tu-Sa 10-5. (D3) 01900 823521.
www.skylarkstudio.bgr.cc

Wordsworth House, Main St. (NT) The Birthplace of William Wordsworth on 7th April, 1770. He was the second son of John and Ann Wordsworth. The house went with John's job as land agent for the Lowther estates. It is a solid Georgian town house built in 1745. The nine rooms are furnished in the C18 style, and there are some personal effects of the poet. Childhood garden with terraced walk. Across the street a sculpture celebrates the poet's life. NT shop. Open Apr-Oct M-Sa 11-4.30. 01900 824805 (D3)
www.wordsworthhouse.com

Where to Eat, Drink & Be Merry in and about Cockermouth...

The Old Stackyard Tea Rooms, Wellington Farm. Tea rooms serving homemade ice cream and cakes plus, with farm shop and local crafts. Open daily 10-5. (D3) 01900 822777
www.wellingtonjerseys.co.uk

Merienda Café, Station Street. Friendly ambience. They serve breakfasts, lunches and coffee. Newspapers and comfy chairs. Live music (jazz) on Friday nights. (D3) 01900 822790

Quince & Medlar, 13 Castlegate. Colin and Louisa have impeccable credentials. They trained at the Sharrow Bay and have brought their creative zest into producing vegetarian meals of excellence. It has a cosy and romantic candlelit dining room. Booking advised. Open Tu-Sa & BH Su from 7pm. (D3) 01900 823579
www.quinceandmedlar.co.uk

Outside Cockermouth...

Kirkstile Inn, Loweswater. One feels immediately at home here. The bar is warm and cosy, old photographs line the walls and if you are short of conversation newspapers are on hand. With a full range of local beers backed up by an award-winning kitchen, life can't be so bad. Accommodation. Dog friendly. (E8) 01900 85219 www.kirkstile.com

Quince & Medlar ss

Gatesgarthdale Beck, Honister Pass

Keswick to **Rosthwaite** to **Honister Pass** to **Buttermere** to **Whinlatter Pass** to **Braithwaite** to **Bassenthwaite Lake** to **Keswick** (44 miles)

This short drive provides an introduction to the northern lakes and passes. Of the former the gem is undoubtedly Derwent Water, and rather than use the lakeside road to the east, the route runs to the west of the lake at a higher altitude through an area of grassy bracken-clad slopes with stupendous views across to Keswick and the mountains beyond. The road descends into Borrowdale amid the towering central peaks, and ascends the formidable Honister Pass. The route then skirts the beautiful lakes of Buttermere and Crummock Water, and after a short stretch of pastoral country we ascend the Whinlatter Pass, a more gentle traverse of the mountains through attractive forested country. Finally, a circuit is made of the quiet and mysterious Bassenthwaite Lake, with fine mountain views on either side.

Keswick. Leave by the **B5289** SP **Cockermouth**. 1 mile out cross bridge and merge with by-pass road. Shortly turn L SP **Portinscale**.

3 miles to **Portinscale**. Keep R through village SP **Grange**.

1 mile to **Lingholm Gardens**. In half a mile fork L SP **Grange**.

4.5 miles to **Grange**. Turn R at T-junction.

1.6 miles to **Rosthwaite**.

1 mile to **Seatoller (not marked)**. Keep R.

2 miles to **Honister Pass Summit**.

4 miles to **Buttermere**. Straight on. In 4.5 miles turn R at T-junction SP **Lorton**.

6.5 miles to **Lorton**. Turn R SP **Keswick**. Straight over next cross-roads.

3.5 miles to **Whinlatter Visitor Centre**.

3 miles to **Braithwaite (unsigned)**. Turn L in village and shortly L again into main road SP **Cockermouth**.

4.5 miles to **Pheasant Inn**. Shortly bear R SP **Castle Inn** and in half a mile turn R over bridge.

2 miles to **Castle Inn**. Turn R at T-junction SP **Keswick**.

3.5 miles to **Mirehouse**. In 3 miles go straight over roundabout SP **Keswick**.

3.5 miles to **Keswick**.

New House Farm ss

Where to Stay in the Bassenthwaite & Cockermouth area...

Highside Farm, Bassenthwaite. The Mawsons are Cumbrian hill farmers offering traditional hospitality. Deborah is a delight and has a flair for the unexpected and an eye for detail with quirky touches in the bedrooms. Her bacon is just yummy and the views from the large, comfy beds are truly memorable. (J3) 017687 76952 www.highside.co.uk

New House Farm, Lorton. If you are seeking luxurious 4-poster beds with bathrooms to match and comfortable lounges to relax in, all within a C17 Grade II listed building look no further. (E6) 01900 85404 www.newhouse-farm.co.uk

The Pheasant, Bassenthwaite Lake. Hostelry, Hotel, Inn? How would one describe what has perhaps the finest bar in Lakeland and some of the finest food? The bedrooms have

The Pheasant ss

been decorated to an extremely high standard. All in all, a true find if you are new to the area. If not, you will know that it has deserved an international reputation for many years. (H3) 017687 76234 www.the-pheasant.co.uk

Willow Cottage, Bassenthwaite. Chris and Roy Beaty along with Henry their golden retriever will extend a warm welcome to their bright and colourful cottage. Double

or twin available. (J2) 01768 776440 www.willowbarncottage.co.uk

Winder Hall, Low Lorton. Jacobean manor formerly known as Lorton Hall lies hidden in the beautiful and often overlooked Lorton Valley. The hotel is small and intimate and once discovered draws in a loyal clientele. It may be just what you are looking for. Perhaps, if passing, drop in for their Lakeland teas served between 1.30-5. (E6) 01900 85107 www.winderhall.co.uk

Derwent Water Marina ss

1917	Dove Cottage opens to the public	1919	Founding of the Forestry Commission
1919	First ascents of Sodom and Gomorrah on Pillar Rock by H M Kelly and C F Holland	1929	Windermere is frozen in its entire length

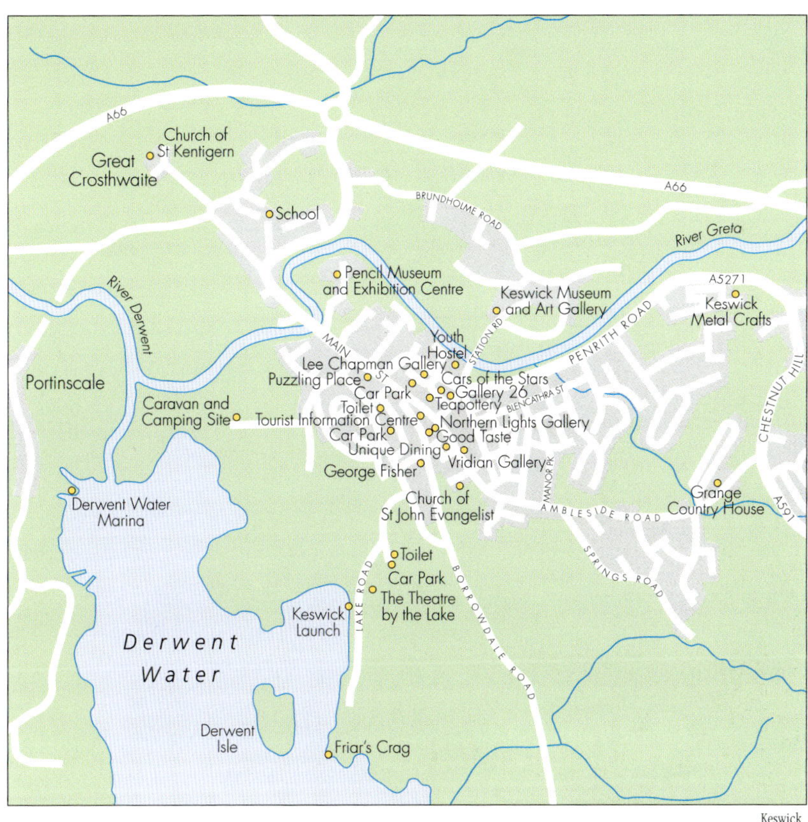

Keswick

KESWICK

This fine town is known as, or has been crowned, 'The Queen of Lakeland'. The town appears to sit in a bowl huddled between the lake, Derwent Water (though barely visible from the town), and the towering mountains, Skiddaw and Blencathra.

The setting is truly magnificent so not surprisingly it is the favourite Lakeland town of many regular visitors. The streets are always busy. It has a profusion of outdoor shops due to being one of England's major walking and climbing centres.

An over abundance of B&Bs have catered for walkers down the years with many now in urgent need of refurbishment. Open-air Saturday market. Moot Hall (TIC). Boats for hire, and trips from Lakeside. (L7)

Special Places to Visit...

Cars Of The Stars Motor Museum, Standish St.

Interesting collection of vehicles from television and films. Open daily East-Nov, W/Es in Dec & Feb 1/2 term, 10-5. (L7) 017687 73757 www.carsofthestars.com

Cumberland Pencil Museum, Greta Bridge.

The discovery of Cumberland graphite in the C16 heralded the production of pencils. The museum traces the history. Children's creative area. Open daily 9.30-5. (L7) 017687 73626 www.pencilmuseum.co.uk

Derwent Water Marina, Portinscale.

RYA courses in sailing and windsurfing. Group and individal lessons in canoeing, kayaking, rock climbing and abseiling, and raft building. Boat hire and sales. Self-catering apartments. 017687 72912 www.derwentwatermarina.co.uk

Gallery 26 at 27, Station St.

Displays a Catholic taste in contemporary and modern art, as well as more traditional watercolours, sculptures, paintings and etchings. Open daily 10-5. (L7) 017687 72090 www.nelsonn.com

Great Crosthwaite Church, St Kentigern.

Impressive late Perpendicular building of C14 origins (north chapel), C16 font and windows dating from the C14-16. There are brasses to Sir John Ratcliff and his wife, 1522. What impresses one is the white marble effigy by Lough of the poet laurcatc, Robert Southey, 1846. who lived at nearby Greta Hall.

Keswick Launch, Lakeside.

Cruises around Derwent Water 'The Queen of the Lakes'. Rowing and self-drive boats for hire. Open all year, times vary. (L7) 017687 72263 www.keswick-launch.co.uk

Rowing boats on Derwent Water

Derwent Water by Alison Critchlow, Northern Lights Gallery ss

Keswick Metal Crafts, 25 Latrigg Close. W C Pepper creates beautiful and ornate objects from stainless steel including plates, bowls, servers and hip flasks. Commissions undertaken. (L7) 017687 73368

Lee Chapman Gallery, 1 Bell Close. With over eighty artists on their books this gallery exhibits a wide range of contemporary art, photography, ceramics, sculpture and original paintings. Open daily from 10. (L7) 017687 71188

Mill Pottery, Goosewell Farm. Jan Burgess creates a wide range of domestic stoneware. Pots are glazed in many subtle colours. Open daily. (M7) 017687 80123

Necessary Angel, Packhorse Court. Specialises in contemporary jewellery made in the UK, all fashioned from various materials, aluminium to zirconium. Open daily from 10-5.30. (L7) 017687 71379 www.artangel.co.uk

Northern Lights Gallery. Unusual and interesting contemporary arts and crafts from Cumbria, Northern England and Scotland. Cafe. Open daily 10-5. 017687 75402 (L7) www.northernlightsgallery.co.uk

Teapottery, Central Car Park Rd, Teapots of every size and shape: hand painted and decorated. Open daily 9-5. (L7) 01768 773983 www.teapottery.co.uk

The Puzzling Place, Museum Square. Where seeing is not always believing; with anti-gravity room, hologram gallery, optical illusions and puzzles. Open daily 10-6. (L7) 017687 75102 www.puzzlingplace.co.uk

Theatre by the Lake, Lakeside. Refurbished into a magnificent venue for the arts. It is home to theatre, drama, dance, comedy, music, film (festivals), exhibitions, literary festivals and special events. Bar and cafe. Open daily from 9.30. (L7) 017687 74411. www.theatrebythelake.com

Thornthwaite Galleries. A rabbit warren of a gallery exhibits the more traditional views of Lakeland, in various media especially watercolours, oils and photography. Teashop. Open daily Mar-Oct 10.30-5. Nov-mid Dec F and W/Es. (J6) 017687 78248 www.thornthwaite.net

Viridian Gallery, 13 St John Street. Mainly features the work of Diane Gainey, a watercolour artist, and other invited artists: ceramics, sculptures and original paintings. Open daily, 10-5. (L7) 017687 71328 www.diane-gainey.co.uk

Viridian Gallery ss

1930   Alfred Wainwright makes his first visit to the Lake District
1930   The Robertson Lamb climbing hut opens in Langdale
1931   Formation of the climbing group known as The Coniston Tigers
1932   The first Bob Graham Round – Ascent of 42 peaks in 24 hours
1932   Ted Scott, editor of The Guardian, capsizes in his yacht on Windermere and is drowned

Clough Head
2166 Calfhow
Sememen
Threlkeld Knotts
Wanthwaite Crags
Salutation Inn
Horse & Farrier Inn
Threlkeld
B5322
Birkett Mire
Birkett Bank
Lowthwaite
Quarry
Beckth
B5322
Bram
Mire Ho.
B5322
4
Hill Top
to A5
Legburt
A66
St. John's Beck
St. John's in the Vale
3
Wanthwaite Bridge
Riddings
2
S
Bridge Ho.
River Grela
Hollin Root
Yew Tree
▲ 1183
Burns
Shundraw
High Rigg
Wescoe
Row End
6
Tewet Tarn
Low Rigg
Shaw Bank
A66
Naddle Beck
Sikes
Bracken
wentfolds
A591
Brundholme
Dale Bottom
Goosewell Fm
Castlerigg Stone Circle
Causeway Foot
Brundholme Wood
P
Nest
A591
7
CASTLE LANE
A66
Rakefoot Pike ▲ 1177
Fieldside
▲ 686
Rakefoot
Brockle Beck
Briery
2
Moor
Castlerigg
P
▲ 1206
Latrigg
Chestnut Hill
A591
Brigham
Wallow Crag
▲ 1234
River Grela
KESWICK
Great Wood
Le
B5289
to Rossth
1
0
P
Ormathwaite
Stable Hills
Keswick Leisure Pool
i
P i
Lords Island
Rampsh
Islan
Friar's Crag
Derwent Isle
Derwent Water
N E S W
Scale
0   500   1000 metres
0   500   1000 yards
St. Her
Islan
scar
to Bothel & A595
to Cockermouth
to A66
A66
A591
B5289
High Hill

The Keswick Railway Path and Castlerigg Stone Circle

9 miles (14km)
3.5 off-road, 5.5 road.

Grade 1.

Riding Time 2 hours.

A short morning or evening ride in stunning surroundings that is excellent for beginners. The Railway Path also makes an easy link from Keswick to Threlkeld to start the Blencathra Round or Old Coach Road circuit. With its rapids and pools, the River Greta beside the old railway is quite beautiful. The Castlerigg Stone Circle has wonderful views. Another good viewpoint is the church of St Johns in the Vale, a short, steep climb up tarmac. Return the same way, or by the A591 variant. No refreshments en route, but plenty in Keswick.

0 Start at Keswick Leisure Pool car-park clearly signed, past the Youth Hostel on Station Lane, close to the town-centre.

1 Turn right onto the well-surfaced Railway Walk. After a level km, the track dips then climbs again, to cross under the A66.

2 After an elevated wooden path the route provides 3km of superb riverside scenery with information boards, seats and shelters.

3 Several gates and bridges then a tunnel leads to two more bridges. Just before the second of these a white arrow directs you right through a bridle gate onto a stretch of single track under the A66 to a minor road.

4 Turn left over the bridge across the river then after 100m Right through an unsigned bridle gate down steps to rejoin the Railway Path for 200m to the end. Descend steps to the B5322, turn right along this for 700m to the first turning right. (100m further on the left the Old Coach Road begins, Signposted Matterdale/Unsuitable For Motors and C2C. See Threlkeld/Troutbeck Route).

5 Turn right, Signposted Keswick 41/4/St Johns in the Vale. Follow the road on past the turning for the church, for another 1km to a t-junction.

S *The alternative route. Take the lane steeply up to the small church. 200m of very steep, winding graveled track leads down from the col west to a tarmac lane. Turn left then right on this to the A591. Right for 700m, then right again on Castle Lane to rejoin normal route just west of the Stone Circle.*

6 Make first of three successive left turns (first two with blue cycle way arrows, Signposted Keswick then Castlerigg Stone Circle, the third unsigned). Follow the lane uphill past Goosewell Farm to the Stone Circle (through gate on left).

7 Straight ahead down to Keswick, steepening to t-junction. Turn left, then immediately right onto the A591. At BP petrol station, either carry up steps onto the Railway Walk to return, or follow the road to the War Memorial at end of the carpark. Turn right into Station Lane.

Derwent Water, 'The Queen of the Lakes' and arguably the most beautiful (though to some, Ullswater might just take the honour). It is one of the largest and most accessible. A circular drive provides breathtaking panoramas, although it's even better viewed from a bike in the quieter times of day. The lake is ringed by towering peaks, green valleys and woodland which sweep down to the water's edge. Skiddaw, and the Derwent Fells, leave their mirror-like reflections for us to record. Easy walks to Friar's Crag and Castle Head. Excellent skating during a winter freeze. Good fishing. Boats for hire, or steam trips from Lakeside. Beside Friar's Crag, a memorial stone to John Ruskin. (L8)

Crummock Water is the Celtic name for crooked, or bent lake. Fine views from Lanthwaite Hill towards Buttermere and Great Gable. Look out for the sound of Scale Force which plummets 100 feet south of Mellbreak into these waters. This lake offers good fishing: rods and boats may be hired from the National Trust. Recommended walks: up Rannerdale Beck, or for the more active, to Mellbreak, through the blooming heather. The battle ground for a victory for the Anglo-Saxons over the Normans. (E9)

Loweswater, 'The leafy Lake' is remote and sometimes forgotten. Park at the southern end for a circular walk. Eastwards are splendid views. Good pub in the village, the Kirkstile Inn. (D7)

Mirehouse ss

Where to Stay...

The Grange Country House, Manor Brow. If you are seeking a traditional Cumbrian house with spacious and elegant rooms tastefully decorated to the highest degree and you seek peace and tranquillity, look no further. The elevated position above the town affords superb views. (M7) 01687 72500 www.grangekeswick.com

Special Places to Visit outside Kewick...

Castlerigg Stone Circle (NT). Set in a quite spectacular position, with mountain views all around. Thirty-eight stones of The Carles (also known as The Druids Circle) make an imperfect circle with ten more grouped inside. Each stone an independent sculpture. Open daily. Park opposite. (M7)

Lodore Falls. Tumbling cascades of water set in woodland with moss and lichen, and slippery rocks. Best visited by boat from Keswick. Honesty box. Commemorated by Robert Southey in verse: 'All at one and all o'er, with a mighy uproar. And this way the water comes down at Lodore'. (L9)

Mirehouse. The home of the Spedding family lies in a most advantageous position overlooking Bassenthwaite Lake. It is a beautiful manor house that dates from the C17 and has many literary connections with portraits and manuscripts of the Poet Laureates: Southey, Wordsworth and Tennyson. You can walk through the rose, herb and walled gardens and amble beside the lake. It is specially geared up for children with an adventure playground, history quiz and an owl hunt. Teas in the Old Sawmills Tearoom. Grounds open daily Apr to Oct 10-5.30. House open Apr to Oct, Su & W 2-5, also F in Aug. (J4) 017687 72287 www.mirehouse.com

Trotters World Of Animals. Rare breeds, Birds of Prey. Hand milking. Open daily mid-Feb to Oct 10-5.30. (H2) 017687 76239 www.trottersworld.com

Whinlatter Forest Park. Run by Forest Enterprise. Centre combines information on forest walks, orienteering and fell walking, trail orienteering for the children. Mountain 'forest cafe'. Adventure playground. Open daily 10-5 (dusk), closed Xmas to mid-Jan. (H6) 01768 778469 www.forestry.gov.uk/whinlatterforestpark

1937	Grizedale Estate acquired by the National Trust	1939	The first "Bluebird" powerboat driven by Malcolm
1939	Wrynose Pass is given its first layer of tarmac		Campbell on Coniston Water sets a new world record
	(before it was an unsurfaced road)		of 141.74 mph

Newlands

Where to Eat, Drink & Be Merry...

Bassenthwaite Lake - The Old Sawmill Tearoom. Belongs to the Mirehouse Estate.

The Farmers Arms, Portinscale. Contemporary interior matches the creatively cut sandwiches and traditional Cumbrian recipes. 017687 73442

Lakeland Pedlar, Hendersons Yard, Keswick. Wholefood vegetarian café and bicycle centre. Laid back and a cool place to be in Keswick. 017687 74492 www.lakelandpedlar.co.uk

Unique, 26 St John Street. Chris Cooper's enthusiasm is infectious and if he achieves his goal the folk of Keswick will be lining up outside to taste his culinary delicacies which change monthly; grilled sea bass fillet, butter fried guinea fowl, pan fried lamb etc. The decor is designed for romantic evenings and the table is yours for the night. Open all evenings except W 6.30-10. (L7) 017687 73400 www.uniquedining.co.uk

Underscar Manor. An impressive Italianate villa of three bays with a centrally placed tower built in 1856- 63 for William Oxley of Liverpool. The restaurant is a popular dining out venue for locals' Special Occasions. The panoramic views from the hotel towards Derwent Water are very fine. Next door, the health spa, Oxleys. (L6) 017687 75000 www.underscarmanor.co.uk

Villages of Interest...

Applethwaite. Small hamlet perched on a terrace overlooking Derwent Water and the half-way point to Millbeck considered by the poet Robert Southey the finest view of the lake. (L6)

Newlands

1940	Haweswater valley flooded to create the reservoir	1948	Francis Coulson opens the Sharrow Bay Hotel to create the
1947	Stone axe factory discovered at Stake Pass, Langdale		first English Country House Hotel

Bassenthwaite.
Norse word for cleared land. The stuff of legend, for Excalibur was apparemtly thrown into this lake. The little church dedicated to St Bega is three miles to the south of the village set in the middle of a field beside the lake. (J2)

Bridekirk. C12 font with superb carvings survives from the original Norman church. (D2)

Grange, Borrowdale.
One of the most popular walking centres. With a cluster of cottages and the ancient stone bridge over the Derwent was once the site of the grange or granary store used by the monks from Furness Abbey. There are easy riverside walks through the Jaws of Borrowdale. Tearoom. (K10)

High and Low Lorton.
Inter-connected village in Lorton Vale famous for the village hall named Yew Tree Hall after the founder of Quakerism, George Fox sat below a yew tree and preached to Cromwell's troops. Lorton Hall is now called Winder Hall. (F6)

Loweswater. The path follows the contour of the terrace above the lake. Start on the Lamplugh side which leads into Holme wood. (D7)

Newlands

Dales & Passes...

Lorton Vale. On entering this lush valley from Cockermouth, one appreciates the three lakes, Loweswater, Crummock and Buttermere, as a rare delight. All can be walked to within a day, and all have fine walks beside the shoreline and on the surrounding fells. (E5)

Newlands Pass (335m/1100ft). The direct route from Keswick to Buttermere. The gentle, pastoral landscape (the setting for Mrs Tiggywinkle) of Newlands Valley soon turns wild, and desolate. At top, a bracing walk leads one to Knott Rigg, affording fine views of Crag Hill's sheer rock face. (J8)

Whinlatter Pass (318m/1043ft). Very easy to manage. Superb views across to Bassenthwaite Lake. Relaxed route to Loweswater, Buttermere and Crummock Water. (H6)

Newlands

The Lakes...

Bassenthwaite. The only body of water in the Lake District to carry the name 'lake', the others are called meres, or waters and the inspiration for Tennyson's 'Morte d'Arthur', and no wonder. At times, the lake has a mysterious and haunting quality. It is best viewed from neighbouring Skiddaw and the Thornthwaite Forest. Access is only possible on the east side at the country house, Mirehouse. To preserve the wildlife, powerboats are banned. There are no public launch sites and little development on the shores. The southern end is popular with twitchers. In April and May the RSPB sets up a 24-hour watch for the osprey. You can watch the birds via field glasses from the osprey viewpoint in Dodd Wood, opposite the entrance to Mirehouse on the east shore. Dinghy sailing is popular due to reliable winds. Pike fishing too. (H3)

1951	Windscale (Sellafield) Nuclear Plant opens	
1952	Alfred Wainwright sets himself a hobby, to climb, map and draw routes for all the major Lakeland fells	

1955	Publication of Wainwright's first Pictorial Guide, The Eastern Fells
1956	Lowther Castle's roof is removed and the house abandoned

Skiddaw

The Mountains...

Skiddaw, 3053ft/931m. This monumental mountain, of Skiddaw Slate, towers over Keswick and Derwent Water. From the top there are fine views to the Isle of Man, the Pennines and Scotland. The climb is easy, straightforward, accessible, and considered relatively safe for family walking but a long slog. Children might get bored. If your family is into peak bagging it's the easiest of the large mountains to conquer.

Route 1. The most popular route starts from Underscar, and leads up to Jenkins Hill, passing Little Man on the left. (M6)

Route 2. Start near the Ravenstone Hotel. Follow path up to Ullock Pike. Follow the ridge of Long Side, and Carl Side to the summit. Return via Broad End (on Northern flank) and Backbethdale. (K4)

Short, Easy Walks...

Dodd Wood (& RSPCA Osprey Lookout). (L9) Start from the Mirehouse car park (tea rooms & toilets) but beware of hazardous, fast moving traffic in opposite direction. A steep path leads up into the wood beside a stream. Bearing right to the RSPCA Osprey Lookout in half-a-mile providing spectacular views over Bassenthwaite Lake.

Ashness Bridge to Watendlath. (L9) This easy, 2 mile/3 km route takes you through a wood and alongside a stream passing Lodore Falls on the way.

Friar's Crag, Derwent Water. (L7) From the Lakeside car park this easy 2 mile/3.2 km circular walk leads you to one of Derwent Water's finest viewpoints beloved of John Ruskin who is commemorated with a sculpture. Take care to avoid the tree roots on the path. Return via Cockshot Wood.

Keswick to Threlkeld Railway Line. (L7) An easy, linear route of 4 miles/6 km suitable for cyclists, prams and wheelchairs. Start from the Keswick Leisure Pool car park on Station Lane just past the YHA. The route then follows a line over the rapids and pools of the River Greta which is particularly beautiful in Spring or Autumn.

Catbells from Hawes End. (L7) Due to the power of TV this once spectacular walk has all but been ruined by its popularity. Heavy erosion of the car park area and the worn paths has prompted the Cumbria CC to advise you to arrive either by the Keswick Launch, or by foot. From Hawes End follow the clear path to cattle grid and ascend the steep zig-zag scramble (on hands and knees) onto Skelgill Bank. There are paths descending off to your left if you can't manage the final ascent of Catbells. Then continue and follow paths to left to return to Hawes End. The views of Derwent Water are stupendous but if you seek solitude, best to walk elsewhere. It can be like the M4 on a bank holiday. The walk is about 3.5 miles/5.7 km.

Whinlatter Forest Trails. (H6) Start from the Visitor Centre. This is England's only mountain forest and is home to a network of easy waymarked woodland paths and junior trails. Sculptures. Gift shop, restaurant and toilets.

Skiddaw

1956	Calder Hall Power Station opens	1963	The steamboat Gondola sinks and is washed ashore following
1960	Re-opening of the T'laal Ratty Railway		a storm. Her hull is half submerged to preserve her
1962	Closure of Greenside Lead Mines, Glenridding	1966	Flooding turns the head of Borrowdale into a lake

Newlands from Catbells

For an industrial and shipbuilding heritage, coastal walks, historic towns and architecture.

For the Lakeland visitor in a rush to explore the lakes and tarns, fells and valleys this corner of Cumbria is often overlooked. But, if your interest is your industrial heritage and the future of nuclear power and its alternatives then a visit to Whitehaven, Workington, Maryport or Sellafield will not go amiss.

Maryport and Whitehaven have a rich history of shipbuilding. And Maryport's maritime museum is worth a visit. If town planning and the origins of the Big Apple (New York) interests you then walk the streets of Whitehaven where you will discover that the Georgian town planners devised a grid system said to be the foundation of New York's Manhattan. Located nearby is also Sellafield with its impressive visitor's centre showing the history and workings of nuclear power.

Cumbria currently has a dozen wind farms - the most notable of which are those of Oldside and Siddick on the Solway Coast, just north of Workington which have been producing electricity since 1996. Visit to decide if wind farms are a blight on the landscape or strangely beautiful.

And, if church architecture be your forte don't miss the Church of St Mary and St Bega at St Bees followed by a stiff walk along the beach to the sandstone cliffs and rocks of St Bees Head.

The Beacon

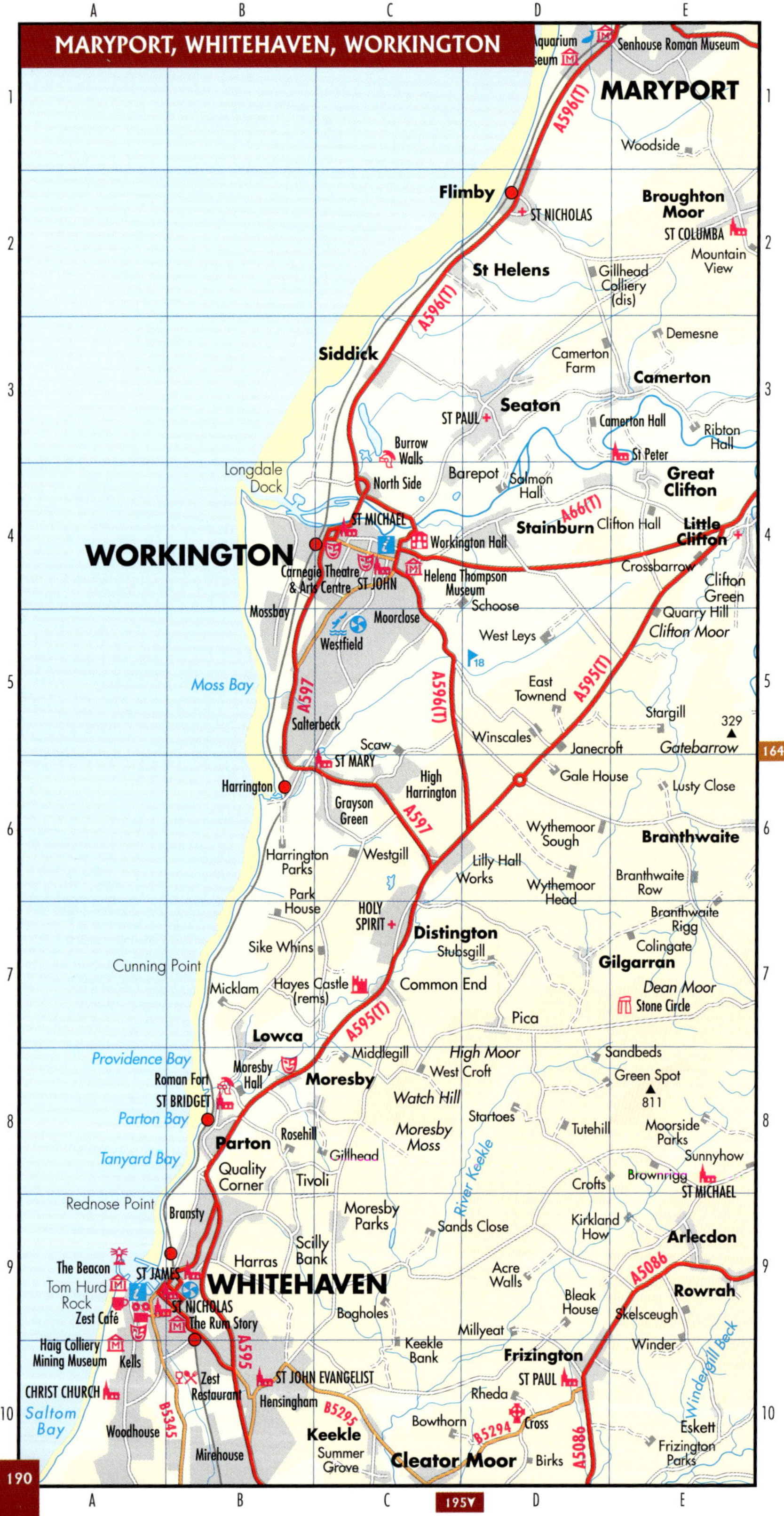
A B C D E
MARYPORT
Aquarium Museum
Senhouse Roman Museum
Woodside
Flimby
ST NICHOLAS
Broughton Moor
ST COLUMBA
Mountain View
St Helens
Gillhead Colliery (dis)
Demesne
Siddick
Cameron Farm
Cameron
Seaton
ST PAUL
Cameron Hall
Ribton Hall
Longdale Dock
Burrow Walls
North Side
Barepot
Salmon Hall
St Peter
Great Clifton
Stainburn
Clifton Hall
Little Clifton
WORKINGTON
ST MICHAEL
Workington Hall
Crossbarrow
Carnegie Theatre & Arts Centre
ST JOHN
Helena Thompson Museum
Schoose
Clifton Green
Mossbay
Moorclose
West Leys
Quarry Hill
Clifton Moor
Westfield
Moss Bay
A597
18
East Townend
A595(T)
Stargill
329
Gatebarrow
164
Salterbeck
Scaw
ST MARY
Winscales
Janecroft
Lusty Close
Harrington
High Harrington
A596(T)
Gale House
Grayson Green
A597
Wythemoor Sough
Branthwaite
Harrington Parks
Westgill
Lilly Hall Works
Wythemoor Head
Branthwaite Row
Park House
Branthwaite Rigg
HOLY SPIRIT
Colingate
Sike Whins
Distington
Stubsgill
Gilgarran
Cunning Point
Micklam
Hayes Castle (rems)
Common End
Dean Moor
Stone Circle
Pica
A595(T)
Lowca
Middlegill
High Moor
Sandbeds
Providence Bay
Moresby Hall
West Croft
Green Spot
811
Roman Fort
Moresby
Watch Hill
ST BRIDGET
Startoes
Tutehill
Moorside Parks
Parton Bay
Parton
Rosehill
Moresby Moss
Sunnyhow
ST MICHAEL
Tanyard Bay
Quality Corner
Gillhead
Tivoli
Crofts
Brownrigg
Rednose Point
Bransty
Moresby Parks
Sands Close
Kirkland How
Arlecdon
The Beacon
ST JAMES
Harras
Scilly Bank
Acre Walls
A5086
Rowrah
Tom Hurd Rock
ST NICHOLAS
WHITEHAVEN
Bogholes
Bleak House
Skelsceugh
Zest Café
The Rum Story
Millyeat
Winder
Haig Colliery Mining Museum
Kells
Keekle Bank
Frizington
ST PAUL
Rheda
CHRIST CHURCH
Zest Restaurant
ST JOHN EVANGELIST
Cross
Eskett
Saltom Bay
Woodhouse
B5345
Hensingham
B5295
Bowthorn
B5294
A5086
Frizington Parks
Mirehouse
Keekle
Summer Grove
Cleator Moor
Birks
River Keekle
Windergill Beck
190
195
A596(T)
A66(T)

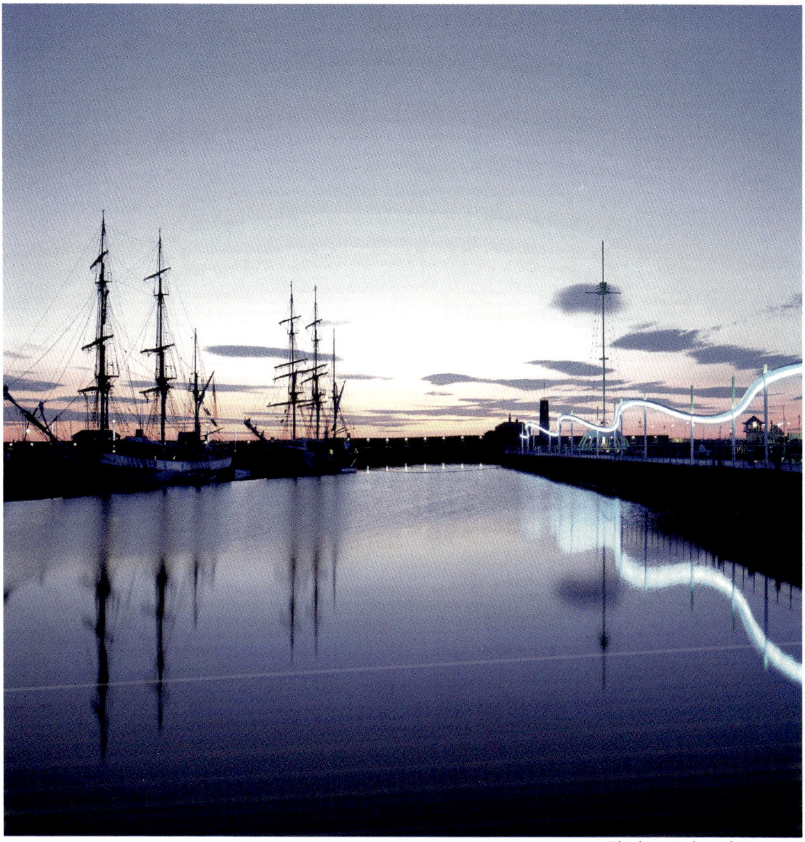

Whitehaven Harbour, The Beacon ss

MARYPORT

Set on the southern edge of the Solway Firth, Maryport has a tradition of shipping and can today boast a fine, deep harbour and modern marina. The harbour serves a small fishing fleet as well as providing shelter for yachts and leisure craft. New buildings (apartments) have sprung up and overlook the sea. It was formerly known as Ellenfoot until 1749. The Elizabeth Dock, the first floating dock of its kind, was built in 1857. Later, Humphrey Senhouse, who built much of Maryport, developed the Senhouse Dock in 1884. Coal and iron ore were the staple industries in the C18 but all this fell away in the 1930s' slump. Walk into the town and you will discover some Georgian buildings and a cobbled square. The history of the town is ably exhibited in the Maritime Museum. (E1)

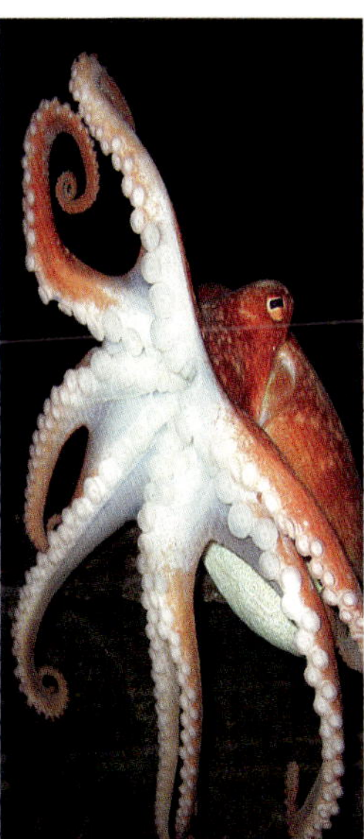

Lake District Coast Aquarium ss

Special Places of Interest...

Lake District Coast Aquarium, Harbourside. An all-weather family attraction with local sealife, cafe, gift shop, crazy golf, adventure playpark and more. Open daily 10-5. (E1) 01900 817760. www.lakedistrict-coastaquarium.co.uk

Maritime Museum, Harbourside. Tells the story of Maryport and her sea-going past. TIC. Open M to Th 10-5, Fri and W/Es 2-5. (E1) 01900 813738

Senhouse Roman Museum. Sculptures and inscriptions from the Roman Fort (Alauna) are believed to be the oldest antiquarian collection in Britain. The museum is housed in the former Naval Reserve Battery that was built around 1885. Open Apr-June Tu, Th-Su 10-5, daily July-Oct, 10-5. Nov-Mar F & W/Es 10.30-4. (E1) 01900 816168 www.senhousemuseum.co.uk

1967	Donald Campbell's fateful run in "Bluebird" on Coniston Water reaches 328 mph but ends in disaster.
1969	Brockhole National Park Centre opens
1970	Rydal Mount opens to the public
1970	Opening of Theatre-in-the-Forest, Grizedale

WHITEHAVEN

Former port and shipbuilding centre of some importance that traded in coal and tobacco and had a long association with America. There are some attractive Georgian buildings. Harbour with fishing boats and pleasure craft. Street markets on Thursday and Saturday. (A9)

Special Places of Interest...

Haig Colliery Mining Museum, Solway Rd. Restored by volunteers, the pit features two steam winding engines, locomotives and mining artefacts. Open daily 9-4.30. (A9) 01946 599949 www.haigpit.com

The Beacon, West Strand.
A fascinating museum that covers a host of local, maritime and industrial history, plus a met-office weather gallery with panoramic views of the town and harbour. There's a massive archive and photographic collection featuring Whitehaven's rich industrial past. TIC. Open Tu-Su & BH Ms 10-4.30. (A9) 01946 592302. www.thebeacon-whitehaven.co.uk

The Rum Story, Lowther St.
Rum is known as the dark spirit of Whitehaven. History of rum covering the Slave Trade, American Prohibition and Royal Navy. Cafe. Open daily 10-4.30. (A9) 01946 592933 www.rumstory.co.uk

Where to Eat, Drink & Be Merry...

Zest, Low Road. Ricky is a chef to take note of and is becoming quite a star in West Cumbria. His modern European dishes such as grilled fish and seared tuna are dearly sort after. Open W-Sa 6.30-9.30 pm. (B10) They also run a funky Café/Bar overlooking the harbour in Whitehaven. 01946 692848 www.zestwhitehaven.com

WORKINGTON

Former port at the mouth of the River Derwent. The town's prosperity relied on coal and ore, and British Steel once had a major plant here, now sadly no more. The town then became a major unemployment black spot until Nuclear Fuels

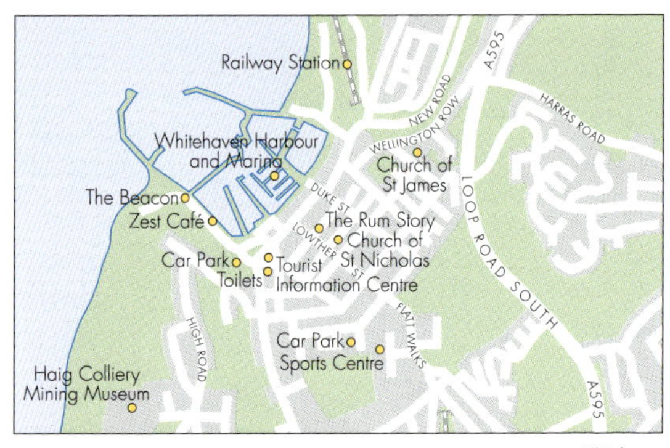

Whitehaven

expanded. There are some massive retail outlets being built on the outskirts which the local council hope will draw in the crowds from West Cumbria. (C4)

Special Place to Visit...

Helena Thompson Museum.
Costumes, decorative art, shipbuilding, social and local history. Open Tu to Su 1.30-4.30, July to Aug 10.30-4.30. (C4) 01900 606155 www.htmworkington.com

CTC Sculpture

Coal Miners, Whitehaven

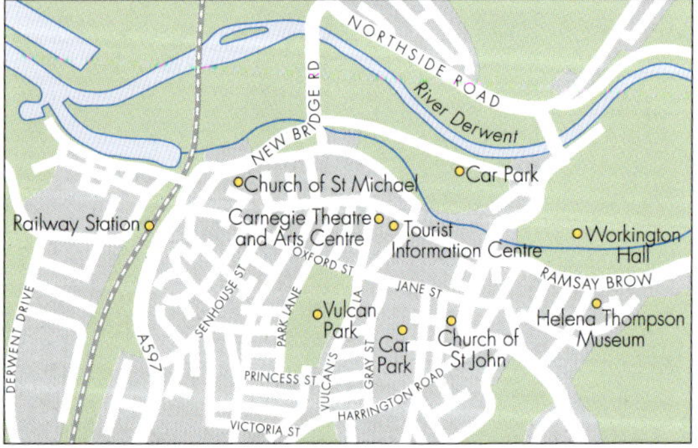

Workington

1974   Modern county of Cumbria created out of Cumberland, Westmorland and part of Lancashire

1975   Jos Naylor (fell runner) of Wasdale sets a new record by traversing seventy-two Lakeland peaks in less than twenty-four hours – extending the Bob Graham round

Holker Hall RT

Entering Whitehaven Harbour by George Nelson jnr

The Beacon

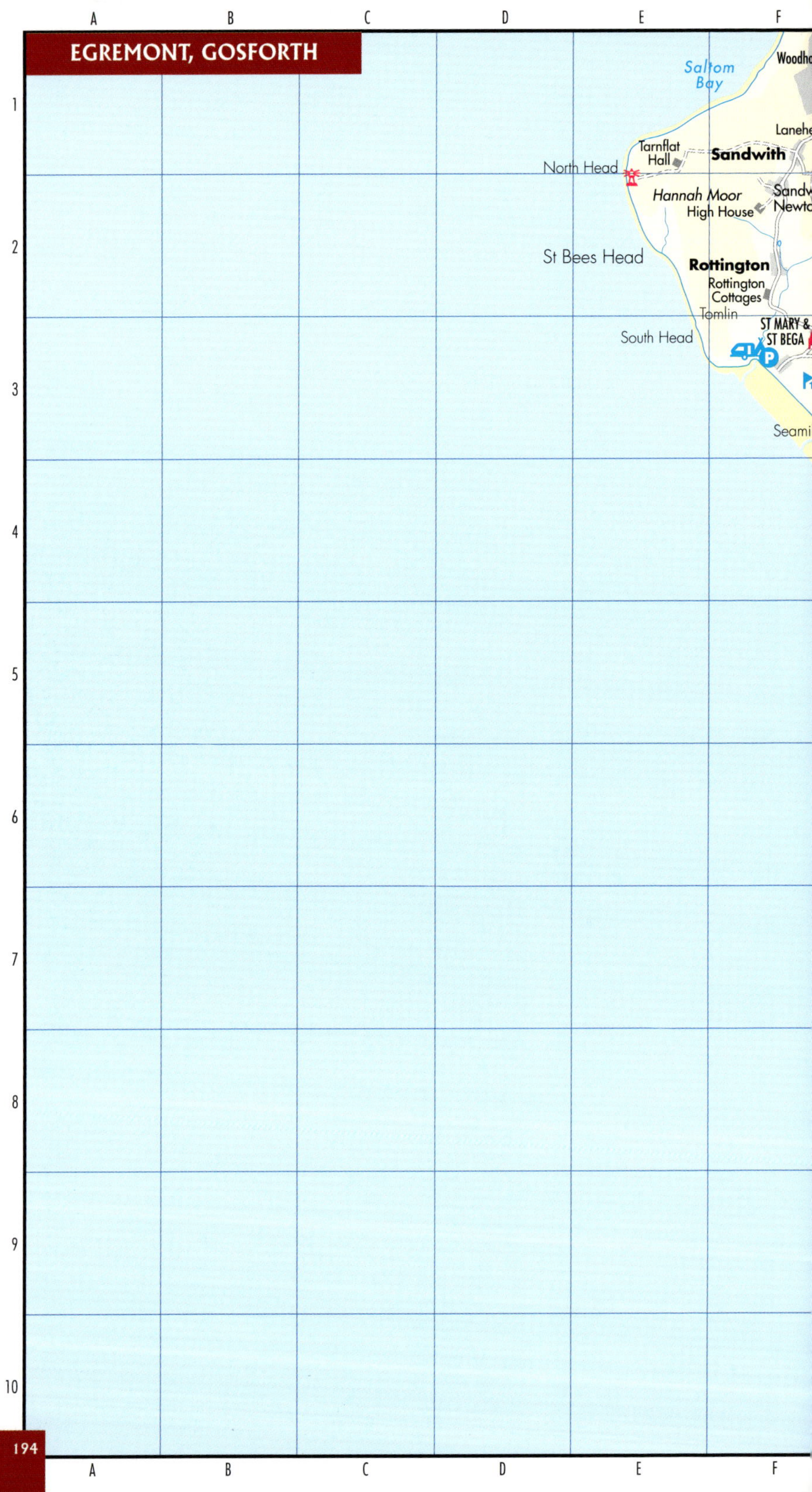
Saltom Bay
Woodho
Lanehe
Tarnflat Hall
Sandwith
North Head
Hannah Moor
High House
Sandw
Newto
St Bees Head
Rottington
Rottington Cottages
Tomlin
South Head
ST MARY & ST BEGA
Seami

G
H
J
190A
K
L
M
Mirehouse
Keekle
Bowthorn
Threapthwaite
Eskett
Hollins
How Hall
B5294
Birks
Frizington Parks
Ennerdale Bridge
ST MARY
Summer Grove
B5295
A5086
Parkside
High Waterside
R. Ehen
Lanefoot
Moorend
Cleator Moor
Scalehill Hall
Cathow
Meadley Res.
Swinside
1
Moor Row
ST JOHN EVANGELIST
Heckbarley
1586
Grike
Stanley
ST JOHN
ST LEONARD
Cleator
Brown Bank
870
Flat Fell
Blakeley Moss
Linethwaite
Springfield
A5595(T)
A5086
Black How
D e n t
Stone Circle
1376
Blakeley Raise
Low Walton
Bigrigg
Woodend
1131
Long Barrow
Sillathwaite
2
High Walton
Southam
Dent Cottage
Cow Field
Uldale Farm
Lankrigg Moss
Pallaflat
Row Foot
Lowther Park
High House
Cobra Castle
Kirk Beck
Latterbarrow Moss
1776
Whangs
Briscoe
Cote Close
Winder
Latter Barrow
Lank Rigg
EGREMONT
St Helena
Wilton
High House
Gill
Kinniside Common
3
Black Beck
Lowes Court Gallery
Brackenthwaite
Simon Kell
Egremont Castle
ST MARY
Oxenriggs
How Hills
1337
How Man
Ashley Grove
River Ehen
Tongue How
Town Bank
Moor Platt
Whitebarrow Head
Side
Worn Gill
4
Coulderton
Black Ling
Carleton
Cold Fell
Side End
Thornholme
t Bees
B5345
Thornhill
Swainson Knott
Middletown
Mine (dis)
Haile
Strudda Bank
Stords
Scalderskew
Rothersyke
A595(T)
Florence Mine
River Calder
Stone Pike
5
Nethertown
Yeorton Hall
Broadleys
Beck Cote
Middle Ethenside
Castle
Blackbeck
Prior Scales
Farmery
Ponsonby Fell
Low Ethenside
Beckermet
ST BRIDGET
Stephney
Abbey Flatts
ST BRIDGET
Calder Abbey
Laverock How
114
Braystones
Calder Bridge
Camp
Lowcrag
Petersburgh
Scargreen
6
Middle Bank
Ponsonby
Blengdale
Whin Garth
Sellafield Visitor Centre
Yottenfews
A595(T)
Bleng Fell
Stirling Castle
Windscale
New Mill
Boonwood
Wellington
British Nuclear Fuels
Sellafield
Newton Manor
Gosforth Pottery
Sowermyrr
7
Calder Hall
Gosforth
Gosforth Cross
Seascale Hall
Fleming Hall
ST MARY
Park Nook
Hall Bolton
Stone Circle
B5343
Tarn How
Meolbank
Seascale How
18
Silver How
Wardwarrow
A595(T)
ST CUTHBERT
Snowder
8
Seascale
Greenlands
Whitriggs Scar
B5343
Burnt Moor
Hallsenna
Greengarth Hall
Irton Cross
Stubble Green
Cookson Place
Summer View
Holmrook
ST PETER
9
Greenside
B5343
Gubbergill
Drigg
River Irt
Barn Scar
DANGER AREA
Hall Carleton
Cumblands
Nature Reserve
Mite Houses
Saltcoats
10
DANGER AREA
Railway Museum
Ravenglass
G
H
J
74
K
L
M
195

EGREMONT

A small market town just off the busy A595 and considered by the town's fathers to be the centre of the Western Lakes although to back up this claim there will need to be some attractive accommodation on offer and I haven't found it yet. Henry III granted the town a Charter. The Crab fair held here since 1267 celebrates the crab apple and greasy pole competition. (H3)

Special Places of Interest...

Egremont Castle.
This early Norman castle of red sandstone was founded by William de Meschines between 1130-40 and is an impressive site. Ruins in public park. (H4)

Florence Mine.
A special place for all industrial archaeologists, for this was sadly the last working deep iron mine in Europe. Underground Tours at W/Es, BHs and daily in school hols. Make sure you take along old clothes and gum boots. Heritage Centre. Coffee shop. Open M-F 9.30-3.30, W/Es & BHs Apr-Oct 10-4 (all year by appoint). (J4) 01946 825830 www.florencemine.co.uk

Lowes Court Gallery, 12 Main St.

C18 building restored to promote the arts. Exhibits of local artists and craftsmen with adjoining craft shop. TIC. Open Jan/Feb M-Sa 10-1. Mar-Dec M-Sa 10-5 (W 10-1). (H3) 01946 820693 www.lowescourtgallery.co.uk

ST BEES

There are three reasons to visit this little town: to educate a child in the small private school, to make a pilgrimage to the church described below, or to admire the fine sandstone cliffs of St Bees Head which are also a bird colony. (F3)

Special Place of Interest...

St Mary & St Bega.
An impressive church famous for the magnificent Norman doorway decorated with rich chevron mouldings, beak heads of man and serpents, and a ram. The shape is Cruciform and constructed in red sandstone. Outside are ancient stones possibly with origins dating back to the C8. These depict St Michael and the dragon. (F3)

Other Special Places to Visit in West Cumbria...

Calder Abbey.
Founded by William de Meschines in 1134 for the Order of Savigny. Later the Savigny united with the Cistercian Order in 1148. It is a unique ruin beside the renovated mansion. Its claim to fame may surprise you, for in 1423 the monks produced the first Royal Jelly Mead. If you are lucky, the reclusive custodians may, just may, show you around their pile. (K6)

Gosforth Pottery.
Busy country pottery. Demonstrations and 'Have a go' sessions. Pottery Courses. Open daily all year, (except Jan-Feb Su-W). Self-catering cottages. (L7) 019467 25296. www.potterycourses.co.uk

Gosforth Cross.
Standing at a height of 15 feet in Gosforth's churchyard is this late C10 cross. Tall and slender with intricate patterns whose meanings are obscure. These have plaited beasts head set above Christ on the Cross, and men on horseback - its origins may be Nordic. (L7)

Sellafield Visitor's Centre.
An impressive, and sophisticated

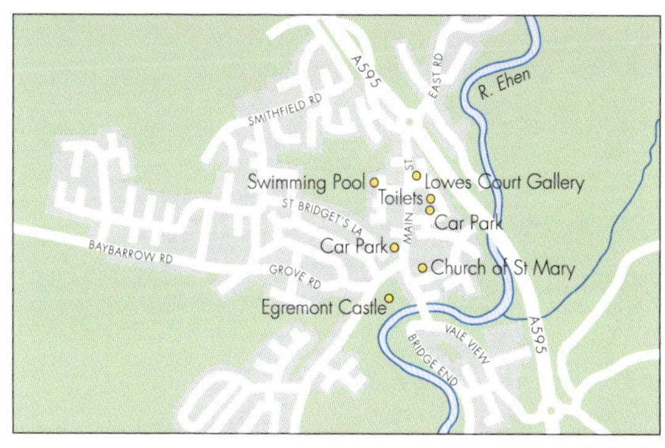

Sellafield when known as Windscale

Egremont

new science - was there ever such a broad divide between the Arts and Science? The Lake District gives you the opportunity to visit both a nuclear site and sites of alternate energy generation (wind farms). Why not do so and join the debate by going to www.greenpeace.org.uk and www.sellafield.com

Villages & Towns of Interest...

Drigg. Although this long village affords fine views of the eastern fells, the reason to stop here must surely be to walk amongst the sand dunes and look out across the salt marshes populated by a colony of black-headed gulls. The nature reserve is visited by Common Arctic and Little terns, shelduck and ringed plover. (L9)

Short, Easy Walks...

St Bees to St Bees Head. (F3) 7 miles / 10 km. Grade is easy to medium on public footpaths. The route is close to unfenced cliffs, muddy and steep in places with spectacular views. Route passes RNLI Bird Sanctuary, before returning via Hannah Moor Lane and rejoining cliff path at Fleswick Bay.

display of salesmanship illustrates the workings of nuclear power. Whatever your position regarding this controversial energy source, a visit here is an education. There are science workshops and interactive experiments on hand. Formerly known as Windscale, the site was an ammunitions factory during World War II, later to have built (under military control) an atomic reactor without the knowledge or permission of Parliament. Britain was in a race to produce the H-bomb and be on equal terms with the Americans within the Transatlantic Alliance. This secret was revealed on the night of October 10, 1957, when the graphic core of the nuclear reactor caught fire and released substantial radioactivity resulting in a major cover up. This was considered the world's worst reactor accident until Three Mile Island in 1979, to be dwarfed by Chernobyl in 1988. Nuclear Power and the safe management of nuclear waste continues to brew controversy. This doesn't appear to be much in evidence in this part of the world for Sellafield has brought much prosperity and safeguarded employment for many in West Cumbria. Given Wordsworth and Ruskin's opposition to the railways, one wonders at their opinion of this

Burnmoor Tarn
Burnmoor Lodge
ESKDALE FELL
Eskdale Moor
▲ 1103
Boat How
Tongue Moor
Low Longrigg
Gill Bank
Stone Circles
Great Barrow
Bel Tarn
▲ 820
Boot
Hows
Hollins
Paddock Wray
Woolpack Inn
Eskdale Youth Hostel
Biranow
Wainhouse Bridge
4
5
Wha Ho.
River Esk
Kepple Crag
▲ 1062
Dow Crag
Long Crag
Penny Hill Fm
Doctor Bridge
6
Low Birker Fm
Tarn Crag
Crook Crag
▲ 160
Birker Force
Low Birker Tarn
Silver How
BIR
FE
Arment Ho.
Gate Crag
Low Birker Pool
Great Arming How
Green How
Smallstone Beck
DALEGARTH STA.
951 ▲
BECKFOOT STA.
Blea Tarn
Dalegarth Hall
7
Stanley Force
Whincop
Birkerthwaite
Highford Beck
Miterdale Head
River Mite
Siney Tarn
Green How ▲ 654
Low Ground
High Ground
Whin Rig
Low Place
Caddy Well
1286 ▲
▲ 1079
Great Bank
Low Holme ▲ 653
Spout Ho.
Milkinstead Mire
889 ▲
The Seat
803 ▲
King George IV Inn
3
River Esk
Forge Bridge
8
Forge Ho.
Garner Bank
▲ 1049
Rough Crag
Eskdale Green
9
ESKDALE GREEN STA.
2
Field Head
Brant Rake
Water Crag
▲ 997
Irton Fell
IRTON ROAD STA.
Hollowstones
Linbeck Gill
Devoke Water
Cubben
Keyhow
10
Muncaster Head Fm
Linbeck
Rowantree How
n Ho.
▲ 438
Plumgarth
Parkgate Tarn
Irton Park
▲ 570
1597 ▲
Woodend Height
White Pike
Yo
Sleathwaite
RAVENGLASS AND ESKDALE RAILWAY
Knott End
Raven Crag 649 ▲
Birkby Fell
The Knott ▲ 1071
nton dge
Mill Ho.
Ross's Camp
▲ 731
Cropple How
Crag
Stainton Beck
Murthwaite
Muncaster Fell
11
High Eskholme
Hinning Ho.
Ancient Settlement ▲ 551
Barnscar
St
Kitchen Ground
River Mite
▲ 757
Hooker Crag
▲ 712
The Intake
Wood End
Chapel Hill ▲ 586
Low Eskholme
Hawbank
Mainsgate
Miteside
Ellerbeck
Black Beck
Stainton
Gasketh
Monument ▲ 428
▲ 556
Samgarth Beck
Whitt
Moorgate
1
Moorend
Muncaster Mill
MUNCASTER
Muncaster Bridge
P
0
Graymains
Nether Stainton
Grange
Carleton Hall
A595
Branken Wall
Muncaster Castle
Rougholme
A595
Bridge End
Woodside
Welcome Nook
Carleton Head
Deer Park
Hall Haberthwaite
Waberthwaite
Bellhill
Thornflatt
Cumblands
Newtown
Beacon 256 ▲
A595
Whitestones
Lane End
Normos
Saltcoats
Ravenglass
GLANNOVENTA ROMAN FORT
P i
Scale
0   500   1000 metres
0   500   1000 yards

Eskdale Circuit

18 miles (29km)
8 off-road, 10 road.

Grade 1.

Riding Time 4 hours

Along the lovely valley of the Esk on quiet lanes, wooded bridleways and farm tracks, often parallel to the tiny Ravenglass Railway. The only real climb is the half-mile of road back to Muncaster Castle (twice as steep and long if the route is reversed). Simple navigation, and easily shortened at several places. (To reverse the route, descend the A595 south from Muncaster Castle to a sharp right hand bend in 500m. Take the bridleway on the left, signposted Muncaster Head/Grizedale passing a white house in 100m.)

0 Start from the car park opposite Muncaster Castle on the A595, 1 km from Ravenglass. Or Ravenglass itself is worth visiting, but more time on an often busy A-road.

1 After crossing the River Esk at Muncaster Bridge, turn left into an unsigned lane. Follow this for 3km to t-junction.

2 Bear left across Forge Bridge (return via bridleway on the right) to t-junction by King George Inn.

3 Turn right, signposted Wrynose and Hardknott Pass and follow road east for almost 3.5km, past Dalesgarth Station, Boot and Eskdale YHA to obvious river bridge.

4 Across the bridge and immediately right through gate, signposted Public Bridleway. Track soon swings away from river for short, steep climb to a junction.

5 Turn right, signposted Penny Hill to pass Penny Green Farm (walking in front of farmhouse), to Doctor Bridge

6 Turn left onto obvious stony track immediately **before** the bridge. Track becomes grassy, climbing to bear right past Low Birker Farm, then alongside river.

7 Bear left at bridleway junction, cross small ford to larger ford and footbridge. Over this, through two gates to wide track. Straight on through metal 5-bar gate, signposted bridleway Eskdale Green, then along grassy bridleway to road at bridge.

8 Turn right (north) on road as before to George Inn. Pass this to railway bridge before Eskdale Green Station.

9 Turn left up track immediately before bridge, signposted Bridleway Muncaster Head/Fells. Where track swings right over railway, left on single track into wood. Exit wood to cross middle of meadow towards left of two oak trees on horizon. Join track bearing left through gorse down to gate above farm.

10 Pass in front of farm to gate on right. Through this onto track along edge of wood, to tarmac lane and cottage.

11 50m after cottages there is a wooden sign for three routes. Take the left of these, signposted Main Road through 5-bar gate to cross golf course and rejoin A595. Turn right for stiff 500m back to the Castle.

OCG Gallery, Ambleside

MY Workshop and Gallery, Staveley

Beckstones Art Gallery, Greystoke

Northern Lights Gallery, Keswick

W G Collingwood, Brantwood

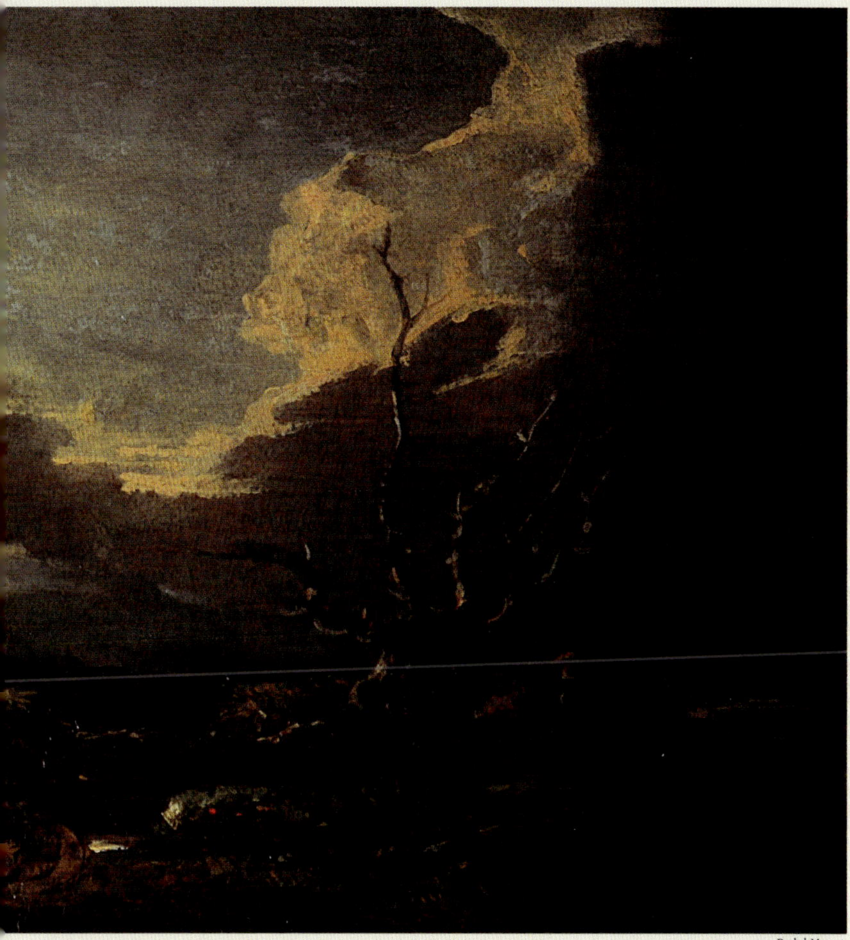

Rydal Mount

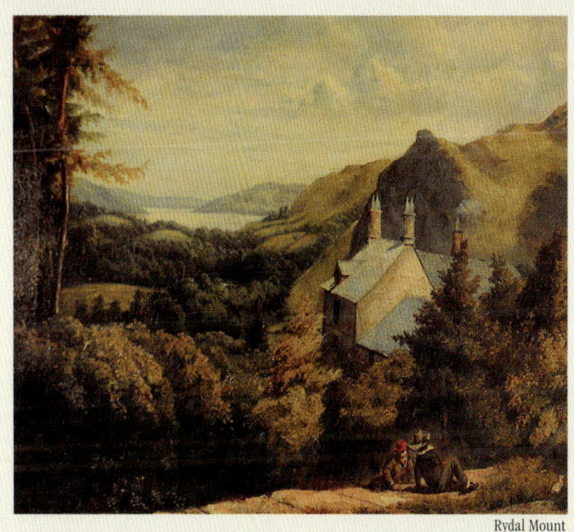

Rydal Mount

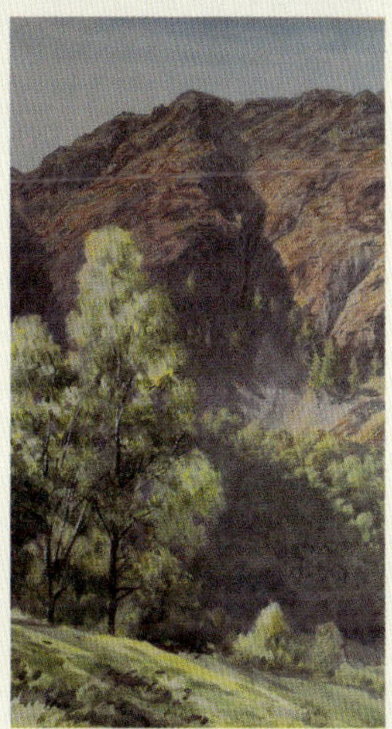

W G Collingwood, Brantwood

These Celebrities are listed by order of birth. They have been selected because they have achieved greatness or notoriety in their chosen fields, sometimes posthumously, and have an attachment to the Lake District either by birth or by choosing to live in the Lake District.

Herdwick Sheep

Introduced by Norse settlers between the 10th and 11th centuries. Known in Old Norse as Herdvyck. They have been described as the Lake District's gardeners. They are born black (as Young Hoggs) and turn to a dark brown-purple colour after twelve months. Their wool is coarse, their meat is of a strong flavour. They can survive on the fells from December to April, and live off little foliage. Their influence has been great for much of the Lakeland dialect refers to sheep husbandry. Beatrix Potter bred them and became President of the Breed Association. Her influence with the National Trust determined their survival for she bequeathed the Trust 4,000 acres with the proviso that they continued to maintain the breed. Sadly, the foot 'n mouth epidemic of 2001 saw 25% of the entire stock of Herdwicks destroyed.

John Kemp of Flanders

In 1331 Edward 11 invited him with "Letters of Protection" to establish a woollen industry in Kendal. He brought men and servants to set up gangs of weavers' apprentices and at the height of the wool trade 300 packhorses left Kendal every week.

The town's motto was "wool is my bread". The trade flourished for another six centuries. However, by 1332 he was living in Cranbrook, Kent where his expertise again came into its own.

Lady Anne Clifford, Countess of Pembroke, Dorset & Montgomery, 1590-1676

Author, Benefactor, Conservationist, Diarist, Landowner, Noblewoman, Restorer of Castles & Churches. Born in Skipton Castle, the third and only surviving child of George Clifford, Earl of Cumberland and his wife Margaret Russell. She led a colourful and eventful life dominated by her fight to maintain possession of the estates left to her by her father. She married twice. First to Richard Sackville, the 3rd Earl of Dorset and lived at Knole, Kent, in great extravagance. The servants at the Lord's Table numbered eight persons, at the Parlour Table twenty-one including Ladies in Waiting, Chaplain, Secretary, pages etc, and at the Clerk's table in the Hall, twenty. Sackville's extravagance and infidelities knew no bounds. He died in 1624. She married her second husband, Philip Herbert, Earl of

Pembroke & Montgomery in 1630. Again, another difficult marriage, but his one redeeming feature was that he encouraged her to regain her father's estates. He was a cad too, and has been described by Bridgman as "vicious, ignorant, and unlettered in a surprising degree, yet strange to say, he was chosen Chancellor of the University of Oxford." He died in 1650. Anne Pembroke (as she liked to be known) bore five children but no sons survived into adulthood. By this time the dissolute behaviour of Herbert had forced her to leave him and on his death she was free to pursue her own interests. By the age of 60 she had inherited the Clifford family northern castles and estates and so decided to move north and set about rebuilding her legacy. With the help of Inigo Jones and others she rebuilt the castles at Appleby, Brough, Pendragon and Skipton, the churches at Appleby-in-Westmorland, Brougham, Mallerstang and Ninekirk, and countless almshouses. The initials AP writ large are often to be found on the buildings she restored. At her funeral she was described as "who while she lived was the honour of her sex and age."

George Fox, 1624-1691
Grazier, Preacher, Prisoner, Quaker, Shoe-maker. Born into yeoman stock in Leicestershire. His father was a weaver. He was apprenticed to a shoemaker and glazier but sought a more simple and ascetic life. Moved to London in 1643 where his religious ideas started to take shape based upon St Peter's Acts of the Apostles 2 & 3. He thus began his ministry, teaching where he could. He believed the Church of England had lost its way and become too institutionalised. He founded the "Religious Society of Friends" (Quakers) but was soon in trouble with the authorities, being imprisoned on numerous occasions for blasphemy and incitement to riot. Oliver Cromwell took an early interest in his affairs, at first, considering him a problem but later agreeing in principle, with his message. During his time in Lancaster gaol he met Margaret Fell who was to become his wife, a woman of social status and wealth. They settled at Swarthmoor Hall on the outskirts of Ulverston.

Sir Humphrey Senhouse of Nether Hall, 1706-1770
Developer, Entrepreneur, Landowner, Mine Owner. He was a local Cumbrian landowner who had seen how successful the Lowther family had been developing the town of Whitehaven, and through an Act of Parliament in 1749 he developed the new town and harbour of Maryport. His plan was to develop shipbuilding and to export coal and iron ore from his Ellenborough Colliery. The town was named Maryport in 1756 in honour of Mary Senhouse. It had formerly been known as Netherhall, and before that, as Ellenfoot.

George Romney, 1734-1802
English Portrait Painter, FRA. He was born and buried in Dalton in Furness. He was apprenticed to his father, a cabinet maker, but in 1755 moved to Kendal to study painting under the tutelage of Christopher Steele. In 1762 he moved to London and was soon accepted by society after his early painting "The Death of General Wolfe" was awarded a prize. Visits to Rome and Parma followed. An obsession with Emma Hart, later Emma Hamilton, dominated his work, painting 60 portraits of her. In1799, after 40 years away from home, he returned to his wife and family.

Sir John Barrow, 1764-1848
Astronomer, Biographer, Linguist, Naval Administrator, Teacher, Traveller. Born in Ulverston, the only son of a journeyman tanner. His expertise in mathematics at an early age took him from a Liverpool iron foundry to participating in a whaling expedition to Greenland, aged 16. An interest in astronomy, exploration and navigation led to his participation on an expedition to China in 1792. As Second Secretary to the Admiralty (1804-45) he was instrumental in promoting many expeditions to seek the Arctic's North-West Passage, exploration in West Africa and the Antarctic. Founder member of the Royal Geographical Society in 1830. The Barrow Monument on Hoad Hill, Ulverston was built in his honour.

Fletcher Christian, 1764-1793
Born in Cockermouth at Moorland Close Farm and educated at St Bees School and Cockermouth Grammar School where he was considered an excellent scholar. He surprised his teachers by joining the Navy. His father was descended from a long line of gentry from the Isle of Man, his mother came from an old established Cumberland family. Aged 18 he sailed aboard HMS Eurydice to India and was quickly promoted from Midshipman to Master's Mate. He then sailed twice to Jamaica with William Bligh. In 1787 Bligh appointed him his Chief Mate. The Bounty was commissioned to transport live breadfruit from Tahiti to the West Indian colonies. The infamous mutiny was prompted by the crew's affection for the female islanders. Christian took the Bounty back to Tahiti then on to the Pitcairn Islands where they established a colony on Tubai. Legend has it that he was later sighted in many ports, but the more likely outcome was that he was killed following a dispute with an islander.

John Dalton, 1766-1844
Chemist, Quaker, Scientist, Tutor. Born Eaglesfield near Cockermouth. He was the son of a weaver born into a Quaker household. He studied physics and chemistry and proposed his pioneering theory on Atomic Theory in 1803 but it was not until his theories were presented in the "New System of Chemical Philosophy" 1808-1827 that his peers took serious note of him.

John Peel, 1776-1854
Father, Hard Drinker, Huntsman. Known throughout the world for the songs they sang about him. He hunted, mostly on foot, three times a week with his own pack of hounds. Lived in the northern fells close to Caldbeck. Aged 20 he galloped off to Gretna Green with his true love, Mary White, and married her much to his mother's displeasure. They brought up 13 children. He was known and loved throughout Cumbria and 3,000 people turned up for his funeral in Caldbeck Church after he died from falling off his horse.

"Dye ken John Peel,

Yes, I ken'd John Peel, with his coat so gray,

He lived at Caldbeck once on a day,

But now he's gone and he's far, far away,

And, we shall ne'er hear his horn in the morning."

Mary Robinson, 1778-1837
The Maid of Buttermere, daughter of the landlord of the Fish Hotel. She was often described as being exquisitely elegant, and nice in manner, and for having long, copious hair. She became, in her own right, quite a tourist attraction promoted by the Romantic poets, but in 1802, as a young girl, she was duped into marriage by the bigamist, and forger calling himself The Hon Alexander Hope MP. The marriage was written up as a great romance by Coleridge in the Morning Post. The bounder was discovered to be one John Hatfield, a bankrupt wanted for forgery, to be immortalised in Wordsworth's Prelude and also in De Quincey's work. Hatfield was later

hanged in Carlisle for forging the King's stamps, a treasonable offence in those days. She later remarried and raised many children, and lies at rest in Caldbeck churchyard. Melvyn Bragg wrote a novel entitled The Maid of Buttermere.

Thomas Arnold, 1795-1842
Churchman, Educational Theorist, Headmaster, Professor. Born East Cowes, Isle of Wight. Educated Winchester and Corpus Christi, Oxford. Headmaster of Rugby School from 1828-1841 where he introduced Modern Languages, Mathematics, Modern History and the Form System which greatly influenced the Public School system of education and independent thinking. His time was documented in the novel Tom Brown's Schooldays. In 1841 he was appointed Regius Professor of Modern History at Oxford. A lifelong friend of S T Coleridge, he was also featured in Lytton Strachey's Eminent Victorians. His summers were spent at Fox How, at Under Loughrigg. There is a memorial window to him on the south side in St Mary's Church, Rydal. His son, the novelist Matthew Arnold, was a friend of William Wordsworth, and wrote of Rydal Mount: "Nowhere on earth have I seen a spot of more perfect and enjoyable beauty."

Harriet Martineau, 1802-1876
Abolitionist, Feminist, Journalist, Novelist, Sociologist. Born in Norwich, the sixth of eight children. Her family were of Huguenot extraction and her father a successful textile manufacturer. Her parents were Unitarians and had progressive views on education. Harriet moved to London in 1829 writing for the Monthly Repository. Her early influences were the writing of John Stuart Mill but it was her book The Illustration of Political Economy, 1832 that brought her financial independence. She travelled widely in the USA and later wrote novels and for many journals notably the Daily News. Her friends and acquaintances were many: George Eliot, Thomas Carlyle, Elizabeth Barrett Browning. Her interests included Darwinism and Malthusian principles of population growth. She was feted

by the Whig Party. She moved to Ambleside in 1845.

James Spedding, MA, 1808-1881
Author, Editor, Scholar. Born in Cumberland. Educated at Bury St Edmunds Grammar School and Trinity College, Cambridge. He joined the Colonial Office and was secretary to various dignitaries. He lived at Mirehouse overlooking Bassenthwaite and counted many writers as friends: Carlyle, Southey, Tennyson and Wordsworth. His major work on the "Life of (Francis) Bacon" took him 30 years to write.

John Ruskin, 1819-1900
Artist, Conservationist, Gardener, Educational Philanthropist, Philosopher, Professor of Art, Social Revolutionary. Born in London and son to a successful sherry merchant (the co-founder of Allied Domecq). He was educated at home, took part-time courses at Kings College, London and at Christ Church, Oxford where he was heavily influenced by the evolutionary sciences of the day. He was soon to turn his hand to writing about art and architecture and became a fervent supporter and advocate of JMW Turner's work, and the new breed of young artists - the Pre-Raphaelite Brotherhood. At the age of 29 he married Effie Gray. The marriage was never consummated and she left him six years later for John Everett Millais. There has been much speculation about this disastrous relationship. Effie claimed that he found her body repugnant. His knowledge of the female form was confined to Greek statues and paintings of the nude. When he came to know his wife, it has been claimed that he was shocked by the reality of womanhood. Tragic, for indeed she was a pretty woman (see Millais' painting The Order of Release). Whatever the real truth, we shall never know. It was a blip in an extraordinary life of a man that some consider one of the great minds of the 19th century. Ruskin then immersed himself in work producing a three-volume study of Venice, and at the heart of this work he contrasted medieval craftsmanship with contemporary manufacturing. From this point of his life he tried to

shape and influence society. However, the momentum of his cause was severely tested when in his 40s he fell in love with Rose La Touche who then died tragically young at 29. He never recovered from this loss, and thereafter fell into regular bouts of depression. His interest in medieval craftsmanship had sparked a friendship with William Morris. This drove the launch of the 'Arts & Crafts Movement'. In 1869 he was appointed Slade Professor of Art at Oxford. His teachings had had a profound effect on Canon Hardwicke Rawnsley (and Octavia Hill) the co-founders of the National Trust. In 1872 he bought Brantwood overlooking Coniston Water and lived there until his death. Ruskin was a man before his time. He championed the Welfare State, Town & Country Planning, Green Belts, Smokeless Zones. More importantly, education for the illiterate and poverty-stricken, believing that only through education could you temper crime. His name is used throughout the world as a symbol of educational philanthropy. He may well have been unlucky in love. He did, however, lead a long and fulfilling life, and he has left a legacy that few, or any of us, could hope to match.

Earl Mayo, 1822-1872
MP, Statesman, Viceroy of India. Born in Cockermouth and educated Trinity College, Dublin. He was known as the Forgotten Earl. Appointed the Viceroy of India by Queen Victoria, he did much to promote agricultural irrigation, developed the railways and other public institutions. During a visit to a penal colony at Port Blair in the Andaman Islands he was assassinated by the convict Sher Ali, who was later hailed as a heroic freedom fighter.

Canon Hardwicke Drummond Rawnsley, 1851-1920
Clergyman, Co-Founder of the National Trust, Conservationist, Oarsman, Poet. Born in Shiplake near Henley-on-Thames and educated at Balliol College, Oxford. His early ambition in life was to become an Arctic explorer but reality took hold and he became a priest in East Anglia. In 1871 he moved to become vicar of Wray Church near

IN MEMORIAM
'WHO BATTLED FOR THE TRUE THE JUST'
H. D. RAWNSLEY
1851 † 1920
VICAR OF THIS PARISH
FOR 34 YEARS
CANON OF CARLISLE
CHAPLAIN TO THE KING.
AND
EDITH HIS WIFE

Ambleside. He met Beatrix Potter in 1882 and encouraged her to draw and write her Peter Rabbit books. In 1883 he moved to St Kentigern's Church at Crosthwaite. His belief in conservation was fundamental to his faith and morality. He fought hard against bungalows and development and was instrumental in founding the Lake District Defense Society (later to become The Friends of the Lake District). Measure the man by his legacy. Small acorns grow into... He was Co-Founder of the National Trust with Octavia Hill and Sir Robert Hunter, a lawyer. They raised money to purchase Brandlehow Wood at the foot of Cat Bells, the National Trust's first property. He was influenced by John Ruskin and wrote a biography of him. He also wrote 30,000 sonnets. In retirement, he bought Wordsworth's old house, Allan Bank which he left to the Trust.

William Gersham Collingwood, 1854-1932

Artist, Biographer, Climber, Professor of Fine Art, Walker. Educated University College, Oxford and the Slade School of Art. He started working in the summer holidays for John Ruskin. He married Edith Isaacs in 1883 and moved to Coniston to be Ruskin's assistant. During this time he met Arthur Ransome who based many of his Swallows & Amazon adventures on life with Collingwood and his children. At the outbreak of WW1 he joined the Admiralty Intelligence division and following the Armistice was asked to design many of the War Memorials. He was made Professor of Fine Art at Reading University. Some of his paintings hang in Ruskin's bedroom at Brantwood (and are illustrated in this bookon page 202).

Beatrix Potter (Mrs William Heelis), 1866-1943

Botanist, Children's Author, Conservationist, Farmer, Feminist, Illustrator, Mycologist, Sheep Breeder. Born in South Kensington, London into a privileged and over-protective household. Her education by a succession of governesses stifled her intellectual development but led her towards an interest in flora, fauna and mycology (fungi). A family holiday to the Lake District awakened a passion for landscape and a meeting with Canon Hardwicke Rawnsley developed her drive for conservationism. In 1902 she had her first book published by Frederick Warne & Co titled The Tale of Peter Rabbit. It sold over 28,000 copies in its first year. Her books have been transformed and told through various mediums: film, ballet, animation and TV. More recently, her early life has been the subject of the film Miss Potter starring Rene Zellwegger and Ewan MacGregor, and this more than doubled the annual visitors to Hilltop Farm. Sadly, it failed to depict her later (and more interesting) years as a passionate conservationist and sheep breeder. She helped to save the Herdwick from extinction and was instrumental in saving hundreds of acres for the National Trust and the livelihood and life of the Lakeland hill farmer from extinction by protecting these farms from developers. Hilltop Farm was very much a depository for her antiques and bric-a-brac and is indeed worth a visit. She died a very rich woman and lived across the fields from Hilltop in Castle Cottage.

Millican Dalton, 1867-1947

Ascetic, Caveman, Climbing Guide, Drop Out, Pacifist, Professor of Adventure, Stoic, Teetotaller, Vegetarian. Born in Neathead, Cumbria and educated at the Quaker School in Wigton. He started his working life as an Insurance Clerk in the City but did what many dream of. He dropped out of society and followed his romantic dreams. He lived in a cave at Castle Crag on the foot of Borrowdale and offered camping, sailing and adventure holidays. He rarely belayed on his rock climbs and surprisingly survived into old age. He made his own clothes, pursued the simple life, and in winter moved south to Epping or the New Forest to live in sheds or under canvas. His motto: "You can't feel lonely with nature as your companion."

Kendal Mintcake, 1869
The original recipe has been credited to Joseph Wiper who lost concentration whilst boiling up some glacier mints which went cloudy. The recipe is naturally a State Secret but the ingredients are generally mixed in copper pans: a mix of sugar, glucose and water. After cooling half-an-ounce of oil of peppermint is added to every 40 pounds of mix. The blend is then poured into shallow trays where it hardens quickly. The result is an immediate source of energy much loved by walkers and mountaineers. The firm of George Romney was established in 1936 by Sam T Clarke and is now managed by the fourth generation. The mintcake has been to the top of Everest in 1953, across the world on motorcycles with Charlie Boorman and Ewan MacGregor, and in most rucksacks that colour the fells.

Abraham Brothers, George 1871-1965, & Ashley 1876-1951
Climbers, Photographers. These two brothers recorded the evolution of Lake District rock climbing. Their images are iconic. Their star climber was Own Glynne Jones from 1896-1899 until his death in the Alps. Apart from the Lakes, they also photographed Snowdonia and the Isle of Sky. Their workshop is now the outdoor store George Fisher in Keswick where a café celebrates their life.

Arthur Ransome, 1884-1967
Author, Bolshevik Sympathiser, Fisherman, Foreign Correspondent, Spy, Yachtsman. Born in Leeds. Educated at a Windermere Prep School, Rugby School and Yorkshire College (Leeds) where he read chemistry for a year before abandoning his studies for London and Bohemia. His first book Bohemia in London, 1907 was followed by a biography of

Oscar Wilde and a libel suit from Lord Alfred Douglas. This action and his disastrous first marriage prompted him to flee England for Russia in 1913. He wrote a guidebook to St Petersburg and studied Russian folklore. In 1914 he became a reporter on the Eastern Front for the radical Daily News; he later covered the Russian revolutions of 1917. During this time he made friends with Lenin and Tolstoy. Fell in love with Tolstoy's private secretary Evgenia Shelepina at the Bolshevik headquarters at Smolny. His activities were not overlooked, first by MI6 and later MI5. He was feeding information to Lenin and may have been a double agent. Following the end of WWI he moved with Evgenia to Estonia, built the cruising yacht Racundra and sailed the Baltic. Racundra's First Cruise is a classic of sailing literature. Returning to England in 1929 he settled in the Lake District, first in Winster Valley, later at Haverthwaite. During these years he wrote his famous children's books, Swallows and Amazons, loosely based around Coniston Water and Windermere, later the Norfolk Broads. He became a "Country Diarist" for The Manchester Guardian writing about fishing. He is buried in St Paul's churchyard, Rusland.

Sir Hugh Walpole, 1884-1941
Biographer, Dramatist, Novelist, Teacher. Born in New Zealand. Son of a Bishop. Educated at King's School, Canterbury and Emmanuel College, Cambridge. He worked for the Red Cross during WW1, then as a teacher before he could afford to live off his writings. He lived in Cumbria from 1924-41 at Brackenburn overlooking Derwentwater. His library amounted to 30,000 books. His famous novels "The Herries Chronicle" (Rogue Herries, Judith Parris) were centred around Borrowdale. He wrote biographies of Joseph Conrad and Anthony Trollop. He never married.

Stan Laurel, 1890-1965
Actor, Comic, Director, Screenwriter. Born Arthur Stanley Jefferson in Ulverston, died Los Angeles, California, USA. Educated at King James 1 Grammar School, Bishops

Auckland and King's School, Tynemouth. His father was an actor-theatre manager. Stan joined Fred Karno's troupe of actors and became a one-time understudy to Charlie Chaplin. By 1924 he was working full-time in films, and was eventually involved in 190 movies. He was the quiet member of the double-act known as Laurel & Hardy. Before his funeral he wrote his own epitaph: "If anyone at my funeral has a long face, I'll never speak to him again". He's buried at Fort Lawn in the Hollywood Hills.

W A Poucher, 1891-1988
Chemist, Landscape Photographer, Perfumer, Writer. He followed in the tradition of the Abraham Brothers and with Leica in hand would spend at least a fortnight every year in May climbing and photographing the Lake District. His books are classics and have recently been re-issued by Frances Lincoln. His early books were pocket-sized. Later, his original publishers developed a large, coffee table book range. His monochrome prints are classics of mountaineering photography, and the originals are much sought after. However, his bestselling book "Poucher's Perfume, Cosmetics and Soap" is still in print today, and has run into its tenth edition. For thirty years he was the Chief Perfumerer at Yardleys. Often teased by his fellow climbing friends because of his profession: "A perfume salesman who wears his wares." He also produced books on the Welsh Peaks, Scottish Peaks and the Isle of Sky. His other passion was fast cars.

Josefina de Vasconcellos, 1904-2005
Centurion, Christian, Composer, English Sculptor, Painter, Poet. Her father was a wealthy Brazilian diplomat. She won a scholarship to the Royal Academy in 1921, later studied in Paris under Antoine Bourdelle, a former assistant to Auguste Rodin. Once her career took shape she was Runner Up at the Prix de Rome contest in 1930. She lived most of her life at The Bield in Little Langdale. Married to the artist and lay priest Delmar Banner, they adopted two children. She retained her father's name for her professional

Wilk, Pheasant Inn, Great Crosthwaite

duties. Her sculptures were an extension of her faith and stand in many cathedrals: notably Coventry, Gloucester, Liverpool and St Paul's, London. A further two can be seen in Cartmel's parish church. Apart from her artistic work her great passion was setting up a school for disadvantaged boy Outpost Emmaus for which she was made an MBE.

"Wilk" John William Wilkinson, 1906-1994.

Artist, Countryman, Foreman Fitter, Walker. A Keswick man all his life who started work at the bobbin mill, then moved to the gas works for 31 years. His main pastime was drawing. He would shelter behind a stonewall at a hunt and talk to the farmers and country folk. Later, in the warmth of The Pheasant Inn at Great Crothwaite he would unroll his characters on to paper amidst great jollity and laughter.

Alfred Wainwright, MBE, 1907-1991

Cartographer, Illustrator, Recluse, Philanthropist. Walker. Born in Blackburn, Lancashire the son of a stonemason. As author and illustrator of the Pictorial Guide to the Lakeland Fells compiled between 1952 and 1966, no one person has done more to change the face of Lakeland exploration than Alf Wainwright and all was researched via the use of the local bus service. Strangely, he never missed the last homeward bus after a day on the fells. As Chairman of the Animal Rescue in Cumbria most of his book's royalties contributed to this charity. His ashes were scattered on his favourite mountain, Haystacks, by his second wife Betty. Following his death the publishers Michael Joseph let his Pictorial Guides go out of print. They were recently re-published under the Frances Lincoln imprint and have received a new impetus in sales with the added help of countless TV series following his walks. His achievements made him famous and shy of publicity. One wonders what sort of a dinner companion he would have been.

A Harry Griffin, OBE, 1911-2004

Countryman, Coniston Tiger, Diarist, Journalist, Rock Climber. Born on Merseyside, brought up in Barrow-in-Furness and educated at the local Grammar School. He became a Club Reporter on the Barrow Guardian, later moving to the Lancashire Evening Post. In 1937 he joined the Manchester Guardian and for 53 years was a Country Diarist writing the "Lakeland Diary". During WWII he was with the Intelligence Corps in the Far East. His diary was read and followed by millions. He captured the moods of the Lakeland hills, the seasonal changes and the thrill of the wild places like no other writer of his generation. His rock climbing endeavours were the stuff of legend and he continued to climb well into his eighties. His book The Coniston Tigers is a classic of mountaineering literature.

Jim Birkett, 1914-1993

Conservationist, Ornithologist, Rock Climber, Quarryman. Born in Little Langdale, the son of a roadman, he was drawn to the fells after a day out with the local fox-hunting pack. He worked by day in the Honister Quarries but on a dry evening he would head for the crags. He dominated Lakeland climbing from the late 30s to the early 50s. Shod in heavy nailed boots and with tremendous finger-strength, he set

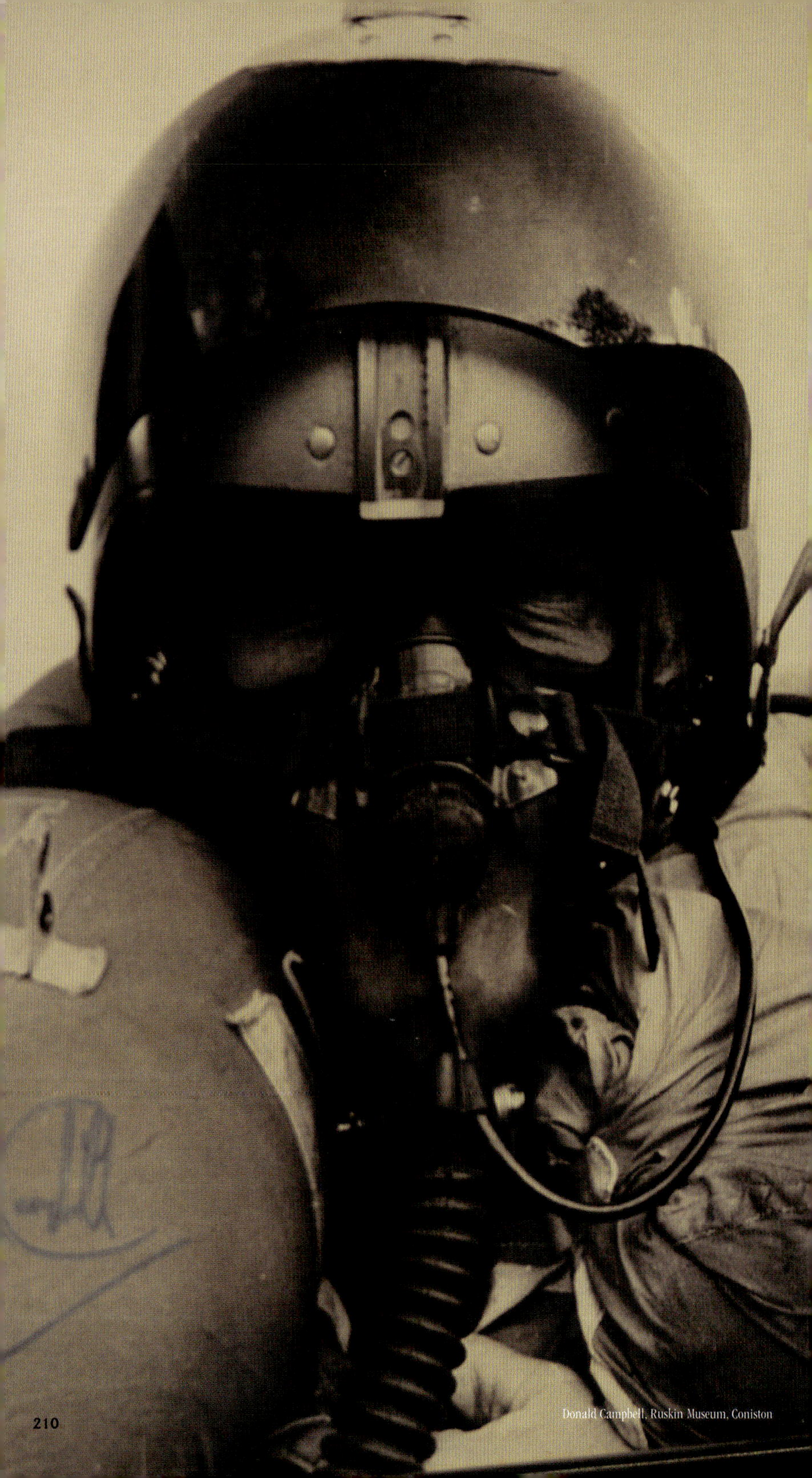

Donald Campbell, Ruskin Museum, Coniston

new standards of routes on Scafell, Dove Crag, Harlot Face (recognised as Lakeland's first Extreme Climb) and Castle Rock, of Triermain. His later years were spent managing Moss Rig Quarry and protecting peregrine falcons' nests for the RSPB.

Norman Nicholson, 1914-1987
Lakeland Poet, Man of Millom. Forever associated with Millom, for he lived in the same terraced house for most of his life bar a time at a sanatorium whilst recovering from tuberculosis. His poetry explored the simplicity of language. His subjects were industry and the grind of daily life. He was inspired, nay bewitched, by the beauty of the Duddon Valley (as was Wordsworth). He married twice and was apparently bisexual. Awarded the Queens Award for Poetry in 1977, and an OBE in 1981.

John Cuncliffe, 1919
Children's Author, Librarian, Teacher. The author of Postman Pat, Rosie and Jim and 200 children's books. The Greendale of Postman Pat is in fact Longsleddale. The TV series has been shown in 50 countries. He has lived in Kendal for many years and researched the books by wandering around the surrounding villages talking to the farmers, shopkeepers and the village postmen.

Donald Campbell, 1921-1967
Boys' Hero, Engineer, Speed Record Holder. Educated Uppingham School. At the outbreak of WWII he volunteered for service in the RAF but was turned down due to a childhood illness. He joined Briggs Motor Bodies as a maintenance engineer. His father was Sir Malcolm Campbell, holder of 13 world speed records in the 1920s and 30s (in the Bluebird cars and boats). It wasn't long before he followed in his father's footsteps. He was to break countless world speed records in his boats K4 and K7 between 1955-64, first on Ullswater at 202 mph, then on Lake Mead at 216 mph. Coniston runs followed in 1958 at 248 mph, and at Lake Dumbleyuns in 1964 at 276 mph. He also achieved land speed records of 401 mph at Lake Eyrie in Australia in 1964. He held both land and sea speed records simultaneously.

His demise came on Coniston Water on January 4th when Bluebird K7 somersaulted. His body and his boat weren't recovered until the 28th May 2001. His body was interred in Coniston Cemetery on 12th September 2001. He married three times. For more information visit the Ruskin Museum, Coniston.

Alan Hankinson, 1926-2007
Broadcaster, Climber, Gurkha, TV Journalist, Writer. Born in Gatley, Cheshire. Educated at Bolton School and Magdalene College, Oxford. Known to all as "Hank". He saw war service with the Black Watch and the Royal Gurkha Rifles, 1944-47. Started his career with the Bolton Evening News, then moved to join ITN News. He was a friend to climbers and mountaineers and would follow their expeditions for the news services and became great friends with Chris Bonington, Doug Scott, Don Whillan and Mick Burke. He wrote some classics of mountaineering literature: The First Tigers, 1972 and Coleridge Walks The Fells. In later life, he moved to Bassenthwaite and worked tirelessly for The Theatre By The Lake.

Sir Chris Bonington, CBE, 1934
Mountaineer, Photographer, Rock Climber, Writer. Born Hampstead, North London. Educated University College School and the Royal Military Academy, Sandhurst. Commissioned into the Royal Tank Regiment in 1956. Lived in Cumbria with his wife Wendy since 1974. His list of achievements as a pioneering climber in the Alps and the Himalayas is immense. His literary output is impressive too, and has run parallel with his expeditions. He is without doubt a legend in his own lifetime. Made a CBE in 1976, and Knighted in 1996. His achievements would fill pages. Better to visit his own website: www.bonington.com

Hunter Davies, 1936
Author, Biographer, Broadcaster, Journalist. He was born in Scotland and brought up in Carlisle and Dumfries. Educated at Carlisle Grammar School and Durham University. He is married to Margaret Forster, the novelist, and divides his time between London and Cumbria. His early novel Here We Go Around The Mulberry Bush about a young man trying to loose his virginity was made into a successful film. His biographies of The Beatles, 1968, Tottenhan Hotspur and ghosted books for Wayne Rooney, Dwight York and Paul Gascoigne have made him a household name. He is President of the Cumbrian Wildlife Trust and has plugged the writings of Alf Wainwright for years. His book "A Walk Around The Lakes" is my favourite Lakeland book.

Margaret Forster, 1938
Biographer, Critic, Mother, Novelist, Teacher. Born in Carlisle and educated at Carlisle County High School for Girls and Somerville College, Oxford. She has written novels featuring heroines struggling with the issues of love and family, and biographies of Daphne du Maurier and Elizabeth Barrett Browning. She is a literary critic for the London Evening Standard and a Fellow of the Royal Society of Literature. She lives part-time in Cumbria and London, and is married to a splendid fellow, one Hunter Davies, father of her three children.

Melvyn Bragg, 1939
Broadcaster, Life Peer, Novelist, Screenwriter, Born in Wigton, Cumbria and educated at the Nelson Thomlinson School, Wigton and Wadham College, Oxford. Joined the BBC as a trainee. He has written countless novels (many set in Cumbria) and screenplays for The Music Lovers, Jesus Christ Superstar and Isodora. He was Controller of the Arts for London Weekend TV and Presenter of The South Bank Show for years. More recently, he has presented the Radio 4 programme, In Our Time. Chancellor of the University of Leeds. He was made a Life Peer by Tony Blair in 1998 - Baron Bragg of Wigton.

Buttermere

Ambleside
Central Buildings, Market Cross,
LA22 9BT
amblesidetic@southlakeland.gov.uk
Website and online booking service
015394 32582

Ambleside Waterhead
Waterhead Car Park, LA22 0EN
waterheadtic@lake-district.gov.uk
015394 42895

Barrow-in-Furness
Forum 28, Duke St, LA14 1HU
touristinfo@barrowbc.gov.uk
01229 876505

Bowness
Glebe Rd, LA23 3HJ
bownesstic@lake-district.gov.uk
015394 42895

Broughton-in-Furness
Town Hall, The Square. LA20 6JF
broughtontic@btconnect.com
01229 716115

Carlisle
Old Town Hall, CA3 8JE
tourism@carlisle-city.gov.uk
01228 625600

Cockermouth
Town Hall, Market St, CA13 9NP
cockermouthtic@co-net.com
01900 822634

Coniston
Ruskin Ave, LA21 8EH
mail@conistontic.org
015394 41533

Egremont
Lowes Court Gallery, 12 Main St,
CA22 2DW
email@egremont-tic.fsnet.co.uk
01946 820693

Grange-over-Sands
Victoria Hall, Main St, LA11 6DP
grangetic@southlakeland.gov.uk
015395 34026

Hawkshead
Main Car Park, LA22 0NT
info@hawksheadtouristinfo.com
015394 36946

Kendal
Town Hall, Highgate, LA9 4DL
kendaltic@southlakeland.gov.uk
01539 725758

Keswick
Moot Hall, Market Sq, CA12 5JR
keswicktic@lake-district.gov.uk
017687 72645 Open all year

Maryport
Town Hall, Senhouse Street,
CA15 6BH
maryporttic@allerdale.gov.uk
01900 702840

Millom
Folk Museum, St Georges Rd,
LA18 4DQ
millomtic@copelandbc.gov.uk
01229 772555

Penrith
Penrith Museum, Middlegate,
CA11 7PT
pen.tic@eden.gov.uk
01768 867466

Penrith - Rheged
Redhills, Penrith, CA11 0DQ
tic@rheged.com
01768 868000

Ravenglass
R and ER Railway Station, CA18 1SW
01229 717278

Sellafield
Visitors Centre, CA20 1PG
david.g.henderson@britishnucleargroup.com
019467 76510

Ullswater
Main Car Park, Glenridding,
CA11 0PA
glenriddingtic@lakedistrict.gov.uk
017684 82414

Ulverston
Coronation Hall, County Sq,
LA12 7LZ
ulverstontic@southlakeland.gov.uk0
1229 587120

Whitehaven
Market Hall, Market Place, CA28 7JG
thebeacon@copelandbc.gov.uk
01946 598914

Windermere
Victoria St, LA23 1AD
windermeretic@southlakeland.gov.uk
015394 46499

Workington
Carnegie Theatre, Finkle St,
CA14 3BD
workingtontic@allerdale.gov.uk
01900 606699

M6 Killington
Killington Lake Services, LA8 0NW
015396 20138

M6 Southwaite,
Southwaite Services, CA4 0NS
southwaitetic@visitscotland.com
016974 73445 Open all year.

Cumbria Tourism
Windermere Road, Staveley,
Kendal LA8 9PL
01539 822222.
stay@cumbriatourism.org.
www.golakes.co.uk

For specific dates please contact the local Tourist Information Centre

March
Ambleside Daffodil and Spring Flower Show
South Cumbria Music Festival, Ulverston
Ulverston Walking Festival
Words By The Water, Theatre by the Lake, Keswick

April
Damson Day, Low Farm, Lyth Valley
Jan Kjellstrom Festival of Orienteering, Graythwaite Est.
Hawkshead Trail Race (PUMA)

May
Barbon Speed Hill Climb (cars)
Cartmel Races
Flag Fortnight, Ulverston
Kendal Medieval Market, Kendal
Keswick Mountain Festival
Keswick Jazz Festival
Carlisle & Borders Spring Show
Hutton-in-the-Forest Plant & Food Fair
Dalton-in-Furness Medieval Market
Holker Garden Festival
Ravenglass Charter Fair

June
Whitehaven Annual Concert
Appleby Horse Fair
Cockermouth Carnival
Dent Folk Festival
Edwardian Festival, Grange-over-Sands
Eskdale Beer Festival
Gummers How Fell Race
Kendal Book Fair, Brewery Arts Centre
Keswick Beer Festival
Holker (Hall) Garden Festival
Lanercost Music & Arts Festival
Lakeland Historic Vehicle Show, Hutton-in-the-Forest
Ullswater Country Fair
Ulverston International Music Festival
Whitehaven Male Voice Choir's 'Annual Concert'
Windermere on Water Festival
Rheged Crafts Festival

July
Ambleside Traditional Lakeland Sports & Rush Bearing
Cartmel Races
Cartmel Antiques Fair
Coniston Country Fair, Coniston Hall
Coniston Water Festival
Cumberland County Show, Carlisle
Cumberland Sausage Day
Cumbria Steam Gathering, Flookburgh
Dalton Pops, Barrow-in-Furness
Furness Traditions Folklore Festival, Ulverston
Lakeland Rose Show, County Showground, Kendal
North Lonsdale Agricultural Show, Bardsea
Penrith Agricultural Show, Brougham Farm
Staveley Carnival

August
Ambleside Summer Flower Show & Craft Fair, Ambleside
Brough Agricultural Show
Carlisle Great Food Fair
Carlisle Live, Bitts Park, Carlisle
Cartmel Agricultural Show
Cartmel Races
Cumbria Guitar Show, Rheged
Dalston Show
Gilsland Show
Gosforth Agricultural Show
Grasmere Sports
Hawkshead Show
Lake District Summer Music Festival
Lake District Sheep Dog Trials
Lakes Chilli Fest, Levens Hall
Lowther Horse Driving Trials & Country Fair
Made in Cumbria Food & Craft Fair, Cockermouth
Millom & Broughton Agri. Show, Broughton in Furness
Muncaster Country Fair
Patterdale Dog Day
Rydal Sheepdog Trials, Rydal Park
Skelton Show, Hutton-in-the-Forest
Silloth Carnival
Threlkeld Sheepdog Trials

September
Ambleside Flower Show
Borrowdale Shepherds Meet, Rosthwaite
Coniston Walking Festival
Egremont Crab Fair
Eskdale Show
Great North Swim, Windermere
Kendal Torchlight Carnival
Kentmere Sheepdog Trials
Lantern Procession, Ulverston
Loweswater & Brackenthwaite Agricultural Show
Lowick Agricultural Show
Ulverston Charter Festival
Ulverston Beer Festival
Westmorland County Show, Crooklands

October
Buttermere Shepherds Meet & Show
Coniston Trail Race (PUMA)
Wasdale Head Shepherds Meet & Show
Westmorland CAMRA Beer Festival

November
Biggest Liar Competition at Bridge Inn, Santon
Carlisle Fireshow
Dark Muncaster
Dickensian Festival, Ulverston
Kendal Mountain Film Festival
Ulverston Art Trail

December
Epic Mountain Bike Events Christmas Party, Kendal
Made in Cumbria Food & Craft Fair, Market Pl, Cockermouth
Whitehaven Male Voice Choir, St Begh's Church

Spot the ball, Ambleside Cricket Club

ACKNOWLEDGMENTS

I would like to thank Mike Taffinder for reading my first and second drafts, and for his impeccable proof reading skills, advice and enthusiasm. The same goes for Caroline, my dear wife, for her encouragement and great help in choosing the final images. Thank you Francis and Avril Creighton for the use of Nettleslack Cottage. Not to be forgotten, all the kind persons at the many attractions, places to stay and eat, for showing me around their establishments and for putting up with my endless questions. Finally, I must thank Chris Dyer (Book Designer) and David Cox (Cartographer) for maintaining a passion for this project. And, thank you to Sebastian Faulks for permitting me to quote your praiseworthy comments on the cover of my book.

Photography

Until the introduction of digital photography most of my images were taken with a Nikon FE, a brilliantly robust and simple manual SLR, ably assisted by my trusty Manfrotto Tripod. I must have got through at least six bodies over a twenty-year period. I was a little hesitant, at first, to be fully sold into the use of digital machines but I have been truly bowled over by the flexibility and practicality of this media for my type of work. I started using a Fuji S1 Pro because of its compatibility with my lenses and because of its wonderful range of colour. Its slowness was a complete bore. I now use a Nikon D300 and despite its 450 page manual I am just about coping with it. Its speed and quality of tone is awesome. I am not a techno freak and have little knowledge of other cameras and their multitudinous effects. I am a firm believer in getting up early and staying out late. If you have the patience you never know what light will unfold. My maxim is: Understand the weather and tides, and swot up on your subjects; be they camellias in spring, or the autumn equinoxes. And, get closer to your subject.

Loan of Images

Goldeneye would like to thank the following for allowing us to photograph their property, or for providing us with an image (s) to illustrate their property: Andrea Grimshaw of Kendal Museum, Andy Airey of George Fisher, Caroline Davy of L'enclume, Castlegate House Gallery, Chris at Jerichos, Chris Lowe of Lakeland Motor Museum, Chris Marshall of New House Farm, Denise King of Holker Hall, Diane Gainey of the Viridian Gallery, Gosia of OCG Arts, Janaki Spedding of Mirehouse, Jeanette Edgar of Lakeland Arts Trust,Jo Wagstaff of Muncaster Castle, Jon Trotman and Alison Critchlow of Blencathra Art, Karen of Beckstones Gallery, Kate Willock of Lucy's of Ambleside, Lady Inglewood of Hutton-in-the-Forest, Lake District Aquarium, Lakeland Wildlife Oasis, Linda Doran of Hill Top, Louise Le Voi of Quince & Medlar, Martin Nargate, Matthew Wylie of The Pheasant, Peter Elkington of Rydal Mount, Pippa Greenwood of Peter Hall & Son, Rachel Litten of Brantwood, Rebecca Heaton Cooper of Heaton Cooper Studios, Sabine Skae of Barrow's Dock Museum, Sam Hall of Sharrow Bay, Sara of Honister Slate Mine, Simon Patterson of Patterson Boatworks, Derwent Water Marina, Sue Steinberg of the Abraham Brothers Picture Library, Susan Denham-Smith of The Beacon Whitehaven, Sylvia of Cartmel Gallery, Steam Yacht Gondola's crew, Ian and Dennis, Venus Griffiths, Zoe Cuncliffe of Gilpin Lodge.

Bibliography & Reference

Church pamphlets are often an invaluable source of local knowledge. Rarely credited to an author they can be bought in the church and will contain a history of the church, its past patrons and a history of the region. My favourite Lakeland book is Hunter Davies' A Walk Around The Lakes, as fresh today as when it was first written in 1978. If climbing is your passion then I recommend A. Harry Griffin's The Coniston Tigers. I doubt if there has ever been a kinder man climbing these crags, than he. For outstanding photography W. A. Poucher was the first of the many Lakeland photographers to find a publisher (never to be seen in remainder bookshops). For a more recent photographic study the books by Rob Talbot and Robin Whiteman have rarely been bettered. For the scholars amongst you a trip to Dove Cottage and the Wordsworth Museum should satisfy your curiosity for they have a mountain of letters, manuscripts and data to appease all apetites.

Aerofilms, The Lake District From The Air, 1991. Barker, Juliet, Wordsworth A Life, 2000. Bavin, Eric, Travelling In Lakeland, 1999. Bicknell, Peter, The Illustrated Wordsworth's Guide To The Lakes, 1984. Brabbs, Derry, Fellwalking With Wainwright, 1984. Davies, Hunter, A Walk Around The Lakes, 1979. Fleming, Fergus, Barrow's Boys, 1998. Gray, Hilary, Cumbria Lake District Life, 1991. Griffin, A. Harry, The Coniston Tigers, 1999. Hughes-Hallet, Penelope, Home At Grasmere, 1993. Ordnance Survey Outdoor Leisure series 4,5,6 & 7. Pevsner, Nicholas, Cumberland and Westmorland, 1967. Pevsner, Nicholas, North Lancashire, 1969. Poucher, W. A. , Over Lakeland Fells, 1948. Talbot, Rob, Lakeland Landscapes, 1997. Talbot, Rob, The English Lakes, 1989. Wainwrights Pictorial Guides to the Lake District. Wallace, Doreen, English Lakeland, 1940. Welsh, Frank, The Lake District Companion Guide. Wordsworth, William, The Prelude A Parallel Text, Penguin Classics 1971

Ullswater

INDEX

Hutton - In - The - Forest ss

MAP SYMBOLS EXPLAINED

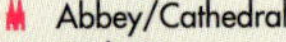

- Abbey/Cathedral
- Battle Site
- Bed & Breakfast Accomodation
- Café
- Castle
- Church/Chapel of Interest
- Cinema
- Craft Interest
- Cross
- Cycleway
- Fun Park/Leisure Park
- Hill Fort/Ancient Settlement
- Historic Building
- Hotel
- Industrial Interest
- Karting
- Lighthouse
- Mining Interest/Engine Houses
- Miscellaneous/Natural Attraction
- Museum/Art Gallery

- Pottery
- Pub/Inn
- Railway Interest
- Restaurant
- Standing Stone/Barrow
- Theatre/Concert Hall
- Tourist Information
- Tumulus/Tumuli
- Viewpoint
- Windmill/Wind Farm
- Airfield
- Aquarium
- Boat Trips
- Camping Site (Tents)
- Caravan Site
- Ferry (Pedestrians)
- Ferry (Vehicles)
- Fishing Trips
- 9/18 Hole Golf Course
- Harbour

- Inshore Rescue Boat
- Leisure/Sports Centre
- Lifeboat
- Parking
- Picnic Site
- Tents & Caravans
- Sailing
- Surfing
- Tourist Information
- Windsurfing
- Youth Hostel
- Agricultural Interest
- Arboretum
- Bird Reserve
- Garden of Interest
- Vineyard
- Walks/Nature Trails
- Wildlife Park
- Zoo
- National Trust Car Park

- 381m.
- 305m.
- 229m.
- 152m
- 76m.

A Road

B Road

Minor Road

Other Road or Track
(not necessarily with public
or vehicular access)

Railway

Cycleway

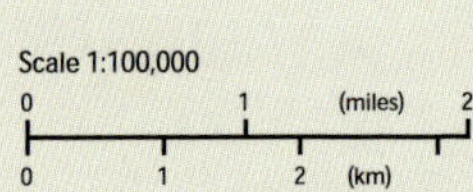

Open Space owned
by the National Trust

Built-up Area

Scale 1:100,000

0   1   (miles)   2

0   1   2   (km)

Kendal Church